SHAKESPEARE'S SATIRE

Shakespeare's Satire

By OSCAR JAMES CAMPBELL

GORDIAN PRESS
NEW YORK
1971

Originally Published 1943
Reprinted 1971

Copyright© 1943
By Oxford University Press
New York, Inc.
Published by GORDIAN PRESS, INC.
By Arrangement With
OXFORD UNIVERSITY PRESS

Library of Congress Catalog Card Number — 74-159036
ISBN 87752-150-6

Contents

Preface

THE idea that the 'gentle' Shakespeare wrote satire of any sort may be distasteful even to those most familiar with his plays. Yet much of the great dramatist's work which has puzzled generations of critics becomes clear only when seen to be based upon that middle ground between comedy and tragedy long occupied by satire. It is true that Shakespeare could not serve as a model for a portrait of your typical satirist, for he never feels the fierce indignation of a Juvenal, nor does he pursue his characters with Ben Jonson's whip of steel. Indeed, he seldom pronounces direct judgment upon his men and women, but prefers to let them all act and speak as they must, without restraint or disapproval from their creator. In this sense Shakespeare's intense interest in life seems to have been disinterested.

However this does not mean that Shakespeare held altogether aloof from his dramatic creations. He was a poet who set every aspect of his world to dancing in the sunlight of his incomparable imagination. His artistic vitality floods the acts and speeches of all his characters. Even his fools and knaves are full of his zest for life. It would be strange indeed if such a dramatist were to display the zeal of a reformer or the laughter of a jealous God.

Shakespeare's view of life was thus expansive rather than critical. Yet everyone knows that he manages to make us laugh at many sorts of folly and stupidity. In the first part of his career his derision was always good-natured. For the absurd in humankind he feels no scorn and displays no reformatory zeal. Satiric commentators like Mercutio or the Bastard in *King John*, characters designed to direct the laughter against others deserving ridicule, were also themselves diverted by what they saw. Their good-natured amusement overwhelmed the indignation expected of the typical satirist. But for all that, Shakespeare so frequently cast these agents of his derision in traditional satiric moulds that they deserve a place in our study of his satire.

During the first decade of the seventeenth century Shakespeare began to give freer rein to his satiric spirit and to grind it to a sharper edge. Indeed some of the dramas that he wrote during these years, notably *Troilus and Cressida, Measure for Measure, Coriolanus,* and *Timon of Athens,* are not only filled with the harsh spirit of formal satire, but in construction they also display distinguishing characteristics of the genre. Consequently their sombre tone and their disillusioned temper have almost always been taken as proof that the author's personal unhappiness has gone so deep as to drive him to the verge of despair. Dowden long ago contributed to this interpretation a happy phrase that did much to prolong its life. Shakespeare, he wrote, during these middle years when he seemed to be buried in gloom was 'in the depths,' and his personal despondency, so the theory ran, became transmuted into the artistic impulse which produced his great tragedies and his 'dark' comedies.

Of late many critics have given up what is after all a gratuitous assumption that Shakespeare was afflicted with a long-drawn-out despair enduring from 1600 to 1609. There is more reason for suspecting that the bitterness of his plays may have been an artistic device, the product of a satiric impulse. Many works of English literature written between 1598 and 1608 are tinged with derision. It is more than likely that Shakespeare, in filling certain of his dramas with a harsh critical spirit, was merely imitating a popular literary fashion. In fact it would have been strange to find Shakespeare im-

mune to the influence of formal satire, one of the strongest
literary movements of his age.

In a work published in 1938, entitled *Comical Satyre and
Shakespeare's 'Troilus and Cressida,'* I showed how the prohibition of poetical satire in 1599 failed to stifle the vigorous
satiric impulse abroad in England. The fact is that the re-
pressive measures merely diverted its stream to flow tumultu-
ously through the plays of Jonson and Marston. In that book
I put forward the idea that Shakespeare in *Troilus and
Cressida* made a highly original contribution to the new
genre of dramatic satire. Since then it has become increasingly clear to me that *Troilus and Cressida* was only one of
the most striking of Shakespeare's triumphs as a writer of
satire. In fact the conviction grew that only by setting the
play in logical relationship to the dramatist's other satiric
productions would its significance in the history of Shakespeare's development become clear. That is the service which
this book attempts to perform. It describes in chronological
sequence the poet's principal satiric achievements.

It is only in larger outline that I have followed this phase
of Shakespeare's achievement. I have avoided the temptation
to discover beneath dramatic figures the sting of personal
lampoons; I have not searched that happy hunting ground
of conjecture for evidence of Shakespeare's personal an-
tipathies. Similarly, I have not seen in Hamlet's advice to
the players the author's scorn of Alleyn's melodramatic por-
trayals in a rival theatre. Nor have I studied *Richard II* to
discover the traits that Shakespeare disliked in Queen Elizabeth. Above all, I have not found Essex lurking behind
Hamlet or any other of the characters in the plays. It has
been my aim to make this study rigorously objective.

I have also tried not to stretch the conventional conception
of satire unjustifiably. Those who assume that only works
which display something of Juvenal's severity can properly
be regarded as satires may be surprised at my detection of

the satiric note in some of the speeches of Launce and Falstaff. They may feel that I believe any sort of ridicule to be
a form of satire. Such is not the case. I have studied only
those forms of derision which satirists, ancient, medieval, or
Elizabethan, had made conventional by Shakespeare's day.
For example, though the clowns and louts in Shakespeare's
early comedies have seldom, if ever, been thought of as
satirists, they are all descendants by direct or collateral line
from the Vice in the Morality plays—a character that surely
was as much satirist as maker of malicious mischief.

Again, we know that the caricature drawn with a few bold
strokes in the first lines of a formal or poetic satire was one
of the invariable characteristics of the genre. But we have
been slow to recognize Falstaff's distorted portraits of his
cronies as his own highly original version of those familiar
satiric sketches. To be sure, Falstaff's descriptions lack the
ill nature and moral zeal informing the works which served
as their models. Yet when, in spite of this important difference, we see them as variations of a well-established satiric
convention, we find that they throw a flood of light upon
Shakespeare's critical temper and also upon his theatrical
resourcefulness.

Launce and Falstaff are but two of the many commentators
in Shakespeare's plays, each one of whom proves to be the
poet's original development of some well-established satiric
convention. The characters against whom Shakespeare directs his ridicule form as significant a cloud of witnesses to
his technical mastery as do these mouthpieces of his raillery.
At first his shafts were directed at figures like Jaques, Nym,
or Dr. Caius, who are but loosely connected with the plot.
The laughter which they arouse is utterly free from anger
or contempt. Yet Shakespeare's good-natured amusement exposes their absurdities as effectively as Ben Jonson's indignation and scorn ever 'stripped naked' the follies of his time.

When Shakespeare begins to incorporate into his plays

some of Jonson's innovations in the field of dramatic satire, his mood darkens. Witness his treatment of Malvolio in *Twelfth Night*. He follows the presumptuous steward with mockery whenever the fellow walks upon the stage, and finally ejects him from the comedy with a burst of contemptuous laughter. Troilus and Cressida are both objects of scorn in a drama ringing with hostile and disillusioned laughter.

The last form of Shakespeare's satiric writing, displayed in *Timon of Athens* and *Coriolanus,* can properly be defined as tragical satire. In designing these plays he followed Jonson into a new region of dramatic activity, which his versatile friend had explored while writing *Sejanus.* That is the reason why Timon and Coriolanus go to their tragic ends hounded by derision. All the characters we have mentioned, and many more, are expressions of a satiric impulse. By themselves they form a gallery of striking portraits. Without them the brave new world created by the poet would lack much of its color and excitement. This study will have served its modest purpose if it has added a cubit to the stature of some of Shakespeare's most familiar creatures. But it has had the further aim of clarifying the structure of some of the plays which down to the present day continue to puzzle the commentators. If there is truth in any of the theories presented in this book, its pages should have widened, if only by a little, our comprehension of the myriad-minded Shakespeare.

The point of view taken in this volume is my own. I am, however, under deep obligation to scholars and critics too numerous to mention here. Those to whom I am most indebted have, I hope, been given due credit in the notes to individual chapters. I am particularly grateful to the Henry E. Huntington Library for permission to rework some of the material on *Troilus and Cressida* which appeared in *Comical Satyre and Shakespeare's 'Troilus and Cressida'* and to reprint parts of an article on Jaques originally appearing in the *Huntington Library Bulletin.* In my quotations of Shakespeare's lines I have followed the text of George Lyman Kittredge's edition of *Shakespeare's Complete Works.*

O. J. C.

Columbia University

SHAKESPEARE'S SATIRE

I

The Clown

SHAKESPEARE's clown was the first of his characters to play the satirist. In the company for which the young dramatist began to write, Will Kemp was the actor to whom this time-honored role was always assigned. By the year 1590 Kemp was so popular and had established so definite a 'line' that Shakespeare had to include among the *dramatis personae* of each of his plays a character calculated to display this actor's distinctive talents.

Kemp's art was largely a development and enrichment of the 'business' of the Vice as he appeared in the morality plays. This figure, representing in a manner all of the seven deadly sins at once, became primarily a farcical mischief-maker. His special delight was to make a laughing-stock of all the other characters, whom he harassed with crude practical jokes and teased with his impudencies. Merry Report in John Heywood's *Play of the Wether* (1535) is a perfect example of the Vice in the role of vulgar jester. In this interlude he is a kind of secretary to Jupiter, presiding, as it were, over the god's outer office or waiting-room. The suppliants can gain access to the god only through Merry Report. On the day of the dramatic action many petitioners appear. Each one has come to beg for the kind of weather that is best for his business and his pleasure. They naturally ask for different sorts. The wind-miller, for example, wants much wind and no rain; the water-miller, much rain and no wind. The launder (washer woman) wants much sunshine; the gentle-woman, who fancies her complexion, little sun. The entire play is satiric in temper and it is the business of the Vice to direct and drive home each attack. Crude and vulgar though they often are, they form satire of a rough and ready sort. Kemp's thrusts often retain some of the horse-play of the Vice.

Sometimes the Vice becomes almost pure fool. Then he takes his place in the vast literature of folly, best represented in English by Barclay's translation of Sebastian Brandt's *The Ship of Fools* (1509) and Sir Thomas Chaloner's translation (1549) of Erasmus' *Praise of Folly*. The wise fool of the latter work in one of his speeches makes it clear why he is so effective an instrument of satire:

> A fool speaketh like a fool (videlicet) plainly—of fools oft times, not only true tales but even open rebukes are with pleasure declared. That what word coming out of a wise man's mouth were an hanging matter, the same yet spoken by a fool shall much delight even him that is touched therewith.

In this passage Erasmus explains the strange popularity of the court, or domestic, fool—a character who usually bores a modern audience. Only an innocent 'natural' could rebuke with impunity those high in the social scale. Only he could express freely the suppressed irritations of the underlings in a patriarchal household. The clown's ability to sugar the bitter pill of satiric correction with absurdity enabled him to fill his office without danger to his back and sides. Kemp's indebtedness to the domestic fool is slight. It is his successor Armin who exploits all the dramatic possibilities of this character.

Part of Will Kemp's business was inherited from a third comic type—the booby, or country lout. The 'natural' who provided hilarious amusement to the people of almost every English village could have supplied an actor like Kemp with much of his nonsense. Before Kemp began to act, however, the actors who played the loutish servant in Italian popular comedy [1] had stylized and systematized its business. One of the characters in the earliest extant scenario of the *Commedia dell' arte* is a stupid rustic. He plays no part in the plot, raising laughter merely by his countrified appearance and his stupidity. His *lazzi*, or farcical tricks, became early stereotyped. Leone di Sommi in a book of dramaturgy written sometime between 1567 and 1590 instructs actors who expect to play the role of the lout as follows: 'If he plays the fool, besides answering off the point (a trick that the author will put into his part) he must be able to act the imbecile, catch flies, kill fleas and perform other foolish acts of a similar sort.' That Kemp relied on the same sort of physical farce we learn from a passage in *The Pilgrimage from Parnassus*. In one scene of this play a character named Dromo enters, drawing a clown in with a rope and explaining that 'Clownes have been thrust into playes by head and shoulders ever since Kempe could make a scurvey face.' In answer to the clown's question, 'But what must I do now,' Dromo says, 'Why, if thou canst but drawe thy mouth awrye, lay thy legg over thy staffe, sawe a peece of cheese asunder with thy dagger, lape up drinke on the earth, I warrant thee theile laugh mightilie.' [2]

Next to this sort of clowning, malapropism became the favorite, indeed the distinguishing, trick of this lout. The first sentence on each of his appearances was likely to contain two or three ridiculous mistakes in words. Another popular piece of business was his impersonation of two or more figures in a farcically acted little duologue.

Kemp displays most of these characteristics in the part of Launce of *The Two Gentlemen of Verona*, apparently the first role that Shakespeare designed for this popular actor. His favorite *lazzi* appear clearly on the first occasion he has the stage to himself. He enters leading his dog Crab on a rope, and his first remarks to the audience form a farrago of verbal confusions: 'I have received my proportion like the Prodigious son,' he begins, 'and am going with Sir Proteus to the Imperial's Court' (II. iii. 3-5). Then with the aid of his wooden shoes, his hat, and his staff, he sets the stage on which he plans to re-enact the scene of his parting with his family. 'This hat is Nan, our maid,' he carefully explains. 'I am the dog. No, the dog is himself and I am the dog. O, the dog is me and I am myself' (II. iii. 22-4). By this time he is thoroughly entangled in his stage properties, but finally extricates himself enough to act out his tragi-comedy.

As Launce's domestic drama unfolds, it proves to be a parody of the scene which has immediately preceded it. There Proteus has taken a lachrymose farewell of his first love, the gentle Julia. Some parody, as we shall see in a moment, is a naïve form of satire. But in this little comedy of Launce's there is virtually none. It is rather in the lout's farcical impersonation of the various members of his family that all the amusement lies.

A little later in a similar sort of parody Launce unmistakably derides his master's baseness. Proteus, deserting Julia, has fallen in love with Silvia, the betrothed of his friend Valentine. His passion drives him to an even deeper infidelity—it makes him betray his friend's plan for an elopement to Silvia's father. Proteus's treachery accomplishes his evil purpose. The Duke decrees Valentine's banishment. Then the deceitful Proteus, pretending anxiety for his friend's life, speeds him out of the city to a place far away from Silvia.

Launce watches all this villainy with wide eyes, and when left alone on the stage soliloquizes as follows: 'I am but a fool, look you, and yet I have the wit to think my master is a kind of knave. But that's all one, if he be but one knave' (III. i. 261-4). This satire is rendered 'toothless' by the apparent witlessness of Launce's last phrase, but conceals beneath its folly a sting of truth. Proteus is so two-faced, so talented a dissimulator, that he really is knave not in one role only, but in all the many parts he is trying to play.

Launce then goes on to remark in his own inimitable way on the rapid transfers of his master's love from one object to another. The servant, like the audience, is in doubt as to 'Who loves whom now?' But his comment is delightfully indirect. He pretends that he too loves a lady, but who it is no one will ever know. 'He lives not now,' he cries, 'that knows me to be in love; yet I am in love. But a team of horses shall not pluck that from me: nor who 'tis I love. And yet 'tis a woman' (III. i. 264-6). This monologue, though it sounds like brainless folly, is a sally into satire. Kemp has learned how to make his clownish parodies yield trenchant comment on the absurd or evil ways of his fellow characters.

Grumio in *The Taming of the Shrew* and Launcelot Gobbo in *The Merchant of Venice* are both characters in Kemp's 'line' and both were probably impersonated by him. But into neither role has Kemp insinuated any satire. Both Grumio and Launcelot mistake the word, and the latter in a dialogue between the Fiend and his Conscience gaily impersonates each of the two interlocutors. The rest of the business of these two louts is silly clowning.

II

In two other plays, however, the tiny seed of satire sown in Launce's part puts forth goodly blossoms. The Bastard in *King John* and Mercutio in *Romeo and Juliet* are satiric commentators developed from the conventions of the lout's role. Few critics have assigned these parts to Will Kemp. They follow T. W. Baldwin in his statement that Kemp was 'crowded almost out of the tragedies.' [8] But this shelving of Kemp would have been stupid business for a dramatist writing for the company. Kemp during the years 1595 and 1596

was as popular an actor as Burbage, so that Shakespeare must
have felt bound to provide those two principal actors with
fat parts in every play he wrote. It is because Baldwin assumes that Kemp never tried any role except that of the
lout that he fails to hit upon any part in the tragedies that
the talented actor might have played.

A strong reason for suspecting that the Bastard was one
of Kemp's parts is the fact that the first time that the character appears he, like Launce, carries on an imaginary duologue with himself. After he has been officially pronounced
to be the bastard son of Richard Coeur de Lion, he pretends
that he meets one of his old friends, now much too insig-
nificant to be recognized by a royal bastard. The friend
begins: 'Good den, Sir Richard,' and he replies, 'God-a-mercy
[i.e. Thank you] fellow.' Then the Bastard continues:

> And if his name be George, I'll call him Peter;
> For new-made honour doth forget men's names:
> 'Tis too respective and too sociable
> For your conversion. Now your traveller,
> He and his toothpick at my worship's mess:
> And when my knightly stomach is suffic'd,
> Why, then I such my teeth and catechize
> My picked man of countries. 'My dear sir,'
> Thus, leaning on mine elbow, I begin,
> 'I shall beseech you.' That is question now,
> And then comes answer like an Absey-book:
> 'O sir,' says answer, 'at your best command,
> At your employment, at your service, sir!'
> 'No, sir,' says question. 'I, sweet sir, at yours!'
> And so, ere answer knows what question would—
> Saving in dialogue of compliment,
> And talking of the Alps and Apennines,
> The Pyrenean and the river Po—
> It draws toward supper in conclusion so.
> But this is worshipful society
> And fits the mounting spirit like myself.
>   (I. i. 184-206)

This is Will Kemp's favorite piece of business presented as an interlude when the Bastard is alone on the stage. Like Launce's dramatization of his farewell to his family, it is parody, this time of the dialogues appearing in the fashionable primers by which conversational French and Italian were taught in Shakespeare's day. The best known of these books were Florio's *First Fruits* (1578) and *Second Fruits* (1591). The dialogues were printed in parallel columns—the Italian or French in one and the corresponding English in the other. The two subjects which the Bastard parodies are the 'exchange of compliments' and 'description of travel.' For example, chapter seven of *First Fruits* is entitled 'To Speak with a Gentleman' and presents a dialogue which begins as follows:

> Wel met my lord.
> How doth your lordship?
> Very wel, at the commaundement of you, and redy to serue you in any thing that I may.
> Verily I yeeld you thanks, make the like account of me.
> Wel my lorde, I goe through this streete, and you.
> No sir, I go through this other, wil you commaund me any thing or not? [4]

The exchange of polite salutation here is fully as long drawn out and fatuous as that in the Bastard's parody. The travel dialogue was also a feature of these modern-language manuals. Florio's fifteenth chapter, called 'To Speak of England,' is a tedious and naïve description of many aspects of English life.

In 1593 John Eliot published a parody of these manuals under the title *Ortho-epia Gallica, Eliots Fruits for the French*. In one of his Dialogues called 'The Painter,' while the interlocutors are examining a map, one of them exclaims: 'Seest thou the Fennes of the Nyle! Lo here the red Sea! Look upon the great Caire! On this side is Europe—Here are

the Alpes, over which we go downe into Italie. There are the
Appenines, and here are the Pyrenaean hills, by which you
may go directly into Spaine.' [5]

The Bastard in his talk of Alps and Apennines, the Pyre-
nean and the river Po, is obviously ridiculing the travel dialogue in Eliot's derisive manner. Both use a similar method
of parody; yet in *King John* the parody is the vehicle of gay
social satire. The lesser art has been put into the service of
the greater. Kemp and Shakespeare together have learned
how to expand and to elevate the role of loutish commentator until it has become a delicate and highly original instrument of satire.

Once established as a satirist, the Bastard practices his new
art on all occasions. He ridicules literary absurdity every
time it appears. For example, a citizen on the walls of Angiers, in threatening the French and English armies who are
about to attack the town, utters the horrendous verbiage that
had become conventional in chronicle history plays. The
fellow thunders:

> The sea enraged is not half so deaf,
> Lions more confident, mountains and rocks
> More free from motion—no, not Death himself
> In mortal fury half so peremptory
> As we to keep this city.
>
> (II. i. 451-5)

This fustian sounds ridiculous to the Bastard, the natural
man, the voice of common sense, and he cries:

> Here's a 'Stay!'
> That shakes the rotten carcass of old Death
> Out of his rags! Here's a large mouth indeed,
> That spits forth death, and mountains, rocks and seas;
> Talks as familiarly of roaring lions
> As maids of thirteen do of puppy-dogs!
> What cannoneer begot this lusty blood?

He speaks plain cannon-fire and smoke and bounce;
He gives the bastinado with his tongue.
Our ears are cudgell'd; not a word of his
But buffets better than a fist of France.
Zounds! I was never so bethump'd with words
Since I first call'd my brother's father dad.

                                         (II. i. 455-67)

This diatribe deflates once and for all the absurd high-
sounding speeches of defiance that formed one of the most
popular of the sonorous conventions of early chronicle histories. Shakespeare never again composes such fustian as that
uttered by the citizen of Angiers.

A moment later the Bastard pays his respects to another
moribund literary convention—that of the Petrarchan conceit. The Dauphin has just looked full into the face of Lady
Blanch; and finding that he can love her, announces his
discovery in the following self-conscious, tortured figures of
speech:
                    . . . in her eye I find
          A wonder, or a wondrous miracle—
          The shadow of myself form'd in her eye;
          Which, being but the shadow of your son,
          Becomes a sun and makes your son a shadow.
          I do protest I never lov'd myself
          Till now infixed I beheld myself
          Drawn in the flattering table of her eye.

                                         (II. i. 496-503)

Against this verbal trifling the Bastard breaks out in scorn:

BASTARD (aside). Drawn in the flattering table of her
     eye,
     Hang'd in the frowning wrinkle of her brow,
     And quarter'd in her heart! He doth espy
     Himself love's traitor. This is pity now!
     That hang'd and drawn and quarter'd there should
     be
     In such a love so vile a lout as he.

                                         (II. i. 504-9)

Into this speech the Bastard puts the amused scorn and the direct rebuke of satire. Yet it remains merry. It contains none of the savage sting of Juvenal and his disciples.

Petrarchan conventions of love and love-poetry had been derided before in Shakespeare's work. He gave it expression first in his sonnets. The 130th sonnet, beginning

> My mistress' eyes are nothing like the sun,
> Coral is far more red than her lips red,

and ending

> And yet, by heaven, I think my love as rare
> As any she belied with false compare

is the best-known example of this ridicule. Many other sonneteers had taken this chaffing tone toward puling lovers and their extravagant praise of their mistresses. Sir John Davies, for example, wrote in 1595 nine 'gulling sonnets' which parodied various Petrarchan conventions. And a character in the anonymous play of *Lingua* (1603) ridicules directly the same sort of extravagance. When Petrarchan lovers talk of their mistresses, 'They make forsooth her hair of gold, her eyes of diamond, her cheeks of roses, her lips of rubies, her teeth of pearl, and her whole body of ivory.' [6] The Bastard, then, in his attack on the Dauphin's methods of courting was taking a familiar position—one suitable for such a clear-eyed realist as he.

At the end of this same scene the Bastard deepens the tone of his satire. He has just watched a deal made between the French and English which will effect a peace. In return for the Dauphin's marriage to King John's niece, the Lady Blanch of Castille, the English king is to return five provinces to King Philip and add thereto:

> Full thirty thousand marks of English coin.

To the Bastard this seems a disgraceful proceeding. It means the sacrifice of right and honor to self-interest, which he calls 'commodity.' So when he finds himself alone on the stage, he attacks expediency with savage directness:

> That sly devil,
> That broker that still breaks the pate of faith,
> That daily break-vow, he that wins of all,
> Of kings, of beggars, old men, young men, maids,
>
>   .   .   .
>
> That smooth-faced gentleman, tickling Commodity.
>
> (II. i. 567-70, 572)

> And this same bias, this Commodity,
> This bawd, this broker, this all-changing word,
> Clapp'd on the outward eye of fickle France,
> Hath drawn him from his own determined aid,
> From a resolv'd and honourable war,
> To a most base and vile-concluded peace.
>
> (II. i. 581-6)

Up to this point the Bastard has spoken like a severe castigator of sin. But now his temper lightens. He drops his severity and laughs at his own railing. He recognizes that his high moral position is itself a form of self-interest:

> And why rail I on this Commodity?
> But for because he hath not woo'd me yet:
> Not that I have the power to clutch my hand
> When his fair angels would salute my palm,
> But for my hand, as unattempted yet,
> Like a poor beggar, raileth on the rich.
> Well, whiles I am a beggar, I will rail
> And say there is no sin but to be rich;
> And being rich, my virtue then shall be
> To say there is no vice but beggary.
> Since kings break faith upon commodity,
> Gain, be my lord, for I will worship thee!
>
> (II. i. 588-98)

This is the last time that the Bastard is in any sense a satirist. On the few occasions on which he appears in the last three acts of *King John* he is an embodiment of English patriotism. And in the last speech in the play he solemnly announces the political lesson which the action was designed to teach. England, he says has never been conquered

>   But when it first did help to wound itself!

In this later role he serves as the mouthpiece of the author, but never is an agent of ridicule. Even while he acts as a satirist, he never entirely forgets to be a merrymaker. His satire always skirts the edge of good-humored laughter. This remained the nature of Shakespeare's low-comedy commentator as long as Kemp played the part and as long as Shakespeare remained untouched by the influence of Ben Jonson.

III

The role of Mercutio in *Romeo and Juliet* is much like that of the Bastard as he appears in the first two acts of *King John*. The satiric spirit of each is suffused with gaiety. Mercutio was probably not played by Kemp. However, if we were not certain that he took the part of Peter, who appears in the same scene with Mercutio, we might hazard a shrewd guess that he played this part—far removed from 'the pompous countrified blundering clown.' The role of Peter is too minor a one to serve as Kemp's. In any case the part of Mercutio is a natural expansion of those parts into which Kemp found it possible to insert his distinctive comic business.

Mercutio first appears as one of a group of maskers on their way to the dance at Capulet's house. Here he is merely a mad adventurer eager to have Romeo join whole-heartedly in their daring escapade. But almost immediately Shakespeare forces the dialogue to a point where Mercutio can deliver a long satiric speech. He describes with gay mischief the activities of Mab, an impish fairy of folk-lore. She loves best of all to flatter and deceive with evil dreams, which she is able to provoke in all whom she tickles in their sleep:

> Sometimes she gallops o'er a courtier's nose,
> And then dreams he of smelling out a suit;
> And sometimes comes she with a tithe-pig's tail
> Tickling a parson's nose as 'a lies asleep,
> Then dreams he of another benefice.
>
> (I. iv. 77-81)

This is satire, but of the merriest sort. No man is wounded or directly pointed at. But it is inartistic as being external to the play, except as it shows Mercutio to be a realist scornful of every sort of affectation and sham. Thus we are ready for his distaste for Romeo's whining love for Rosaline. 'Alas, poor Romeo,' he exclaims, 'he is already dead! stabbed with a white wench's black eye; shot through the ear with a love song; the very pin of his heart cleft with the blind bow-boy's butt-shaft' (II. iv. 13-17). His alliteration on the explosive 'b' in the last phrase gives a gay fillip to his contempt.

As soon as Romeo appears, Mercutio continues his ridicule of his friend's sentimental attitudinizing—this time with renewed energy:

> O flesh, flesh, how art thou fishified! Now is he for the numbers that Petrarch flowed in. Laura, to his lady, was but a kitchen wench (marry, she had a better love to berhyme her), Dido a dowdy, Cleopatra a gypsy, Helen and Hero hildings and harlots, Thisbe a gray eye or so, but not to the purpose.
>
> (II. iv. 41-7)

Being a strong partisan of the good old English ways, he cannot abide the methods of sword-play employed by Tybalt, who has learned to duel in the affected manner of Italian teachers of the art:

> . . . He fights as you sing pricksong—keeps time, distance, and proportion; rests me his minim rest, one,

two, and the third in your bosom! the very butcher of
a silk button, a duellist, a duellist! . . . The pox of
such antic, lisping, affecting fantasticoes—these new
tuners of accent! 'By Jesu, a very good blade! a very
tall man! a very good whore!' Why, is not this a la-
mentable thing, grandsir, that we should be thus afflicted with these strange flies, these fashion-mongers,
these pardona-mi's . . .
                                    (II. iv. 21-5, 29-35)

Before he receives his mortal wound in the first scene of
the third act, Mercutio finds time to paint a satiric portrait
of his companion in arms, the pugnacious Benvolio:

Thou! why, thou wilt quarrel with a man that hath a
hair more or a hair less in his beard than thou hast.
Thou wilt quarrel with a man for cracking nuts, having no other reason but because thou hast hazel eyes.
What eye but such an eye would spy out such a quarrel? Thy head is as full of quarrels as an egg is full of
meat; and yet thy head hath been beaten as addle as
an egg for quarrelling. Thou hast quarrell'd with a
man for coughing in the street, because he hath wak-
ened thy dog that hath lain asleep in the sun. Didst
thou not fall out with a tailor for wearing his new
doublet before Easter? with another for tying his new
shoes with old riband? And yet thou wilt tutor me
from quarrelling!
                                    (III. i. 18-33)

In Mercutio nothing of the lout remains. To be sure, in
his impersonation of Tybalt, particularly in imitating his
affected speech, Mercutio takes a leaf from Kemp's manual
of comic business. But Mercutio has abstracted from the trick
all of its low absurdity. His tirade against Tybalt shows
clearly the transformation which Shakespeare has effected in
the lout. Mercutio is a satiric commentator full of bold
gaiety, a fellow of infinite zest, whose vitality contributes
lavishly to the life of the play. In no other dramatic development of his early career does Shakespeare show such profuse
originality.

IV

To see in Falstaff's antics traces of this role of merry satirist may seem queer. But in some of his most famous speeches they are clearly evident. As everyone knows, many dramatic traditions converge and unite in his opulent figure. He is part braggart soldier, part tavern denizen, a popular character in all Prodigal Son plays, and so at home in this drama of a royal prodigal. He is also a Puritan fallen from grace, who conveniently remembers the pious tags from sermons which he has heard years ago. These he delights in using in outrageously inappropriate contexts. But more than all these he is an acute and merry commentator on the absurdities of other characters.

Henry David Gray has argued persuasively that Falstaff was one of Kemp's parts.[7] Kemp was still one of the most important members of the Chamberlain's company in the years 1597 and 1598 and for an actor so popular Shakespeare would still have been compelled to provide a substantial role. In the *Henry IV* plays Falstaff was the only 'fat' part at all suitable for Kemp. Baldwin's notion that the role must have been written for some member of the company who had become fat is singularly literal. Skillful padding made even so slight a man as Maurice Evans round enough for the part. However, whether Kemp played Falstaff or not, the role belongs to the same tradition as that of the Bastard and Mercutio.

It is at the immortal gathering in Boar's Head Tavern that Falstaff first plays the part of satiric commentator in Kemp's jolly fashion. After the Prince has exposed the fat rogue's cowardice at the Gadshill robbery and the gross lies by which he seeks to deny the fact, Falstaff decides it is time to force his royal crony to drop this embarrassing subject. He suggests putting on a 'play extemporale' in which he will impersonate Prince Hal's father, the King.

He begins his game by setting the stage as carefully as did Launce in *The Two Gentlemen of Verona,* with his staff and his old shoes. 'This chair,' says Falstaff, 'shall be my state, this dagger my sceptre, and this cushion my crown' (II. iv. 415-17). Immediately he brings the Hostess, who is giggling at his side, into the play. She shall be his Queen. With a flourish in her direction he gives the royal command:

> For God's sake, lords, convey my tristful queen;
> For tears do stop the flood-gates of her eyes.
>
> (II. iv. 434-5)

This sally enchants the Hostess. 'O Jesu!' she exclaims, 'he doth it as like one of these harlotry players as ever I see.' If Kemp did not improvise this scene, it was designed by an actor who had learned how to exhibit successfully Kemp's favorite farcical business of dramatic impersonation.

The speech which Falstaff delivers in the person of the King is not parody or satire of the King's ways of speech. It is direct ridicule of euphuism, still regarded by some great ones of Shakespeare's day as the proper courtly speech. Falstaff begins, after tossing off a cup of sack to make his eyes water:

> Harry, I do not only marvel where thou spendest thy time, but also how thou art accompanied. For though the camomile, the more it is trodden on, the faster it grows, yet youth, the more it is wasted, the sooner it wears . . . If then thou be son to me, here lies the point: why, being son to me, art thou so pointed at? Shall the blessed sun of heaven prove a micher and eat blackberries? A question not to be ask'd. Shall the son of England prove a thief and take purses? A question to be ask'd. There is a thing, Harry, which thou hast often heard of, and it is known to many in our land

by the name of pitch. This pitch, as ancient writers do
report, doth defile; so doth the company thou keepest.

(II. iv. 439-44, 448-58)

Falstaff is also skillful at drawing satiric portraits of his
companions. The sight of Bardolph's bulbous red nose drives
him into unrestrained expenditure of his large fund of odd
figurative language. 'Thou art our admiral,' he begins,

> thou bearest the lantern in the poop—but 'tis in the
> nose of thee . . . I never see thy face but I think upon
> hell-fire and Dives that lived in purple; for there he
> is in his robes, burning, burning . . . O, thou art a
> perpetual triumph, an everlasting bonfire-light! Thou
> hast saved me a thousand marks in links and torches,
> walking with thee in the night betwixt tavern and
> tavern.

(III. iii. 27-49 passim)

This speech, unlike formal satire, has no reformatory aim.
Falstaff seeks only to entertain himself with a purely artistic
excursion of his own imagination. Yet the portrait is a caricature made, as was the fashion of the satiric commentator,
with outrageously appropriate figures of speech.

Falstaff's description of the pitiful ragamuffins whom he
has impressed into military service has a more sober satiric
purpose. In recruiting, he chooses first men of substance and
urgent business, who are willing and able to bribe him to let
them off. Hence his company is made up of indigent scare-
crows, whom he describes with his accustomed gusto. But his
best satiric thrust comes in his reply to Prince Hal's remark
that he has never seen such pitiful rascals as Falstaff's recruits.
'Tut, tut,' Falstaff answers, 'good enough to toss, food for
powder, food for powder; they'll fill a pit as well as better.
Tush, man, mortal men, mortal men' (IV. ii. 71-4). This comment nonchalantly tossed off is a more devastating exposure
of the hollowness of the glories of battle than acres of solemn
protests against rearing boys to become cannon fodder.

The deflation of all the pomp and circumstance of glorious war is completed in Falstaff's famous catechism on honor:

> Well, 'tis no matter, honour pricks me on. Yea, but how if honour prick me off when I come on? How then? Can honour set to a leg? No. Or an arm? No. Or take away the grief of a wound? No. Honour hath no skill in surgery then? No. What is honour? A word. What is that word honour? Air. A trim reckoning! Who hath it? He that died o Wednesday. Doth he feel it? No. Doth he hear it? No. 'Tis insensible then? Yea, to the dead. But will it not live with the living? No. Why? Detraction will not suffer it. Therefore I'll none of it. Honour is a mere scutcheon—and so ends my catechism.
>
> (v. i. 133-44)

Of this and similar speeches of Falstaff Mark Van Doren says:

> Falstaff understands everything; so is never serious . . . His native speech is casual, yet pure . . . We hear it, however, but seldom. Most of the time it is buried under heaps of talk delivered from a hundred assumed personalities, a hundred fictitious identities.[8]

Mr. Van Doren thus emphasizes the delight which Falstaff takes in playing many parts. And the question-and-answer form of the catechism on honor proves that Falstaff, like Launce, played for the laughter he could wring out of a dialogue carried on with himself. It reminds us that Falstaff stands at the end of the tradition that began with Launce.

The catechism is also deflation of the tremendous tirades on honor which more than once stream from the lips of Prince Hal. Yet in spite of the apparent nonchalance of Falstaff, his satire is more than parody. It questions the chivalric ideals which made war regarded as the noblest activity of an Elizabethan gentleman.

In the second part of *Henry IV* Falstaff merely repeats all of his characteristic provocations to laughter. At first they seem less spontaneous and less sparkling. The sight of his little page in attendance on his rotundity provokes his sense of the ridiculous as had Bardolph's nose. The first sentence that he devotes to the situation is one of his best. 'I do here walk before thee like a sow that hath overwhelmed all her litter but one.' But thereafter his tropes seem forced, not filled with his highest spirits.

The truth is that Falstaff's wit remains blunted until Justice Shallow appears. Then it becomes again both keen and hilarious. Falstaff is made to illustrate the evils of recruiting this time by impressing the feeble and impecunious and taking bribes to release the strong and prosperous. All this scandalous behavior we see with our very own eyes. Shakespeare evidently intended to have this conduct wean our affection from Falstaff, so that we could assent to Prince Hal's rejection of his fat friend at the end of the play. But by this time the rogue has been too amply endowed with charm. The foolish Master Shallow proves too keen a whetstone to his wit. For the benefit of his loutish cousin Silence, the starved Justice recalls with Sir John the wild dissipations of his youth. 'Jesus, the days that we have seen' is the text of his reminiscences. Falstaff encourages him in these fictitious memories. But when he is left alone on the stage he tells the truth about the squeaking old man in a caricature which at once bites and tickles.

> Lord, Lord, how subject we old men are to this vice of lying! This same starv'd justice hath done nothing but prate to me of the wildness of his youth and the feats he hath done about Turnbull Street; and every third word a lie, duer paid to the hearer than the Turk's tribute. I do remember him at Clement's Inn, like a man made after supper of a cheese paring. When 'a was naked, he was for all the world like a fork'd radish, with a head fantastically carved upon it with a knife; 'a was so forlorn that his dimensions to

any thick sight were invincible. 'A was the very genius
of famine; yet lecherous as a monkey, and the whores
call'd him 'mandrake.' 'A came ever in the rearward
of the fashion, and sung those tunes to the over-
scutch'd huswives that he heard the carmen whistle,
and sware they were his Fancies or his Good-nights.

(III. ii. 325-43)

A scene between Shallow and his servant Davy also provokes Falstaff to satiric comment. The servant with cere-
moniousness befitting the associate of a country justice per-
suades Shallow to 'let off' a great knave because he is his
friend. 'I have served your worship truly, sir, this eight years,'
he begins his plausible plea, 'and if I cannot once or twice
in a quarter bear out a knave against an honest man, I have
but little credit with your worship. The knave is mine honest
friend, sir. Therefore I beseech you let him be countenanced'
(v. i. 51-7). The Justice has nothing to say against this human appeal and without question grants his servant's request.

This little scene is itself a good-natured satire of a familiar
sort of injustice. But Falstaff's comments are principally directed against the ludicrous way in which Shallow's servants
have come to imitate him and the way in which he insensibly
has grown to be like them. Falstaff remarks:

> If I were sawed into quantities, I should make four
> dozen of such bearded hermits' staves as Master Shal-
> low. It is a wonderful thing to see the semblable co-
> herence of his men's spirits and his. They, by observ-
> ing of him, do bear themselves like foolish justices, he
> by conversing with them, is turned into a justice-like
> servingman. Their spirits are so married in conjunc-
> tion with the participation of society that they flock
> together in consent, like so many wild geese.

(v. i. 69-79)

This Shallow will also serve him in his efforts to keep in
the good graces of the Prince. He expects to devise enough

matter out of him to keep Hal in continual laughter. But
poor Falstaff has not reckoned with the change of temper
which the responsibilities of kingship have wrought in the
once madcap Prince. The King publicly rejects his overtures
of boon companionship and banishes him from his presence.
But we are as unwilling as Shakespeare's audiences were to
lose him forever. And of all his many ways of entertainment
we miss not least his long passages of always good-natured,
sometimes rollicking satire.

Shakespeare promises in his epilogue to *II Henry IV* to
find a place for Falstaff in his next play in which he will
show us Prince Hal as *Henry V*. But he does not keep his
promise. Instead Dame Quickly in *Henry V* reports his death
in one of the quaintest mixtures of tenderness and ineptitude in all literature.

Many reasons have been given for Shakespeare's failure to
give Falstaff another chance to disport himself for our entertainment. A possible reason is that the part had become so
closely identified with Kemp that when Kemp left the Company in 1599 Shakespeare felt that the character must disappear with him. At any rate Shakespeare never created another representative of the genial hilarious satiric commentator. The development of the role could go no further than
it had in Falstaff. In him and, to only a little lesser degree,
in the Bastard and Mercutio, Shakespeare filled satire so full
of zest and merriment that its critical and corrective function
almost entirely disappeared. It struck a new note, one of the
fullest and most resonant in Shakespeare's immense diapason
of expansive mirth.

II

Love's Labor's Lost

Love's Labor's Lost is unquestionably a court play. There
is every reason to suppose that it was designed for an audience which included Queen Elizabeth and her ladies in waiting.[1] The comedy celebrates the triumph of love over the
ideals of cloistered learning and pedantry. And the love to
which honor is paid is neither passion nor romantic devotion, but love which becomes the theme for courtly banter
and conversational wit. It is, in short, the kind of love which
flourished at the court of the Virgin Queen, the kind which
Spenser describes in 'Colin Clout's Come Home Again':

> . . . Love most aboundeth there:
> For all the walls and windows there are writ,
> And full of love, and love, and love my dear.
> And all their talk and study is of it.
>
> (II. 785-8)

With this love the ladies and gentlemen in *Love's Labor's
Lost* play merrily in their 'civil war of wits.' The substance
of this game would have seemed immaterial to any general
public, and the wit folly, but to the Queen and her courtiers
the whole thing must have been exquisite fooling. They
would expect the play to make graceful sport of their social
preoccupations and to allude amusingly to personal, political, or intellectual matters which only those in the know
would catch.

A dramatist writing comedies for the court would seek to
satirize whatever concerns of the coterie he had marked for
ridicule, only with occasional and oblique thrusts. If he were

24

Shakespeare, he would attack with consummate subtlety. He would make his characters reminiscent of this and that person, but never fashion them into rounded portraits of anyone living or dead. Nor would his topical references combine to present a thorough analysis of any folly or abuse. As Dover Wilson has said, 'Shakespeare was a dramatic artist, not a journalist, and above all he was subtle. He hardly ever goes out of his way to make a topical allusion; but he glances at the business in passing, rather than by overt reference.' [2]

This is the way he ridicules in *Love's Labor's Lost* matters which lie buried in the ephemeral interests of the early 1590's. The play satirizes openly a group of gentlemen living at the court of Ferdinand, the King of Navarre. Under his patronage the Lords Biron, Longaville, and Dumain have decided to establish a little 'academe,' the members of which will devote themselves to contemplation and to philosophical and scientific speculation. These studies are to be carried on in monastic seclusion from life. In particular the gentlemen swear for three years:

> Not to see ladies, study, fast, not sleep.

The prohibition against association with women is the most stringent. No woman is to be allowed to come within a mile of Navarre's court, on pain of losing her tongue, and 'if any man be seen to talk with a woman within the term of three years, he shall endure such public shame as the rest of the court can possibly devise' (i. i. 130-33).

All are convinced of the wisdom of this procedure except Biron. He is frankly skeptical. Wisdom, in his opinion, is not gained by poring painfully upon a book.

> Small have continual plodders ever won
> Save base authority from others' books.

And he includes among his pedants certain diligent students of astronomy, for in his view

These earthly godfathers of heaven's lights
That give a name to every fixed star
Have no more profit of their shining nights
Than those that walk and wot not what they are.

(I. i. 88-91)

In spite of his reservations, however, he insists upon taking
the vows at the very moment at which a French princess,
accompanied by a flying squadron of ladies, is knocking at
the gates of the palace. She and her suite have come on a
diplomatic mission. Biron intimates that the necessity of
keeping this forgotten appointment will make the academicians swiftly forsworn; but since he realizes that, if need be,
he can offer 'necessity' as an excuse for breaking his vow, he
too signs away his freedom with a flourish.

The Prince then goes to meet the Princess in the park, but
refuses her request to be conducted to his court, explaining
that his vow forbids her entrance into the palace. Though
thus denying her 'fair harbor in his house,' he tells her that
'here' without—that is, in the park—she shall be received as
though she were lodged in his heart. And in the park the
ladies and gentlemen entertain each other while the experts
in diplomacy are discussing the political questions at issue.
The ladies are coy and fleering, but adroit in all the arts of
verbal trifling. In spite of their oaths the men fall in love,
all four of them, each with a different one of the four ladies.
And the King, Longaville, and Dumain each in turn is over-
heard reading a love poem addressed to his lady. Biron, having witnessed the discomfiture of all three, confesses that he,
too, is in love—with the dark-eyed Rosaline. Then realizing
that his initial scorn has been justified, he gives eloquent
expression to the idea that vital knowledge comes not from
books but from life, particularly from the love light in a
woman's eyes—in his case from the glances of the dark-eyed
Rosaline.

Biron's capitulation to love he himself finds to be intensely ironic, for he has always been contemptuous of all the fashionable paraphernalia of courtship, particularly of the exaggerations of the Petrarchan sonneteers. His amazement at the change Rosaline has wrought in him forms excellent satire of the most extreme conventions of the anti-Petrarchists:

> And I—
> Forsooth in love? I that have been love's whip!
> A very beadle to a humorous sigh,
> A critic, nay, a night-watch constable,
> A domineering pedant o'er the boy,
> Than whom no mortal so magnificent!
> This wimpled, whining, purblind, wayward boy,
> This senior-junior, giant-dwarf, Dan Cupid,
> Regent of love-rhymes, lord of folded arms,
> Th'anointed sovereign of sighs and groans,
> Liege of all loiterers and malecontents,
> Dread prince of plackets, king of codpieces,
> Sole emperator and great general
> Of trotting paritors—(O my little heart!)
> And I to be a corporal of his field,
> And wear his colours like a tumbler's hoop!
> What I? I love? I sue? I seek a wife?
> A woman, that is like a German clock,
> Still a-repairing, ever out of frame,
> And never going aright, being a watch,
> But being watch'd that it may still go right!
> Nay, to be perjur'd, which is worst of all;
> And among three to love the worst of all—
>
> (III. i. 176-197)

Yet Biron has from the first been no ascetic. What he has suspected would happen has happened. Life and nature have defeated the austere conception of learning which Ferdinand had forced him to adopt. Confirmed in his scorn for those who withdraw from the adventure of living, he takes another satiric thrust at cloistered study. Leaden contemplation, he cries, dries up the sources of life:

> Why, universal plodding prisons up
> The nimble spirits in the arteries,
> As motion and long-during action tires
> The sinewy vigour of the traveller.
>
> (IV. iii. 305-8)

Having thus shown his contempt for 'universal plodding,' he turns to celebrate love as the supreme revelation of reality:

> For valor is not Love a Hercules
> Still climbing trees in the Hesperides?
> Subtle as Sphinx, as sweet and musical
> As bright Apollo's lute, strung with his hair.
> And when Love speaks, the voice of all the gods
> Makes heaven drowsy with the harmony.
>
> (IV. iii. 340-45)

In these exquisite lines Shakespeare presents with rare eloquence the humane ideal of those who have learned that pedantry is folly. The best school of life, Biron says, is not monastic contemplation but direct experience of the world, in which woman and her love play the principal part.

But Biron's avowal of love does not put an end to the embarrassments of the gentlemen. The ladies continue to tease them and to mock their amorous advances:

> . . . Their conceits have wings
> Fleeter than arrows, bullets, wind, thought, swifter things.

The elaborate game of persiflage which they play with so much skill seems foolish to Biron. The ladies' wit, so he says, makes

> Wise things seem foolish, rich things poor.

Then he announces his intention of giving up the elaborate verbal juggling of the courtly wooing carried on by the ladies and gentlemen. But he still attacks with the proper urbanity:

Taffeta phrases, silken terms precise,
  Three-pil'd hyperboles, spruce affectation,
Figures pedantical—these summer flies
  Have blown me full of maggot ostentation.
I do forswear them; and I here protest,
  By this white glove (how white the hand,
    God knows!),
Henceforth my wooing mind shall be express'd
  In russet yea's and honest kersey no's.
And to begin: wench, so God help me, law!
My love to thee is sound, sans crack or flaw.
                              (v. ii. 406-15)

This sweeping rejection of the euphuistic and other mannered arts of conversation does not convince the ladies that
Biron has been permanently converted. He has been 'too
replete with music,' too 'full of comparisons and wounding
flouts,' to purge himself thus on a sudden. Time and a radical regimen must complete Biron's reformation. So Rosaline
postpones her answer to even his honest kersey wooing for a
year. In the meantime he is to go every day to

Visit the speechless sick and still converse
With groaning wretches; and your task shall be,
With all the fierce endeavor of your wit
To enforce the pained impotent to smile.
                              (v. ii. 860-63)

Only by such desperate remedies can Biron's gibing spirit be
forever silenced.

So Jack hath not Jill and the play does not end as a
comedy. On the contrary, the scoffing spirit of the piece expresses itself most vividly in the ladies' rejection of their
lovers. Yet the temper of the finale is harmonious with that
which pervades the entire drama and establishes its mood not
of comedy but of good-natured satire.

II

The meaning and force of all this ridicule is perfectly clear in and by itself. However, the audience for which the play was written must have caught in the characters and events of the comedy references to contemporary situations. Even now some of the topical allusions can be understood. The little academe established at Navarre by the king and his gentlemen is probably a satiric equivalent of a coterie—organization is too strong a word—of gentlemen scientists and astronomers grouped about Raleigh and referred to in *Love's Labor's Lost* as The School of Night.[3] Biron confesses that he is in love with the 'black' lady Rosaline. Since brunettes were not accounted beautiful in Elizabethan England, the king exclaims

> O paradox! Black is the badge of hell.
> The hue of dungeons and the school of night.
> (IV. iii. 254-5)

One of the subjects that Navarre and his attendant lords plan to study during their three years of monastic seclusion, as we have seen, is astronomy. And the comedy is filled with references to the sun, the moon, and the stars. There are also innumerable hits at mathematical pretension. The editors of the New Cambridge Shakespeare were the first to note that 'None of the fantastics in this play can count, even upon their fingers.'[4]

The play, with its wealth of astronomical and mathematical allusion, points an accusing finger at the informal group assembled by Raleigh and known now by Shakespeare's nickname, The School of Night.[5] Those who disapproved of the men and their activities gave it a harsher name, first applied to it by the Jesuit Father Parsons—'The School of Atheism.'[6] The intellectual master of the group was the mathematician

Thomas Harriot. He was first a kind of tutor to Sir Walter Raleigh, and at his patron's suggestion went as geographer with the second expedition to Virginia in 1585. Harriot's account of this journey, *A Brief and True Report of the New Found Land of Virginia* is the work upon which his popular reputation is founded. Another scientific member of the group was Lawrence Keymis, a mathematician and geographer. He accompanied Sir Walter on his voyage to Guiana in 1595 and remained thereafter in his service. Other members of the school were the Earl of Northumberland, also a patron of Harriot's and the poets Chapman, Marlowe, and Matthew Royden.

It was Raleigh's interest in navigation that turned the attention of the group to the study of mathematics and astronomy. The impact of the Copernican system and of the even more startling conception of an infinite universe upon these bold minds led them to the free religious speculations which unjustly earned them the name of atheists. The group was thus fair game to a satirist. Moreover, Raleigh was the political rival of the Essex-Southampton faction, with which Shakespeare had some associations. Hence in ridiculing Raleigh's 'school' the dramatist would be feeding the prejudices of his patrons.

The reputed skepticism of Raleigh's coterie, the phase of their speculations which most outraged their contemporaries, Shakespeare completely ignores. It is rather their intellectual pretension that he derides. To him the most ridiculous aspect of these academicians was their assumption of intellectual superiority to everyone else. Their notion that they should live in a world from which women were rigorously excluded was both pedantry and ignorant pride.

Shakespeare's disapproval of the anti-feminism of Navarre and his fellow academicians struck at another important tenet of the creed of the School of Night. Its members regarded the Petrarchan worship of woman as absurd, and eager submission to love as destructive of the intellect. The Earl of Northumberland, to name only one, wrote an essay [7] explaining how he came to give up love for learning, or, as he phrases it, how he forsook his 'finite Mistress' and dedicated himself wholly to his 'infinite worthy mistress.' By making this change he abandoned 'mindes disquiet, attendant servitude . . . loss of time, passion without reason' and other similar tortures, for 'mind's quiet, soul's felicity . . . free from passions, of nothing fearful, in all things happy.' Giordano Bruno, the Italian philosopher who seems to have associated with this group while he was in England, is much more violent on the subject. He opens his *De gli eroici furori*, 1585 (Heroic Enthusiasts), with a headlong attack on the worship of woman. He records 'the perpetual tortures, the heavy torments, the weary thoughts and speeches, the bitter meditations generated beneath the tyranny of an unworthy imbecile, infatuated, wanton, filthy wretch of a woman.' [8]

This attitude we have seen was heresy at the Court of the Virgin Queen. Consequently derision of the systematic attempt of Raleigh and 'his compeers by night' to divorce learning from other and equally important accomplishments of a courtier must have filled with delight the courtly audience for whose entertainment *Love's Labor's Lost* was designed. For such spectators the general satire of pedantry was barbed with the satisfaction of seeing punished the antifeminist contempt of a group of pretentious rebels against the approved conduct of a courtier.

III

The low-comedy figures attached to the plot also display various affectations of learning. The two most important are Holofernes and Armado. Each is a version of one of the masks of Italianate popular comedy, and each displays the

conventionalized qualities of the type.[9] Holofernes is the
'pedante' [schoolmaster] and like his Italian prototype is fond
of uttering proverbs, Latin, and other foreign phrases, and
strange ink-horn terms. In particular, he delights in stringing
together long lists of synonyms. He says that Armado is 'too
pricked, too spruce, too affected, too odd, as it were, too
peregrinate' (v. i. 14-16). He speaks of his own talent for
rhyming as 'a gift that I have, simple, simple; a foolish extravagant spirit, full of forms, figures, objects, ideas, apprehensions, motions, revolutions' (IV. ii. 67-70).

On occasions he talks exactly like a Latin-English dictionary: 'Ripe as the pomwater [a sweet apple], who now hangeth
like a jewell in the ear of *cælo,* the sky, the welkin, the
heaven, and anon falleth like a crab on the face of *terra,* the
soil, the land, the earth' (IV. ii. 3-6). This verbal flourish
throws Sir Nathaniel into an ecstasy of feigned admiration.
'Truly, Master Holofernes,' he cries, 'the epithets are sweetly
varied, like a scholar at the least.' The word 'epithets,' as
Dover Wilson reminds us, 'was a technical term for the synonyms which the master required his boys to supply in as large
a number as possible for the Latin words he might give them
in class.'[10] Thus Holofernes loads his polite conversation
with the routine of the grammar-school classroom. Sometimes he even thinks in grammar. When the country wench
Jaquenetta approaches him and Nathaniel, he turns to the
curate and remarks 'a soul feminine saluteth us' (IV. ii. 83).
He derives even his terms of abuse from his profession. When
Moth, his serving boy, enrages him, he shouts, 'Thou con-
sonant' at him.[11]

Shakespeare's thrusts at the absurd pedantry of an English
grammarian proves that he intended Holofernes to be more
than the stock pedant of the Italian popular comedy. He is
an English schoolmaster, a fellow who spends his life stuffing young boys—and girls, too—with Latin. His school is
called a 'charge-house'; so it is clearly some kind of nonde-

script private venture. His students, unlike those of a grammar school, pay tuition. And it is the follies and stupidities
of such an English schoolmaster that Shakespeare ridicules.
He makes the fellow complacent, pompous, pretentious, iras-
cible, and fatuously susceptible to flattery. The fellow fairly
gulps down the compliments paid him by his hanger-on
Nathaniel, the village curate, although the sycophant's adulation is obvious and crass. When Holofernes has finished
one of the most jejune of his lists of 'epithets,' Nathaniel pretends to be so much impressed that he pulls out his notebook
and writes them down—for future use.

A second conversation between the two old cronies parodies another favorite classroom method of teaching Latin,
one to which Shakespeare himself must have been subjected.
The boys were taught to speak Latin through the oral use
of Latin colloquies or dialogues between master and pupil.
Sir Nathaniel falls into the routine of one of these school
exercises when he begins 'Laus Deo, bone intelligo.' But the
careless pupil has made a mistake and the teacher Holofernes
corrects him in a characteristically pedantic fashion. 'Bone?—
bone for bene! Priscian a little scratched, 'twill serve.' (Priscian, it must be remembered, was a grammarian and the
god of the idolatry of all of his Elizabethan kind.)

> [Enter Armado, Moth and Costard]
> Nathaniel. Videsne qui venit?
> Holofernes. Video et gaudeo.[12]
>   (v. i. 30-34)

A curious dialogue between Moth and Holofernes is based
on a well-known device for teaching little boys the five
vowels. It first appears in one of the most widely used of
these collections of colloquies—the one written by the Spanish educationist Juan Luis Vives and called *Linguae Latinae
Exercitatio*. Vives points out that all five vowels are found in
the Spanish word for sheep, *oveia*. Moth, while teasing Holo-

fernes, gets him to say 'ba.' He then asks Holofernes to re-
peat the five vowels:

> MOTH. The last of the five vowels if 'you' repeat them,
> or the fifth if I.
> HOLOFERNES (*speaking slowly*). I will repeat them—
> a, e, i.
> MOTH. The sheep! The other two concludes it [that is,
> concludes the Spanish word for sheep]—o, u

Moth is trying to get Holofernes to say 'I' so that he can
answer 'o u [sheep]. The jest is labored, but not pointless if
we know that Shakespeare is poking fun at a foolishly ingenious method of teaching a simple matter.

But Holofernes is not only a conceited pedant, he is also
an ignorant one. And his ignorance extends to just those subjects of which he fancies himself a master. He misquotes a
line from one of Mantuan's eclogues—a passage as familiar
to the schoolboys of Shakespeare's generation as *Arma virum-
que cano* is to the modern prep-school boy.[18] Holofernes'
knowledge of music, the elements of which were taught in
every grammar school, is also very faulty. He cannot even
sing the hexachord correctly. 'Re, sol, la, mi, fa' is the confused order in which he hums it. His ideas on etymology
are also grotesquely wrong. 'For the elegancy, facility, and
golden cadence of poesy,' he exclaims. 'Ovidius Naso was the
man. And why indeed Naso, but for smelling out the odor-
iferous flowers of fancy, the jerks of invention' (IV. ii. 126-30).
In this outburst he illustrates also his own powers of invention, the product of his own 'extravagant spirit,' which he
informs the admiring Nathaniel is 'full of forms, figures,
shapes, objects, ideas, apprehensions, motions, revolutions'
(V. ii. 68-70).

But it is his ideas about the correct pronunciation of current English that write him down indelibly as the eternal
learned ignoramus. Being a mere grammarian, he regards

every change in pronunciation as a vulgarism. In particular he abhors simplifications which obscure what he believes to be the Latin etymology of words. He stigmatizes as 'rackers of orthography' those who pronounce 'doubt' and 'debt' with the 'b' silent. 'D-e-b-t not d-e-t,' he exclaims in exasperation. 'Neighbor vocatur nebour,' he continues, 'this is ab-homina-ble, which he would call abbominable' (v. i. 24-8). Holo-fernes resembles the long line of his direct descendants in harassing everyone who uses freely his mother tongue. Like them he asserts clamorously the bogus controls of archaic spelling and of false Latin etymologies over the pronuncia-tion of living speech.

In a series of ruthless strokes like these Shakespeare paints a full-length portrait of a pedantic master of a grammar school. With Holofernes he uses the same satiric method that he employs elsewhere in the comedy. It is the manner of caricature and parody rather than that of formal satire. Each character ridicules himself by the words that issue from his own mouth.

Certain pedants well known to Shakespeare's audience probably suggested some of the characteristics of Holofernes. Since the middle of the eighteenth century [14] John Florio has been the likeliest candidate for this doubtful honor. He is known to us chiefly as the translator of Montaigne. To his learned contemporaries he was the author of an Italian-English dictionary, but to the great mass of Elizabethans he was a fashionable teacher of Italian and the author of hand-books for teaching language by the direct method of typical conversations. From the first this identification of Florio with Holofernes was regarded as improbable. But of late it has been put forward again with new arguments.[15] And it may very well be that on occasions throughout the play Holo-fernes did recall Florio to all who knew the self-important Anglo-Italian.

However, it is a mistake to speak of Florio or anyone else [16] as the 'original' of Holofernes. Shakespeare never devised a character to serve as a portrait or even as an obvious caricature of any of his contemporaries. He may have characterized Holofernes in such a way as to remind a contemporary audience now of Florio, now of Gabriel Harvey, and now of someone else. But Holofernes was primarily an original character, type of the eternal grammarian and pedant, a caricature of the bookish fool who is incapable of learning anything from any of his contacts with reality. As such he enriches the main satiric theme of *Love's Labor's Lost*.

IV

Armado is also both a type figure of Italian comedy and a phenomenon of Elizabethan England. Though he is called a braggart, he displays few characteristics of the farced *miles gloriosus*. He never boasts of warlike achievements, nor of his easy conquest of women. To be sure, he admits he is in love 'and as it is base for a soldier to love, so am I in love with a base wench.' To assuage his amorous torment he has Moth, his boy, enumerate the great men of old who too have been in love. When Moth mentions Samson, Armado exclaims, 'O well-knit Samson! strong-jointed Samson! I do excel thee in my rapier as much as thou didst me in carrying gates. I am in love too' (I. ii. 77-9), and makes similar comments on the ensnared Hercules.

Such shreds and patches of the *miles gloriosus* cling lightly to Armado. They affect in no way his career in the play. The plot does not expose him as a poltroon or as a tricked lover. On most occasions

> Armado is a most illustrious wight,
> A man of fire-new words, fashion's own knight.
> (I. i. 178-9)

He is a refined traveller of Spain,

A man in all the world's new fashion planted,
That hath a mint of phrases in his brain.

(I. i. 164-6)

In these aspects of his character he is the Spanish braggart,
who first grew to comic stature in popular Italian comedy.
In Italy it was inevitable that the braggart soldier of Plautus
and Terence should become a Spaniard. During most of the
sixteenth century, parts of Italy were occupied by the Spanish army. Naturally the native population detested the soldiers of these garrisons, and dramatists writing for its entertainment employed an age-old stage figure as a means of
satirizing the hated Spanish soldier. They converted the
Latin braggart into a Spanish swash-buckler. Since the Cas-
tilian seemed to all other people an absurdly haughty and
ceremonious fellow and a master of grandiloquence, the Italian dramatists chose to deride just these qualities.

Armado, then, is satirized principally because he seems to
have been at some great feast of language and to have stolen
the scraps. His favorite words are polysyllabic, and his favorite phrases smell of the ink-horn. 'Sir,' he says to Holofernes,

> it is the King's most sweet pleasure and affection to
> congratulate the Princess at her pavilion in the pos-
> teriors of this day, which the rude multitude call the
> afternoon . . . For what is inward between us, let
> it pass. I do beseech thee remember thy courtesy.
> I beseech thee apparel thy head . . . For I must tell
> thee it will please his Grace (by the world) sometimes
> to lean upon my poor shoulder, and with his royal fin-
> ger thus dally with my excrement, with my mustachio
> —but sweetheart let that pass.

(v. i. 92-111 *passim*)

Every word of this bombast betrays pompous self-conceit.
In deriding Armado's polysyllabic extravagance, Shakespeare was joining a crusade in which many critics of the
sixteenth century took part. Puttenham in *The Arte of Eng-*

lish Poesie (1589), a treatise that Shakespeare clearly had studied, warns poets against

> inkhorne terms so ill affected brought in by men of learning as preachers and schoolmasters: and many strange termes of other languages by Secretaries and Merchants and travellers and many dark words and not usual or well sounding though they be daily spoken at Court.[17]

Armado, in the speech just quoted, is guilty of all three breaches of good usage. Thus in a manner Shakespeare takes the conservative position of Puttenham and others of like mind, who were determined to prevent the recruitment of the English vocabulary from foreign sources, particularly from Latin and Greek. Importations from the classical tongues to them smelled most of pedantry and were in particular disfavor. George Gascoigne went so far as to urge writers to avoid all polysyllables. 'The more monosyllables that you use,' he says, 'the truer Englishman you shall seeme, and the lesse you shall smell of the Inke horne.' [18]

But Shakespeare's ridicule of Armado is more than a mannered cry of 'Down with the Ink-horn word.' It is his amused comment on a fool's inept imitation of the hospitality extended to new words by nearly every Elizabethan writer. Shakespeare's age was a time of almost complete chaos in its world of words.[19] The coinage of new terms became a kind of conversational sport. Every educated or half-educated person exhibited a passion for verbal experimentation, for lavish importation of foreign expressions. This linguistic freedom greatly enriched the language. Many of the innovations which must have sounded strange to Elizabethan ears are now household words: 'scientific,' 'method,' 'function,' 'refine'—to mention but four of a host. Shakespeare's own verbal inventions, many of which have also become familiar to everyone, were many. But his delight in this ingenuity did not prevent his laughing at those who used the universal linguistic license for display of their own verbal virtuosity. Armado indulges in this sort of ostentation. Only a man with no ear, a man utterly devoid of taste and one ignorant of the genius of his mother tongue to boot, could bring himself to say, 'Dost thou infamonize me among potentates?' (v. ii. 684) for 'Dost thou slander me in this royal presence?' or to address the King in the following outlandish fashion: 'Anointed, I implore so much expense of thy royal sweet breath as will utter a brace of words' (v. ii. 523-5). No wonder the deliberately homely comment of the Princess on this verbal flourish is, 'A speaks not like a man of God his making' (v. ii. 528-9).

Some of Armado's characteristics may have suggested those of a fellow known to some members of Shakespeare's audience. Boyet once describes Armado as

> A phantasime, a Monarcho, and one that makes sport
> To the Prince and his bookmates.
>
> (IV. i. 101-2)

A number of years before (1594-5), the date at which this play was first presented, a fantastic Italian called Monarcho haunted the English Court. As Professor Kittredge says, 'He was a harmless and amusing madman—who was dead by 1580. His resemblance to Armado must have been merely generic.' [20] The suggestion of a likeness between the two was but a flash to bring a fleeting smile to the lips of the courtly audience. It implied no carefully wrought resemblance between the two eccentrics.

Armado, then, was principally the representative of a kind of pedant which was only too familiar to the audience for whom *Love's Labor's Lost* was designed. He adds his grotesque note to the chorus of perverse and self-conscious learning which announces at frequent intervals the theme of the comedy. The intelligent spectator would perhaps be re-

minded now of Raleigh's School of Night, now of the furious
debate between Harvey and Nashe on which was the better
school for authors—academic learning or direct experience
of life. The eccentrics might now and then bring to mind
John Florio, Gabriel Harvey, the Monarcho, or even Tom
Nashe. But Shakespeare intended the minds of his hearers
to be led far beyond such particular identifications as these.
The low comedy characters, like everything else in *Love's
Labor's Lost,* were designed to emphasize the satiric point of
the comedy. They, too, are perspective glasses through which
Shakespeare lets his audience see the absurdity of fanatical
devotion to learning. It cuts the devotee off from the society
of cultivated men and women, where alone the delightful
routines of humane living are to be learned. So these boors
and fools become fit objects of the silvery laughter of Shakespeare satire.

V

Love's Labor's Lost is thus much more than a skillfully
concocted collection of topical references. It establishes
Shakespeare securely on the popular side of the widespread
Renaissance conflict between nature and art. In the play he
laughs us into acknowledging that an ounce of fresh human
experience is worth more than pound upon pound of learning. To be sure he does not take sides in the thorough-going
fashion of the scientists of the new school, who boldly asserted that knowledge comes by observation not by authority. As one of their number announced: 'The true Bible to
read is Nature itself—things as they are are,—not the printed
pages of Galen or another.' Such an adept of the new learning saw that there was an enormous difference between the
abstract speculation of the schools and even the most un-
practical scientific investigation.

The ordinary man, however, in his revolt against pedantic
poring over the authorities, turned against all knowledge

which had no useful end. In this attitude he was encouraged by many of his enlightened teachers. Vives, for example, thinks that a useful inquiry—one that will attend to man's needs—is far more suitable and worthy than 'an investigation as to the measure of the material of the heavens.' [21] Fulke Greville in his crabbed poem 'Treatie of Humane Learning' expresses the same idea in a form more nearly like Shakespeare's own:

> What a right line is, the learned know;
> But how availes that him, who in the right
> Of life, and manners doth desire to grow? [22]

Shakespeare belongs to this popular branch of the new philosophy. He ridicules those who forsake the 'Nature' of experience for the 'Art' of theory, tradition, authority and speculation:

> Small have continual plodders ever won
> Save base authority from others' books.
>
> (I. i. 86-7)

Yet to him scientific astronomers were no less absurd than learned schoolmen. For they, too, completely withdrew themselves from the affairs of living men and women. Though their learning was written in the stars instead of in ancient tomes, it was no less a form of pedantry. Shakespeare, then, revolts against the worship of authority not in the name of the humanism that exalted learning, but of the humanism that exalted humane living. Any sort of learning or wit which became entangled in its own toils was fair game for Shakespeare's ridicule. The spirit in which he derides all self-entertainments of a brain that has ceased to preside over the whole life of man is the same as that expressed in one stanza of Raleigh's poem, *The Lie:*

> Tell wit how much it wrangles,
> in tickle points of nycenesse,

Tell wisedome she entangles
herself in over-wisenesse.
And when they doe reply,
straight give them both the lie.[23]

In *Love's Labor's Lost*, Shakespeare carries out Raleigh's instructions, doubtless to the infinite satisfaction of the Queen and her entourage. The playwright paid off intellectual pretension and pedantry right enough. Besides, he had the tact to hurl his barbed shafts of ridicule against the enemies of the gracious ways of life which the Virgin Queen fostered and glorified in her Court. *Love's Labor's Lost* thus overlays some of the soundest wisdom of the Renaissance with laughter congenial to devotees of regally approved social artifice.

III

As You Like It

In *As You Like It* (1600) and *Twelfth Night* (1601), we enter a brave new world of comedy. These plays reveal a larger poetic reach and an ampler view of human absurdity than Shakespeare's earlier comedies. In them, too, the dramatist seasons romance with a liberal admixture of satire. Two events in the world of letters at the turn of the century suggested to Shakespeare ways of making pungent his satiric spice.

The first was the order of 1 June 1599, already referred to, which suppressed the formal satires of a number of authors mentioned by name and prohibited the further printing of any satires or epigrams.[1] Despite these vigorous efforts at suppression, the ecclesiastical censors did not succeed in forcing into duress the satiric spirit then abroad in English literature. Almost immediately dramatists, led by Ben Jonson, devised a form of comedy which preserved the subject matter, the salutary purpose, and the methods of the proscribed literary form. Shakespeare was perfectly familiar with this contest between ecclesiastical authorities and rebellious artists. He observed the struggle with the detachment of a great artist and transformed into high comedy some of the issues of the quarrel. He went even further, and adapted to his own uses the devices which Jonson invented to circumvent the angry suppression of the bishops.

While Shakespeare was composing *As You Like It,* a change took place in the personnel of his company which exerted almost as much influence upon his methods of writing comedy as did the progress of the satiric movement. In 1599 Will Kemp left the Lord Chamberlain's Men to be succeeded by Robert Armin. As we have seen, Shakespeare had provided Kemp with parts filled with more and more amusing ridicule of folly. Beginning as the conventional type figure of the stupid lout, the talented comedian had gradually been promoted to parts like the Bastard and Falstaff, in which he could give rein to a keen spirit of joyous satire. Kemp's successor, Robert Armin, by the time he entered the company had developed a different clownish line. Hence Kemp's departure forced Shakespeare to abandon one of his most successful forms of comic invention in order to create parts better suited to Armin's peculiar talents.

For these reasons the satire in *As You Like It* is quite different from that which Shakespeare had introduced into his earlier comedies. An informed reader of the play soon realizes that the dramatist was thoroughly familiar with the temper and achievements of the satiric movement in poetry which came to an abrupt end in 1599. As for the low comedy in *Twelfth Night,* that reflects a later development of the satiric movement, its successful invasion of comedy.

Though disturbed social conditions in England gave the initial impulse to the satiric movement, once launched, it slavishly imitated Latin satire, particularly the work of Persius and Juvenal. Some members of this English school—Sir John Davies, Sir John Harington, Thomas Bastard, and John Weaver—wrote only epigrams. Though their master Martial composed epigrams of many sorts, they seem to have been aware only of his satiric vein. Hence an epigram to them was merely a short satire, less severe in tone. It attacked social absurdity rather than sin.

The self-declared satirists were guilty of no such mildness. They assumed the role of ardent reformers dedicated to the exposure of vice. In their efforts to approximate the *saeva indignatio* of Juvenal, they struck attitudes of exaggerated severity. They pretended to wield the lash and the scourge or to operate the rack and the strappado—all instruments of legal torture or punishment. The following lines from Joseph Hall's collection of satires, called *Virgidemiarum* (a harvest of rods, i.e. blows), describes the methods of the entire group:

> The *Satyre* should be like the Porcupine,
> That shoots sharp quilles out in each angry line,
> And wounds with blushing cheeke, and fiery eye
> Of him that heares, and readeth guiltily.[2]

Men dedicated to this high task seldom tried to provoke laughter, for they had marked themselves as melancholy's own. They were proud to be malcontents, proud to voice their profound dissatisfaction with life in bitter diatribes against the state of man. Yet they found the conduct of fools absurd enough to move them to a kind of mirthless laughter which offered momentary relief to their gloomy boredom. Marston knew how to lighten his discontent in this way:

> From out the sadness of my discontent,
> Hating my wonted jocund merriment,
> (Only to give dull time a swifter wing),
> Thus scorning scorn, of idiot fools I sing.[3]

The members of this English school repeatedly asserted that their satires were always impersonal, that they attacked not individuals but general faults. Therefore only those guilty of the follies assailed were justified in taking umbrage at any particular charge. Lodge, in a preface to *A Fig for Momus,* thus explains the significance of the poems in the volume: 'In them (under the names of certain Romaines) where I reprehend vice, I purposely wrong no man, but observe the lawes of that kind of poeme [that is, a satire]. If any repine thereat, I am sure he is guiltie, because he bewrayeth himself.'[4] Such a pronouncement was intended to close the mouths of everyone who objected to any expression of the wrathful spirit then abroad. Jaques, we shall see, represents

Shakespeare's idea of one of these satirists of the old school. In characterizing him the dramatist expresses his opinion of the entire group. But Jaques' temper is quite unlike that which establishes the tone of *As You Like It*. It is just because his sour comments on life are discordant with the spirit of Arden that they are so arresting.

The comedy, as everyone knows, is the dramatization of a very popular pastoral romance, Thomas Lodge's *Rosalynde*, first published in 1590. It should be, therefore, completely romantic in key. To be sure, heroic adventures told at length in the novel do not appear in the comedy. Such incidents as the capture of the heroine by a band of robbers and her subsequent rescue by the hero and her brother were obviously too violent for the atmosphere of a pastoral play. But Orlando is the typical love-shaken, sonneteering lover of romance. Rosalind and Celia are the perfect friends of idealistic fiction. That they are women is a late Renaissance variation of the conventional theme. Adam is the extravagantly loyal retainer of medieval tale, representing 'the constant service of the antique world.' The play is also filled with surprising adventures and strange incidents, and it ends, as all romantic comedies should, with marriages galore.

II

Yet as a reader explores more deeply the meaning of the play, he finds in it much besides the high spirits and thoughtless gaiety of pure romance. Externally the setting is that of a conventional pastoral play. The forest is full of shepherds, foresters, and other creatures who could live together only in an Elysium of escape from the real world. But the Forest of Arden is no mirage of wish-fulfilment. It is not like the world of Italian pastoral romance, not a country in which the longings of those bored with city life were realized. It is an actual English woodland through which real winds blow, a region near the haunts of Robin Hood and his merry men.

This is the place to which Orlando and Rosalind flee when driven away from society by injustice and tyranny. They hope to find in the Forest of Arden that life in accord with nature which they had read about in some Italian pastoral. The escapist return to nature was the theme of Sannazaro's *Arcadia* and of Tasso's *Aminta*. The authors of these works celebrate a natural habitat of dreamy indolence and idyllic freedom, where none of the restraints and artifices of society prevail. Erasmus in his *Praise of Folly,* taking the side of nature as against art, writes, 'Nature hates all false coloring and is ever best where she is least adulterated with art.' [5]

It is the Nature imagined by such writers that Orlando and Rosalind seek in the Forest of Arden. And what creatures do they find there? They meet characters who belong to the most artificial of all worlds of fiction, the pastoral romance. Silvius, the sighing love-sick swain, is there, and Phebe, the obstinately chaste shepherdess. So are William and Audrey, neither of whom has ever been washed by the romantic imagination or any other known cleansing agent. They are the shepherd and his lass as they really are, ignorant dirty louts— simple folk who know nothing but what Nature has taught them. 'Here,' says Shakespeare, 'are two authentic children of Nature.' This is the heterogeneous company to which Rosalind and Orlando must belong if they prefer Arcadia to the artifices of civilized life. The play thus ridicules the belief that life close to Nature is best. The comedy is, as Joseph Wood Krutch says, a 'playfully satiric fantasy on the idea of the simple life.'

III

In this utopian pastoral world the fugitives also come upon the melancholy Jaques. He has no counterpart in Lodge's novel; he is entirely Shakespeare's invention. Because his only part in the comedy is to stand aloof from the action and

make satiric comment upon all that happens, critics have
been tempted to regard him as Shakespeare's mouthpiece.
Many readers have therefore mistaken the famous soliloquy
beginning 'All the world's a stage' for a succinct revelation
of the pessimism which captured Shakespeare's mind about
1600. Life to him, they say, had then become just the pageant
of futility of the melancholy Jaques' vision.

This is a naïve view of a highly effective dramatic figure—
one that had become a popular stage type. Jaques is Shakespeare's representative of the traveller recently returned from
a sojourn on the continent, laden with boredom and histrionic pessimism.[6] His melancholy is artificial and his disgust
with everything at home is a pose.

John Marston in his second satire portrayed in Bruto one
of the earliest representatives of the fraternity. The fellow has
come home from abroad to view every phase of English life
with a jaundiced eye:

> Look, look, with what a discontented grace
> Bruto, the traveller doth sadly pace.
> 'Long Westminster! . . .
>
> .   .   .
>
> And now he sighs: 'O thou corrupted age,
> Which slight regard'st men of sound carriage!
> Virtue, knowledge, fly to heaven again;
> Deign not 'mong these ungrateful sots remain! [7]

This bilious scorn arouses the righteous anger of Marston,
the censor. Pointing the finger of scorn at Bruto, he accuses
him of having lived the life of a libertine while abroad and
of mistaking his sick venom for moral indignation:

> .   .   . O worthless puffy slave!
> Did thou to Venice go ought else to have,
> But buy a lute and use a courtesan,
>
> .   .   .
>
> Well, then exclaim not on our age, good man,
> But hence, polluted Neapolitan.[8]

Bruto's morbid scorn is the distinguishing bias of the malcontent traveller; and Marston's attitude toward him is the exasperated disapproval of the formal satirist. To be sure Bruto displays none of the foppery which frequently characterized the type. Nor does he exhibit the usual hotch-potch of foreign fashions in dress and in manners. But the harvest of his travels has been even more corrupting. He has learned all about the graces of Venetian courtesans and the newest forms of old vices, but nothing of the new humanism. In fact his experiences have polluted both his mind and his body. This is the reason that he is bored with London life, that he scorns everything English. This is the reason that melancholy has settled down upon him like a cloud.

It is true that in Shakespeare's day melancholy was thought often to be an affectation, an imitation of a foreign fashion. Shakespeare makes Prince Arthur in *King John* say:

> Yet I remember, when I was in France,
> Young gentlemen would be as sad as night
> Only for wantonness.
>
> (IV. i. 14-16)

But the travellers' melancholy was sometimes clearly a mental disorder produced by the diseases they had contracted while abroad. It was an unnatural melancholy [9] caused by what the Elizabethans called adustion, but what we should diagnose as a persistent fever. The doctors believed that a melancholy disposition heated by high temperature produced that mixture of understanding and imagination which made its possessor prone to figurative and sententious utterance.[10]

Jaques exhibits all the characteristics of the type, except the foppery. His licentious life abroad has fired his naturally phlegmatic nature to a point at which he can make pithy comment upon the ridiculous spectacle of life even as it is lived in the Forest of Arden.[11] Being by temperament averse to action, he has plenty of leisure for meditation upon the ways of mankind. And his pathological melancholy renders him incapable of taking delight in anything he sees or hears. Life, so he believes, is nothing but folly and futility. In brief, Jaques is a malcontent traveller anatomized according to the approved psychology of Shakespeare's day.

Jaques' utterances resemble those of the typical returned traveller, except that they are directed not so much against the corrupted age as against all human life. Moreover Shakespeare's superior eloquence gives Jaques' tirades a poetic sincerity which is easily mistaken for the author's passionate convictions. This has been particularly true of his most famous soliloquy, a speech which expresses more than the disillusionment of an old roué. Its pessimism, though profound, is relieved by flashes of humor. The whining schoolboy creeping like snail unwillingly to school; the lover sighing like furnace; the justice full of wise saws and modern instances; the futility of each of these human creatures is drawn with broad ludicrous strokes. The satire levelled against them is seasoned with laughter.

It should now be clear that, like all of his fellow malcontent travellers, Jaques is usually the object of his author's ridicule, but on occasions he is just as clearly the mouthpiece of Shakespeare's own satiric comment. In playing this dual role he combines the functions of two characters who had appeared in some plays written just before *As You Like It* was produced, notably Labesha and Dowsecer in Chapman's *An Humorous Day's Mirth*.[12] The first was a social would-be who affected melancholy because the pose was fashionable. The second was a man of strong native intelligence whose mind had nevertheless been invaded by melancholy. As a result, his intellect had been put into the service of a misanthropic spirit. His insight enabled him to ferret out hidden abuses in society and absurdities in human beings. But his persistent low spirits filled his just comments with so much bitterness that they seemed ludicrously exaggerated. Jaques is an amalgam of the two types. He is both affected malcontent and true melancholiac.

In the first role Jaques is self-conscious about his melancholy and proud of its singularity. He warms to self-analysis when he explains his humor to Rosalind:

> 'I have neither the scholar's melancholy, which is emulation; nor the musician's, which is fantastical; nor the courtier's, which is proud; . . . but it is a melancholy of mine own, compounded of many simples, extracted from many objects; and indeed the sundry contemplation of my travels, in which my often rumination wraps me in a most humorous sadness.'
>
> (IV. i. 10-20)

It is his travels on the continent, of this he is sure, that have reduced him to habitual gloom and melancholy reflection. Rosalind immediately recognizes him as a disillusioned traveller:

> 'Farewell, Monsieur Traveller,' she cries. 'Look, you lisp and wear strange suits, disable all the benefits of your own country, be out of love with your nativity, and almost chide God for making you that countenance you are; or I will scarce think you have swam in a gondola.'
>
> (IV. i. 32-7)

Like Bruto and the rest of his kind, Jaques has been a libertine and the Duke attacks him for his career of vice as sharply as Marston had his Bruto. No more unworthy incentive to satire, asserts the Duke, could be found:

> Most mischievous foul sin, in chiding sin.
> For thou thyself hast been a libertine,
> As sensual as the brutish sting itself;
> And all the embossed sores and headed evils
> That thou with license of free foot hast caught,
> Wouldst thou disgorge into the general world.
>
> (II. vii. 64-9)

IV

Jaques, then, is for the most part Shakespeare's portrait of
a familiar satiric type. But on occasions he becomes something much more significant. He stands forth as an amusing
representative of the English satirists whose works streamed
from the press during the years from 1592 to 1599 inclusive.
Jaques enunciates the critical doctrines of these writers in a
form only a little exaggerated.

The satirists took great pains to justify the critical freedom
which they assumed by insisting that their satire was all impersonal. They attacked the vice, not the individual. Sir
John Davies in one of his epigrams states this principle with
becoming terseness:

> But if thou find any so grosse and dull,
> That think I do to private taxing leane,
> Bid him go hang, for he is but a gull
> And knowes not what an epigramme doth meane:
> Which taxeth under a particular name,
> A general vice that merits publike blame.[13]

Marston in his prose epilogue to *The Scourge of Villainy*
protects himself in a still more unassailable manner: 'Let this
protestation satisfy our curious searchers; so may I obtain my
best hopes, as I am free from endeavouring to blast any private man's good name. If anyone (forced with his own guilt)
will turn it home, and say, " 'Tis I" I cannot hinder him;
neither do I injure him.' [14]

Jaques in one of his soliloquies expands and illustrates this
tenet of the satiric school with his characteristic imaginative
reach.

> Why, who cries out on pride
> That can therein tax any private party?
> Doth it not flow as hugely as the sea
> Till that the wearer's very means do ebb?
> What woman in the city do I name

When that I say the city woman bears
The cost of princes on unworthy shoulders?
Who can come in and say that I mean her,
When such a one as she, such is her neighbour?
Or what is he of basest function
That says his bravery is not on my cost,
Thinking that I mean him, but therein suits
His folly to the mettle of my speech?
There then! how then? what then? Let me see wherein
My tongue hath wrong'd him. If it do him right,
Then he hath wrong'd himself. If he be free,
Why, then my taxing like a wild goose flies,
Unclaim'd of any man.

(II. vii. 70-87)

The formal satirists also filled their work with expressions
of fierce zeal to purge the world of its foulness. Asper's threat
in *Every Man Out of his Humor* is a succinct expression of
the mood:

> I'll strip the ragged follies of the time,
> Naked, as at our birth.[15]

Marston in the Prologue to *The Scourge of Villainy* goads
himself into a fury of punitive enthusiasm:

> Now grim Reproof, swell in my rough-hued rhyme
> That thou mayst vex the guilty of our time.
> (Satire III. ll. 1-2)

> I bear the scourge of Just Rhamnusia,
> Lashing the lewdness of Britannia.
> Let others sing as their good genius moves,
> Of deep designs or else of clipping loves:
>
> .   .   .
>
> But as for me, my vexèd thoughtful soul
> Takes pleasure in displeasing sharp control.[16]

All of the satirists at frequent intervals echo these expressions of moral fervor. And Jaques joins their chorus, crying:

> . . . Give me leave
> To speak my mind, and I will through and through

Cleanse the foul body of the infected world,
If they will patiently receive my medicine.

(II. vii. 58-61)

These resemblances between Jaques and the English satirists have led some critics to believe that he is portrait of Sir
John Harington,[17] Ben Jonson,[18] or some other author famous at the moment. But Jaques is not a caricature of any
one satirist. He is merely a character through whom Shakespeare expresses his unfavorable opinion of the entire group.

The dramatist manipulates his dramatic action in such a
way that Jaques' sour generalities are immediately shown to
be ridiculously false. The wretched malcontent urges Orlando 'to rail against our mistress the world and all our
misery' just before the lover meets his Rosalind for a joyous
antiphonal. The poet also places the famous soliloquy of the
seven ages of man in a context which neutralizes its tone and
contradicts all its assumptions. Adam's hunger and Orlando's
desperation stimulate Jaques' cynical review of the seven
futile stages of man's life. But the Duke's sympathy and
benevolence turn the woeful pageant into a scene of content-
ment and joy. Amien's song which follows undergoes the
same transformation. He begins with a lyric variation on
Jaques' eternal theme.

> Blow, blow, thou winter wind,
> Thou art not so unkind
> As man's ingratitude.
>
> (II. vii. 174-6)

But this mood artfully reminiscent of court life cannot sur-
vive in the sunlight of Arden. It cannot persist to the end of
any of the stanzas ostensibly dedicated to lamentation. They
all close with:

> Then, heigh ho, the holly!
> This life is most jolly.

In such indirect ways the play at every turn is made to contradict the skillfully turned phrases of the pessimist. Events reveal him as blind to the realities of the world into which he has intruded. Shakespeare's ridicule of Jaques is in this way much more significant than derision of a roué's scorn of life in England. It is amused disapproval of the head-long moral ardor which the satirists in both poem and play felt or pretended to feel. Such a temper, Shakespeare says, is ridiculous and utterly destructive to the comic spirit.

v

Touchstone's name suggests that he and not Jaques is the sound critic of folly. He serves as a motley measure of the actions of everyone else in the forest. Shakespeare almost surely designed the part for Kemp, but was forced to insert into the role opportunities for Robert Armin to display his peculiar talents. Accordingly Touchstone's part gives scope to the characteristic business of both of these different impersonators of the clown. While providing business for Will Kemp Shakespeare allows Touchstone to ridicule through travesty. In one of his first encounters with Jaques he parodies the malcontent's pessimistic philosophical bent. The clown, too, knows how to 'moralize every spectacle.' A glance at his timepiece is enough to set him off on a train of gloomy reflections quite in Jaques' manner:

> And then he drew a dial from his poke,
> And looking on it with lack-lustre eye,
> Says very wisely, 'It is ten o'clock.
> Thus we may see,' quoth he, 'how the world wags.
> 'Tis but an hour ago since it was nine,
> And after one hour more 'twill be eleven;
> And so, from hour to hour, we ripe and ripe;
> And then from hour to hour we rot and rot,
> And thereby hangs a tale.'
>
> (II. vii. 20-28)

This sally makes Jaques' lungs 'To crow like chanticleer' to think 'That fools should be so deep contemplative.' Obviously he would not have laughed at all if he had realized that Touchstone's soliloquy was a bold caricature of his own dry strictures on mankind.

Touchstone also discovers a way to turn our laughter against Jaques' languid recollections of his life in the great world. He pretends that he too has been a courtier. The account of his adventures in high society forms a brief appendage to the vast body of literature devoted to satire of the court. 'I have trod a measure,' he boasts, 'I have flattered a lady; I have been polite with my friend, smooth with mine enemy, I have undone three tailors; I have had four quarrels, and like to have fought one' (v. iv. 44-8). Then he proceeds to show that he knows how to quarrel 'in print'; 'For courtiers,' says he, 'learn the art of quarreling, as they learn good manners, from books.' He makes elaborate distinctions between the 'Retort Courteous,' the 'Quip Modest,' the 'Reply Churlish,' and so forth, parodying Italian handbooks on duelling which enumerated the quarrels properly leading to a challenge.

Shakespeare almost surely had one particular treatise in mind when he penned these absurd speeches of Touchstone. It was the second volume of Vincentio Saviola's book on duelling, the title of which was translated into English as 'Of honor and honorable quarrels.' [19] To this, as to all Touchstone's sallies made in Jaques' presence, the malcontent plays the condescending patron, completely unaware that his histrionic melancholy is being ridiculed by every word that his protégé utters.

Touchstone is also greatly amused at the proofs that the lovesick shepherd Silvius gives of the authenticity of his passion for Phebe. Silvius laments:

If thou rememb'rest not the slightest folly
That ever love did make thee run into,
Thou hast not lov'd.
Or if thou hast not sat as I do now,
Wearing thy hearer in thy mistress' praise,
Thou hast not lov'd.
Or if thou hast not broke from company
Abruptly, as my passion now makes me,
Thou hast not lov'd. O Phebe, Phebe, Phebe!

(II. iv. 33-41)

This complaint reminds Touchstone of the courtly homage
he once paid to his rustic sweetheart, Jane Smile:

I remember, when I was in love I broke my sword
upon a stone and bid him take that for coming a-night
to Jane Smile; and I remember the kissing of her bat-
let, and the cow's dugs that her pretty chopt hands had
milk'd; and I remember the wooing of a peascod instead of her, from whom I took two cods, and giving
her them again, said with weeping tears, 'Wear these
for my sake.' We that are true lovers run into strange
capers; but as all is mortal in nature, so is all nature in
love mortal in folly.

(II. iv. 41-50)

In even grosser fashion he parodies Orlando's love poem to
Rosalind:

If a hart do lack a hind,
Let him seek out Rosalinde.
If the cat will after kind,
So be sure will Rosalinde.
Winter garments must be lin'd,
So must slender Rosalinde.
They that reap must sheaf and bind,
Then to cart with Rosalinde.
Sweetest nut hath sourest rind,
Such a nut is Rosalinde.
He that sweetest rose will find
Must find love's prick, and Rosalinde.

(III. ii. 99-110)

His wooing and final marriage with Audrey is a caricature
of the lavish inappropriate mating which, in the manner of
all romantic comedies, takes place at the end of *As You Like
It*. Leading in the loutish Audrey, he explains in his own
inimitable manner why he has chosen her: 'I press in here,
sir, amongst the rest of the country copulatives, to swear and
to forswear, according as marriage binds and blood breaks.
A poor virgin, sir, an ill-favored thing, sir, but mine own.
A poor humor of mine, sir, to take that that no man else will.
Rich honesty, dwells like a miser, sir, in a poor house, as
your pearl in your foul oyster' (v. iv. 53-60). This speech is
better evidence than the appearance of Hymen himself that
Shakespeare was poking fun at the hurry-scurry unions usually made in the last scene of a romantic comedy. When
Hymen announces:

> Here's eight must take hands
> To join in Hymen's bands,

what mortal can resist? When Touchstone crowds in among
'the country copulatives' with Audrey, who can still believe
that the marriages with which a romantic comedy winds up
its sentimental business were made in Heaven?

Touchstone, as the Duke says, 'uses his folly like a stalking
horse and under the presentation of that he shoots his wit'
(v. iv. 111-13). This remark suggests that Touchstone is in
part the kind of court fool which Robert Armin liked best
to impersonate. Since Shakespeare before he finished *As You
Like It* knew that Touchstone would be played not by Kemp
but by Armin, he revised the part by inserting into it some
of the witty nonsense which was Armin's forte.

Armin in a book called *Foole upon Foole or Six Sortes of
Sottes* [20] reveals a fascination for this type of innocent that
must have been life-long. He describes the antics of six sim-
pletons, five of whom were jesters attached to great households or to royal courts. One of them, Jemy Camber, dis-

ported himself in the Scottish court; another, Will Sommers, was King Henry VIII's natural jester. The sixth member of the fraternity, 'John of the Hospital,' was no court-fool at all, but a fellow whom Armin calls 'an innocent idiot.' When this John was but a 'foole of a childe,' he used to lead a poor blind woman named Alice about the streets of London. When Alice became helpless, the city provided asylum for her and John in Christ's Hospital; and after Alice's death he was allowed to stay there as a 'fostered fatherless child.' The follies of this idiot were nothing but crass stupidities like the following: The sexton of Christ's Church 'would often set John aworke, to towle the bell to prayers or burials, wherein he delighted much.' Once when the sexton was not on hand Jack got hold of the bell-rope and pulled it lustily. When the people came to discover who was dead 'They saye, "Wherefore towles the bell, John?" "I know not." "When dyed hee?" "Even now." "Who, John, who?" "My mistress' chicken," quoth he, and laughes.' [21]

This sort of good-natured stupidity Armin thought just as entertaining as the studied jesting of a court-fool. A sentence in which Armin describes 'the fat foole,' Jemy Camber, explains the pleasure which our ancestors extracted from their colloquies with the fools. 'They reason with him,' he writes, 'to understand his wit, which indeed was just none at all, yet merry and pleasing, whereat the King rejoiced.'

This sentence proves that the unintentional stupidities of the jesters formed but a small part of their professional stock in trade. In their less spontaneous moments they propounded riddles, as did Will Sommers when he was at his wit's end to dispel King Harry's melancholy. When practicing their art most happily, they turned the Socratic method of catechizing to their own merry purposes. They were skillful in trapping their interlocutors into assenting to trenchant personal and social satire. Robert Armin, we know, used to impersonate naturals like one of his six sorts of sots. He in-

troduced Jack of the Hospital into his play *The Two Maides
of Moreclacke* with the idea of casting himself in the role.
It was inevitable then, that, when Shakespeare began to write
parts for Armin, he should invent characters able to capi-
talize the special talents of his new actor.[22] It is also natural
that Shakespeare should have extended and deepened the
satiric and comic possibilities of the court-fool.

Viola in *Twelfth Night* describes the nature of the comment that Shakespeare designed for Armin:

> This fellow is wise enough to play the fool,
> And to do that craves a kind of wit.
> He must observe their mood on whom he jests,
> The quality of the persons and the time;
>
>   .   .   .
>
> . . . This is a practice
> As full of labor as a wise man's art;
> For folly that he wisely shows, is fit.
>
>   (III. i. 67-70, 71-3)

Antonio in Marston's *Antonio's Revenge* emphasizes another
characteristic of the fool's ridicule—its apparently complete
freedom from emotion:

> He is not capable of passion
> Wanting the power of distinction,
> He bears an unturned sail to every wind.
> Blow east, blow west, he stirs his course alike.
> I never saw a fool so lean. The chub-faced fop
> Shines sleek with full-cramm'd fat of happiness
> Whilst studious contemplation sucks the juice
> From wisards' [wise-men's] cheeks.[23]

Touchstone in a few scenes arouses laughter by Armin's
favorite devices. Like Will Sommers and the rest of Armin's
ninnies in their better moments, Touchstone seeks to amuse
by a combination of impudence and verbal shiftiness. And
beneath his carefully prepared catechisms, satire invariably
lurks. The following colloquy is completely typical:

CEL. Were you made the messenger?

TOUCH. No, by mine honour; but I was bid to come for you.

ROS. Where learned you that oath, fool?

TOUCH. Of a certain knight that swore by his honour they were good pancakes, and swore by his honour the mustard was naught. Now I'll stand to it, the pancakes were naught, and the mustard was good, and yet was not the knight forsworn.

CEL. How prove you that in the great heap of your knowledge?

ROS. Ay, marry, now unmuzzle your wisdom.

TOUCH. Stand you both forth now. Stroke your chins, and swear by your beards that I am a knave.

CEL. By our beards (if we had them), thou art.

TOUCH. By my knavery (if I had it), then I were. But if you swear by that that is not, you are not forsworn. No more was this knight, swearing by his honour, for he never had any; or if he had, he had sworn it away before ever he saw those pancakes or that mustard.

CEL. Prithee, who is't that thou mean'st?

TOUCH. One that old Frederick, your father, loves.

(I. ii. 62-87)

This apparent nonsense contains ridicule of swearing and forswearing with a final thrust at the perfidy of Duke Frederick.

Some of Touchstone's encounters with the simple creatures of the Forest of Arden are cast in just this key. When he seeks to discover whether Corin has any philosophy in him, his object is not so much to make a fool of the old shepherd as to take a fling at the pretensions of court life. And he does so by ironical praise:

TOUCH. . . . Wast ever in court, shepherd?

COR. No, truly.

TOUCH. Then thou art damn'd.

COR. Nay, I hope.

TOUCH. Truly thou art damn'd, like an ill-roasted egg, all on one side.

COR. For not being at court? Your reason.

TOUCH. Why, if thou never wast at court, thou never saw'st good manners; if thou never saw'st good manners, then thy manners must be wicked; and wickedness is sin, and sin is damnation. Thou art in a parlous state, shepherd.

(III. ii. 33-45)

With Audrey, too, he takes the same tack. He begins, talking ostensibly to her but really for the benefit of Jaques, who is eavesdropping on the pair:

TOUCH. When a man's verses cannot be understood, nor a man's good wit seconded with the forward child, understanding, it strikes a man more dead than a great reckoning in a little room. Truly, I would the gods had made thee poetical.

AUD. I do not know what poetical is. Is it honest in deed and word? Is it a true thing?

TOUCH. No, truly; for the truest poetry is the most feigning, and lovers are given to poetry; and what they swear in poetry may be said, as lovers, they do feign.

AUD. Do you wish then that the gods had made me poetical?

TOUCH. I do truly. For thou swear'st to me thou art honest. Now if thou wert a poet, I might have some hope thou didst feign.

AUD. Would you not have me honest?

TOUCH. No, truly, unless thou wert hard-favour'd; for honesty coupled to beauty is to have honey a sauce to sugar.

(III. iii. 12-31)

This is more than big talk designed to confuse and baffle poor Audrey. It is jesting at the expense of poets—the jesting of a fellow whose wit cavorts like a clown among the dancing words of his vocabulary.

The presence of Jaques and Touchstone in the Forest of Arden makes it a sort of satirists' haven from which they can hurl comment back upon the artificial world from which they have happily escaped. The natural world of Arden is no sylvan Paradise. The natives of the forest are either literary types exaggerated out of all possible human semblance, or crude earthy rustics. In such a motley company the melancholy Jaques, a burlesqued representative of the English satirists, does not seem out of place. In Arden his histrionic pessimism, wounding no one, is clearly presumptious and irrelevant to the life he observes. It is patently an infirmity of his jaundiced eye. Touchstone's comments, on the other hand, harmonize with the spirit of Arden. His taxing 'like a wild goose flies unclaimed of any man.'

Shakespeare in *As You Like It* has added a new interest to romantic comedy by providing his spectators with satiric glasses which distort all the characters and all that they do. The faces even of Jaques and Touchstone seem slightly awry as we behold them through these lenses, for even these figures have been fashioned to fit into the whimsically conceived life of Arden. Like their truly pastoral companions, they are thus twice removed from the harsh world of reality. The follies which they half represent and half deride arouse no bitterness. Their satire, devoid of the venom distilled by human envy, is mollified to harmonize with Shakespeare's characteristically humane spirit of ridicule. It does not submerge the love story; it only gives it the charm of psychic distance. *As You Like It,* enriched by a union of romance with a joyous critical attitude, stands forth as a romantic comedy to please both the simple and the subtle-minded among the spectators composing an audience either in Shakespeare's day or in ours.

IV

'Humor' Characters

THE first agents of Shakespeare's satire were, as we have seen, his louts and clowns. The first objects of his systematic ridicule were 'humor' figures. In selecting these somewhat mechanically conceived eccentrics for his victims, he followed the lead of certain dramatists who began to write in the last decade of the sixteenth century, notably George Chapman and Ben Jonson. Employing the world-old psychological theory of humors, they developed a very effective comic technique for ridiculing absurd human beings.

The term 'humor' seems to have come into common use about the year 1592 as a substitute for 'temperament' or 'complexion,' words which up to that time had been used to denominate the distinguishing characteristic of a man's nature.[1] The theory that the personality of a human being was sanguine, phlegmatic, choleric, or melancholy, as one of the four humors predominated in his bodily composition, was as old as Galen, the celebrated Greek physician of the second century. The system, still universally accepted in Shakespeare's day, was thoroughly expounded in the many handbooks of medicine, one of which was a cherished possession of almost every middle-class Elizabethan household.

In popular parlance the term 'humor' did not long retain its technical meaning of psychological master-bias rooted in the very nature of the individual. It came more often to describe a mere eccentricity or foolish mannerism. But the most common meaning of the word was that explained by Cash in *Every Man in His Humour*. To Cob's question,

'What is this humour?' 'It's some rare thing I warrant,' Cash replies, 'Marry I'll tell thee what it is (as 'tis generally received in these days): it is a monster bred in a man by self-love and affectation, and fed by folly.' ²

A 'humor' figure thus came to be a man impervious to everything in the world except the folly which dominated him. He was a creature ridden by idiosyncrasy. Characters much like these 'humorous' figures first appear in some of the morality plays. Abstract vices or virtues, as soon as they became only a little humanized, developed a family likeness to humor types. For example, in Lodge's *Wits Miserie* (1596) a character called Scandale and Detraction, who begins as a personification of Detraction, becomes our familiar malcontent traveller, obsessed by his humor to find fault with everything in England.

Humor characters with this mixed ancestry began to appear frequently in every type of literature written during the 1590's, but the first work properly called a humor play was George Chapman's *An Humorous Day's Mirth* (1597). The structure which Chapman gave this play was modeled on that of John Heywood's *Play of the Wether* (1535). As the Vice Merry Report in Heywood's farce, partly to satisfy his appetite for vulgar jesting and partly to amuse his master Jupiter, points with a leer at the folly of each petitioner for the kind of weather he needs, so Lemot, the King's witty minion in Chapman's comedy, exploits and exposes the humor of many an eccentric fellow at the royal court.

Early in the play Lemot announces, for the benefit of all, just what he expects to do: 'Thus will I sit and point out all my humorous companions.' Though he thus clearly designates himself as the principal scoffer at folly, he has been provided with a sprightly assistant named Lavel. The two together contrive the half-comic, half-satiric incidents in the drama by manipulating the humor figures into situations in which they egregiously display their follies.

Chapman's method of fitting his eccentrics into the dramatic structure of *An Humorous Day's Mirth* is clearly illustrated in his treatment of Dowsecer, a young count resident at the Court. Before he appears, the King paints his portrait, only a little tinged with ridicule:

> They say the young Dowsecer
> Is rarely learned, and nothing lunatic
> As men suppose,
> But hateth company and worldly trash;
> The judgment and the just contempt of them
> Have in reason arguments that break affection
> (As the most sacred poets write), and still the roughest wind
> And his rare humour come we now to hear.
>
> (Sc. vii, 15-22)

Dowsecer proves to be a weeping philosopher, a melancholy fellow who finds all the uses of this world stale, flat, and unprofitable. His attitude is partly pose. Every object that meets his eye automatically starts a train of cynical reflections and looses a flood of misanthropic comment. To expose this humor Lavel deliberately places in Dowsecer's path a picture, a pair of large hose, a codpiece, and a sword. Then the fellow enters uttering a string of absurdly pessimistic comments on life, which are diverted into a new channel by each object which he sees. When this exhibition is over, Lemot turns to the King and asks, 'How like you this humour yet, my liege?'

Dowsecer also has a zany, Labesha, who grows 'marvellous malcontent upon some amorous disposition of his mistress' and imitates the humor of Lord Dowsecer. Some of the low-comedy characters set 'a mess of cream, a spice-cake, and a spoon' in the gull's path in order to provoke him to pessimistic comment on each one of these objects. No sooner have the articles of food been properly placed than Labesha enters. Spying the cakes and cream, he makes an absurd effort to utter melancholy reflections on these comestibles. 'But oh, sour cream,' he exclaims, 'wert thou an onion, since Fortune set thee for me, I will eat thee, and I will devour thee in spite of Fortune's spite' (Sc. xii, 48-50). Labesha's tormentors have concocted their scheme in order to work 'a rare cure on his melancholy.' When they let him know what a fool they have made of him he is shamed indeed, and, we infer, ready to give up his silly affectation.

In similar ways Lemot or Lavel involves the other humor figures in embarrassing situations which force them amply to display their follies. Lemot also sets the scene for a final exhibition and subsequent deflation of all the humoᵣ figures. He assembles the principal characters in the play at the tavern of Verone. There, while the King and his court look on, he contrives to make each humor-ridden figure see his obsession for the absurdity it is and to renounce it.

The final scene is shot through with gaiety. It is utterly devoid of moral severity. No one is rebuked. The King in his final speech invokes the festive spirit in which comedy has always tried to leave the spectators. He invites all the *dramatis personae*:

> Home to my court, where with feasts we will crown
> This mirthful day, and vow it to renown.
>
> (Sc. xiv, 368-9)

II

About a year after *An Humorous Day's Mirth* had been produced at the Rose Theatre, Jonson's *Every Man in His Humour* was brought out by Shakespeare's company.[3] By adopting practically all the distinctive features of Chapman's play, Jonson, as it were, fixed the conventions of a typical humor comedy. The main purpose of this new form of dramatic satire was the exhibition of the humorous characters. The sole function of the plot was to relate them to each other and to provide effective methods of ridiculing them.

Jonson improved on Chapman's structure. He followed his predecessor in giving his mischief-maker Brainworm an important part in the display of his eccentrics. But Jonson, already practiced in the fashioning of comedies, notably *The Tale of a Tub* and *The Case is Altered,* on Plautine models, gave Brainworm's roguery more point than Lemot's. Hence Brainworm plans his disguises and other deceits not out of sheer contempt for the fools in the play, but to bring the romantic plot to a successful end. His roguery enables the young Knowell to secure Bridget for his bride. *Every Man in His Humour* thus avoids the extreme looseness of structure which disfigures *An Humorous Day's Mirth.*

Jonson ends his comedy exactly in Chapman's manner. The mischief-maker sends most of the characters to the house of a water-bearer, Cob, anticipating the merriment which their simultaneous appearance there will produce. Then Doctor Clement, a mad justice in motley, appears to pass judgment, in a buffoonish spirit, on everyone. In this atmosphere of revelry the humor characters recognize their eccentricities as absurd and give them up. Then the merry doctor, like the King in *An Humorous Day's Mirth,* invites all to celebrate at his house their happy escape from folly. He cries, 'And now to make our evening happiness more full; this night you shall be all my guests, where we'll enjoy the very spirit of mirth' (v. iii. 441-3).

Another feature of Chapman's play that Jonson retains and develops is the relation of the gull to the sham gentleman whom he chooses to imitate. The cream of the jest is that the gull becomes a fool's zany. The gull as a type was created by the formal satirists of the 1590's. They made him a simpleton who desired to be a social exquisite, but who, in choosing a model, could not distinguish the true from the fraudulent gentleman. Labesha in his witless aping of Dowsecer is pure gull. Matthew, Jonson's city gull in *Every Man in His Humour,* is ridiculous in just the same way. His rapturous admiration of Bobadill and his efforts to learn the soldierly qualities of a gentleman by imitating the sham captain write him down as the typical zany.

Stephen, the country gull, is a combination of natural fatuity and ignorance of city ways which a fellow just come up to town from the country would show. He wishes desperately to become a man of fashion, yet he knows so well that his efforts are inept that he suspects everyone of laughing at him behind his back. He compensates for this embarrassment by bluster, and in so doing becomes very like Labesha. Like him he takes refuge in evasions when he is called upon to make good his swaggering boasts and threats.[4] To reveal his fatuity Stephen needs but the ear of anyone who will listen. The egregious ass will expose his humor indecently without the aid of any roguish intrigue, of fabricated situations, or of booby traps.

Kitely and Downright display the humor of jealousy and anger respectively, yet both are citizens of Jonson's world. Even the characters who come into the play with the Plautine plot have their traditional business enlivened with contemporary circumstance. Thus old Knowell is in type the unsympathetic and choleric father of Latin comedy, who is depressed at his son's suspected wildness. Yet he is also an Elizabethan of the old school, a firm believer in thrift in both emotional and material expenditure. Jonson makes him play still a third role—that of satiric expositor. In rebuking folly, he paints incisive portraits. Note how his attack on Stephen's passion for hawking etches the gull's follies in our minds:

> Go to, you are a prodigal, and self-willed fool,
>
>   .   .   .
>
> What? Have you not means enow to wast
> That which your friends have left you, but you must
> Go cast away your money on a buzzard.
>
> (I. i. 46, 49-51)

Young Knowell also is a typical Plautine figure—the ardent lover of a girl of whom he fears his father will disapprove. But Jonson endows him with qualities which distinguished a cultivated university man of his day. He is witty, urbane, and, following the fashion of Elizabethan gentlemen, is devoted to the pursuit of poetry. *Every Man in His Humour* thus represents Jonson's perfection of humor comedy. Though based on comic conventions of Roman comedy and orthodox according to the canons of classical theory, it drew its incidents from contemporary life and its spirit from the English satire still free and vigorous in 1597.

III

Shakespeare first showed the influence of the 'humorous' conception of character after Jonson's comedy had enjoyed a success on the stage. Since Shakespeare had acted one of the principal roles in this drama, he obviously knew just what parts of it Elizabethan audiences had received with most delight. It is not surprising, then, to find that humor characters first play important parts in *Henry V* and *The Merry Wives of Windsor,* plays written shortly after the production of *Every Man in His Humour.*

In both those dramas the eccentrics lurk on the edges of the main plot and so provide the spectators with only incidental satire. In *Twelfth Night,* however, they take charge of the important sub-plot and so make the story of Sir Toby, Sir Andrew, and Malvolio a humor comedy in the manner Jonson had adopted in *Every Man in His Humour* with conspicuous success.

Neither *Henry V* nor *The Merry Wives* is built on the lines typical of humor comedy. Shakespeare devoted neither play to a systematic exposure of any fool. Instead he begins to draw his first humor figures in an amused offhand manner. Nym, one of Falstaff's three 'conny catching rascals' in *The*

Merry Wives, becomes perhaps the first heir of this phase of his creator's invention. As soon as he opens his mouth, he makes it clear that he is dominated by a humor. His first words are an answer to Justice Shallow's accusation that he, Falstaff, Bardolph, and Pistol have 'beaten his men, killed his deer, and broke open his lodge.' The Welsh chaplain Evans, who makes fritters of English, tries to allay the dreaded anger of Falstaff by crying, 'Pauca verba, Sir John, goot worts' (I. i. 123). The priest's excited efforts to keep the peace provokes Nym's scornful retort: 'Slice, I say, Pauca! Pauca! Slice! That's my humour' (I. i. 134-5). This orphic utterance shows us that Nym, as the page in *Henry V* says, 'Hath heard that men of few words are the best men.' Hence his humor is to terrify by deliberate understatement and vague hints of the dark deeds he could do if he would. By stuffing the word 'humour' at least once into every sentence he utters, he derides what had apparently become a ridiculous over-use of the term among Shakespeare's contemporaries.

Nym's affectation is made the funnier through its continuous contrast with the humor of Pistol. His is an irresistible impulse to form horrendous speeches out of half-remembered tags from old plays written in 'Cambyses vein.' Pistol had already appeared in the second part of *Henry IV*, which was written at least after Shakespeare's company had accepted *Every Man in His Humour* at his advice, for so tradition has it. Pistol lurches into the inn where Falstaff is dallying with Doll Tearsheet and the Hostess. These females know Pistol's reputation for 'swaggering,' and his stormy entrance congeals them both with terror. Though Falstaff assures the women that Pistol will 'not swagger with a Barbary hen if her feathers turn back in any show of resistance' (II. iv. 107-9), they are all a-tremble when he begins to threaten Doll in high astounding terms. The Hostess beseeches him 'to aggravate his choler,' but her terror only stimulates Pistol

to unlock his word-hoard. 'These be good humours indeed,'
he begins, opening the attack on the use of the word 'humour,' which Nym is soon to take over:

> Shall pack horses
> And hollow-pampered jades of Asia
> Which cannot go but thirty miles a day
> Compare with Caesars and with Cannibals,
> And Troyan Greeks? Nay rather damn them with
> King Cerberus, and let the welkin roar!
> Shall we fall foul for toys?
>
> (II. iv. 177-83)

'These are very bitter words,' cries the Hostess—bitter words
which sound like a wild travesty of Marlowe's style or that
of the crassest of his imitators. But they are only Pistol's idea
of heroic speech. However, this verbal thunder does not
frighten Falstaff. Knowing Pistol of old, he realizes that the
swaggerer is the one man in London whom he can bluff.
This he proceeds to do with a fine show of quiet competence. He draws his sword and incontinently drives Pistol
downstairs, thus deflating him and shaming him in the eyes
of the Hostess and Doll.

When Pistol next appears—this time at Justice Shallow's
house in Gloucestershire—he is bursting with the news that
the King is dead and Prince Hal has succeeded to the throne.
But his excitement so far exaggerates his rhetorical fervor
that he is utterly unintelligible. He begins:

> And tidings do I bring, and lucky joys,
> And golden times and happy news of price.

Falstaff interrupts with:

> I pray thee now deliver them like a man
> of this world.

But Pistol's vocabulary cannot be tamed, and he continues:

A foutra for the world and worldlings base!
I speak of Africa and golden joys.

So Falstaff falls into his vein and parodies his speech to good
effect:

> O base Assyrian Knight, what is thy news?
> Let King Cophetua know the truth thereof.
> (v. iii. 99-106)

Pistol, as his name suggests, is a humor figure. His humor
is a whim, a mannerism of speech. He shoots off his store
of verbal ammunition at the slightest provocation. Twice in
this first play in which he appears his folly is exposed; but
no audience expects reform to come to so great a fool. Both
his humor and that of Nym appear to best advantage when
they are shown together in *The Merry Wives of Windsor* and
Henry V. The contrast between them is so deeply marked
that the folly of each 'sticks more fiery off indeed.' The high
point of this display is the quarrel which they stage in the
second act of *Henry V*. The Hostess, though 'troth-plight' to
Nym, has married Pistol, and stirred in Nym's soul deep impulses to revenge. Nym, while waiting for the newly married
couple to appear, intimates in oracular language the revenge
he intends to take on his old crony: 'Things must be as they
may. Men may sleep, and they may have their throats about
them at that time, and some say knives have edges' (ii. i. 22-5).
When Pistol and the Hostess appear, Nym and Pistol each
draws his sword, and each gives a magnificent exhibition of
his humor:

> NYM. Pish!
> PIST. Pish for thee, Iceland dog! thou prick-ear'd cur
>   of Iceland!
> HOST. Good Corporal Nym, show thy valour, and put
>   up your sword.
> NYM. Will you shog off? I would have you solus.
> PIST. 'Solus,' egregrious dog? O viper vile!
>   The 'solus' in thy most mervailous face!

The 'solus' in thy teeth, and in thy throat,
And in thy hateful lungs, yea, in thy maw, perdy!
And, which is worse, within thy nasty mouth!
I do retort the 'solus' in thy bowels;
For I can take, and Pistol's cock is up,
And flashing fire will follow.

NYM. I am not Barbason; you cannot conjure me. I
have an humour to knock you indifferently well. If
you grow foul with me, Pistol, I will scour you with
my rapier, as I may, in fair terms. If you would walk
off, I would prick your guts a little in good terms, as
I may, and that's the humour of it.

PIST. O braggard vile, and damned furious wight,
The grave doth gape, and doting death is near.
Therefore exhale!

(II. i. 43-66)

In spite of his verbal thunder neither has any appetite for
actual fighting. So at Bardolph's command, they both sheath
their swords with absurd eagerness. Shakespeare clearly intended his audience to wax merry over this encounter without feeling much scorn at the exposure of the vociferous
coward.

Later in the play, however, Pistol is as contemptuously deflated as any humor figure in Elizabethan drama. Gower is
the first of his comrades in arms to discover Pistol's cowardice and his thievery. He tells Fluellen, who up to this moment has been completely taken in by Pistol's flood of words,
that the fellow is 'a gull, a fool, a rogue, that now and then
goes to the wars to grace himself, at his return into London,
under the form of a soldier' (III. vi. 70-73).

Fluellen, thus enlightened, determines to take no more
insolence from the 'rascally, scauld, beggarly, lousy, pragging
knave.' So when Pistol next appears 'swelling like a turkey
cock,' Fluellen, to the accompaniment of blows on the pate,
makes him eat a leek—a Welsh delicacy about which Pistol
had taunted him—to the last morsel. The ceremony com-

pleted, Pistol shouts, 'All hell shall stir for this!' But Gower
turns upon him with savage contempt: 'Go, go. You are a
counterfeit cowardly knave' (v. i. 73-4). Then in a final soliloquy Pistol heaps still fouler dishonor upon his own head:

> Old I do wax, and from my weary limbs
> Honour is cudgell'd. Well, bawd will I turn,
> And something lean to cutpurse of quick hand.
> To England will I steal, and there I'll steal;
> And patches will I get unto these cudgell'd scars
> And swear I got them in the Gallia wars.
> (v. i. 89-94)

This is the conventional exposure and contemptuous rejection which is always the fate of characters ridiculed in
satire. Pistol being a typical humor figure is derided because of an eccentricity which he displays every time he sets
foot on the stage. His humor at first seems to be a mere
form of grandiloquent speech, a parody of a crude style of
dramatic fustian. But, as we become more familiar with his
bombast, we see that it is a grotesque mask which conceals
cowardice and baseness.

In his contemptuous treatment of Nym and Pistol, Shakespeare was probably attacking a type of petty sharper familiar
to anyone who walked the streets of Elizabethan London.
Pickpockets and cut-purses, by posing as deserving but neglected soldiers just home from the wars, were able to ply the
trades of swindler and petty thief with great success.[5] Many
in Shakespeare's audiences would therefore immediately recognize the pair of rogues as members of a well-known fraternity of vagabonds, and would fill the laughter which the
humors of the two provoked with scorn and detestation.

IV

The Merry Wives of Windsor, and to a greater degree
Henry V, abound in national types comically presented.

Fluellen is a stage Welshman; Captain Jamy, a stage Scotch-
man; Macmorris, a stage Irishman. Each is distinguished by
one ruling mental peculiarity. Fluellen is a pedant continually seeking to justify the maneuvers of the British army by
an appeal to Roman military precedents. Captain Jamy is
forever searching for firm bases for properly conducted arguments. And Macmorris takes immediate umbrage at fancied
slights to Ireland. At first acquaintance all three seem to be
humor figures dressed up in national costumes and made
picturesque by their native dialects. But the distinctive qualities of no one of the three are enough exaggerated to be
natural objects of satire. As a matter of fact Shakespeare
makes each of these national figures an admirable part of his
Empire army.

Even Sir Hugh Evans in *The Merry Wives,* though his dialect is an absurd distortion of the King's English, is nowhere
made an object of contempt and nowhere exposed as a fool.
To be sure, the quiz in Latin grammar which he gives to
young William is turned into risqué farce by Dame Quickly's
absurd misunderstanding of Latin words.[6] For example,
when William accurately recites the genitive plural of *hic,
haec, hoc* as *horum, harum, horum,* she cries out, 'Vengeance
of Jenny's case! Fie on her! Never name her, child, if she
be a whore' (IV. i. 63-5). However it is not any characteristic
of Sir Hugh that is derided in this scene, not even his Welsh
distortion of Latin sounds.

Dr. Caius, the French doctor in *The Merry Wives,* is, however, a typical humor figure, one that has clearly been made
an object of satire. His dialect may be a no more ridiculous
deformation of English than that of Sir Hugh, but he is the
slave of a humor which is presented derisively. Every time
he appears he is almost insanely excited and choleric. And
his grotesque accent makes his fluster the more preposterous.
At his very first entrance he makes clear just what his humor
is. Dame Quickly, who in this play has become his house-

keeper and maid-of-all-work, defines his eccentricity as 'old abusing of God's patience and the King's English' (I. iv. 5-6). The doctor comes home to discover that Quickly has hidden Simple, Master Slender's servant, in his medicine closet. The stupid fellow has been sent by Sir Hugh Evans to urge Quickly to speak a good word for Slender with Mistress Anne Page. But Caius is also a suitor of the same lady, and when Simple blurts out the nature of his errand the excitable doctor bursts into a characteristic display of his humor. 'You jack'nape,' he shouts to the terrified servant, 'give-a dis letter to Sir Hugh. By gar, it is a shallenge! I vill cut his troat in de Park; and I vill teach a scurvy jack-a-nape priest to meddle or make! . . . By gar, I vill kill de Jack priest; and I have appointed mine host of de Jarteer to measure our weapon. By gar, I vill myself have Anne Page' (I. iv. 113-16, 121-5).

The duel never takes place, for the Host has a plan for making the French doctor ridiculous. In completing arrangements for the encounter he sends Dr. Caius to one place and Sir Hugh to another. Then the Host, Shallow, and Slender go to the field near Windsor where Caius is boiling with impatience to meet his enemy. The Host deliberately drives the irate doctor into an extravagant display of his humor by praising his valor in wildly extravagant and purposely nonsensical terms. 'Thou art a Castalion-King-Urinal! Hector of Greece, my boy' (II. iii. 34-5). These high-sounding terms of approbation fill Caius with swelling self-approval. As the Host leads him to the place where Sir Hugh is waiting under the pretext that he is to take the doctor 'where Mistress Anne Page is at a farmhouse feasting,' Caius exudes farcical confidence in his success as a duelist and as a lover. 'By gar,' he shouts, 'me vill kill de priest, for he speak for a jack-an-ape to Anne Page.' And he promises to repay the Host for his aid, once he has secured Mistress Anne. 'By gar, me danck you vor dat. By gar, I love you; and I shall procure-a you de good guest—de earl, de knight, de lords, de gentlemen, my patients' (II. iii. 85-6, 94-7).

This is a point which must be reached in the career of every humor figure, the scene in which a rogue succeeds in prodding the eccentric to a supreme display of his folly. It is a dramatic preparation for his deflation, for the first exposure of his fire-eating pretensions. When he confronts Sir Hugh, the two in whispered asides assure each other of their willingness to compose their differences, even while aloud they threaten each other in the proper fustian. When they are left alone, they forget their quarrel and its cause in pretended amusement at the deception of which they have been the victims. To the audience, however, Dr. Caius' bluster has been revealed as a hollow pose. As clearly as Pistol, he has been deflated.

The French doctor hereafter becomes almost wholly lost in the intricacies of the double plot of *The Merry Wives*. He retains a minor importance as one of the conventional three suitors of the amorosa, the one favored by Anne's mother. At his few appearances, however, he continues to exhibit the expected irritable excitement. In the final scene his amorous discomfiture is complete. He walks off to be married with a page, whom he has been led to believe is Miss Anne in disguise. And in a final burst of frantic exasperation he rushes out of the play for good. 'Vere is Mistress Page? By gar, I am cozened. I ha' married oon garsoon, a boy; oon pesant, by gar, a boy! It is not Anne Page. By gar, I am cozened' (V. v. 217-20).

This career of Dr. Caius, though merely sketched, is a typical satiric treatment of the humor figure. His excitability often seems to be little more than a Gallic mannerism. Yet it proves to be the mask of ridiculous conceit and pretension. In tearing it off, Shakespeare shows no indignation and no zeal for reform. The discomfiture of the stage Frenchman at the exposure of his pretensions created all the laughter that Shakespeare desired. Each individual spectator could season it with as much scorn as he chose.

The ridicule of Dr. Caius, no less than that of Pistol, had a topical interest in Shakespeare's day. Foreign physicians, particularly Frenchmen, were held in absurdly high esteem, especially by high-born and fashionable Englishmen. Caius boasts of the earls, knights, lords, and gentlemen whom he can number among his patients. In the second part of the anonymous play *The Return from Parnassus* (1601), Philomusus, a rogue, disguises as a French doctor and has Studioso disguise as a doctor's servant. He explains his deceit as follows: 'And first to my plot for playing the French Doctor, that shall hold: with those shredds of French, that we gathered up in our hostess house in Paris, we'll gull the world.' [7] In this university play the medical pretensions of the French physician are ridiculed. In *The Merry Wives* it is rather his volatile excitement that is satirized; for Shakespeare preferred to deride what he clearly felt was the most ridiculous characteristic of a Frenchman, whether doctor or prince.

v

The humor figures in *Henry V* and *The Merry Wives* have proved to be mere oddities almost wholly independent of the action of the comedies in which they appear. Their follies are little more than personal eccentricities. In *Twelfth Night* Shakespeare places two humor characters at the center of his low-comedy underplot and in so doing first applied to his own work all the lessons that he had learned while acting in Jonson's *Every Man in His Humour*.[8]

Acute critics have long recognized the similarities between *Twelfth Night* and Jonson's first humor comedy. Herford calls it 'the most Jonsonian comedy of Shakespeare.' [9] C. R. Baskervill is also aware of the general relation of both this comedy and *The Merry Wives* to what he calls 'the humor

trend that was associated with satire.' [10] And two American
scholars have worked out many of the details of Jonson's
influence upon the construction of *Twelfth Night*.[11] The
characters in the comedy who are most obviously Jonsonian
are Sir Andrew Aguecheek and Malvolio.

The former is a gull, who imitates Sir Toby Belch as mechanically as Labesha aped Dowsecer, or as Matthew did
Bobadill. Sir Andrew also possesses some of the characteristics
of Stephen, Jonson's country gull. The two are alike in being
unadulterated fools and in their countrified imitation of
what they believe to be the manners of a gentleman. Before
Sir Andrew's first appearance Sir Toby and Maria collabo-
rate in sketching a satiric portrait of the gull:

> MARIA. . . . He's a very fool and prodigal.
> TOBY. Fie that you'll say so! He plays o' the viol-de-
> gamboys, and speaks three or four languages word
> for word without book and hath all the good gifts
> of nature.
> MARIA. He hath, indeed, almost natural! for, besides
> that he's a fool, he's a great quarreller; and but that
> he hath the gift of a coward to allay the gust he
> hath in quarrelling, 'tis thought among the prudent
> he would quickly have the gift of a grave.
>
> (I. iii. 24-35)

Sir Andrew then enters immediately to belie every word
of Sir Toby's encomium and to illustrate every detail of
Maria's detraction. He understands no foreign language and
only the simplest of English words. Sir Toby's suggestion
that he 'accost' Maria, he mistakes for her surname and calls
her 'Good Mistress Mary Accost.' He asks whether *pourquoi*
means 'do or not do'; then sighs 'I would I had bestowed that
time in the tongues that I have in fencing, dancing, and
bear-baiting. O, had I but followed the arts' (I. iii. 96-9). This
speech gives Sir Toby the idea of prodding him to display
his grotesque inability to dance.

But most of the time Sir Andrew needs no urging to exhibit his fatuity. Like Stephen in *Every Man in His Humour*
he requires only an ear into which to pour his fat-witted talk.
He echoes every remark of his hero. To the Clown's exclama-
tion that Sir Toby is 'in admirable fooling,' Sir Andrew
proudly replies, 'Ay, he does well enough if he be disposed
and so do I too. He does it with a better grace, but I do it
more natural' (ii. i. 87-9). Yet when he hears the graceful
compliments which Viola pays Olivia, he is greatly impressed
and determines to learn by heart all her most glowing words:

> VIOLA. Most excellent accomplished lady, the heavens
> rain odors on you.
> ANDREW [*aside*]. That youth's a rare courtier. 'Rain
> odors'—well!
> VIOLA. My matter hath no voice, lady, but to your own
> most pregnant and vouchsafed ear.
> ANDREW [*aside*]. 'Odors,' 'pregnant' and 'vouchsafed'—
> I'll get 'em all three ready.
>
> (III. i. 95-102)

This perfectly simple dramatic method serves admirably
for the display of Sir Andrew's fatuity. But Shakespeare
clearly felt that the unmasking of his cowardice demanded
more artifice. Accordingly he falls back upon a booby trap
which he has Sir Toby and Fabian set. They urge the gull to
send an eloquent and insulting challenge to Cesario, his apparent rival for the hand of Olivia.

> Be curst and brief . . . Go about it! Let there be gall
> in thy ink though thou write with a goose-pen, no
> matter.
>
> (III. ii. 52-4)

The challenge in which he covers his fear in bluster is even
more absurd than that of Stephen, Jonson's country gull.
Having thus emboldened Sir Andrew, Sir Toby turns to
Fabian and tells him for the enlightenment of the audience:

> For Andrew, if he were opened, and you find so
> much blood in his liver as will clog the foot of a flea,
> I'll eat the rest of his anatomy.
>
> (III. ii. 64-7)

Then Sir Toby takes charge of the plot which is to expose Sir Andrew's cowardice. He praises the rage, skill, fury, and impetuosity of each of the duelists to the other, and so frightens them that when they meet they almost 'kill one another by the look, like cockatrices.' Andrew is willing to do anything to avoid the combat:

> Plague on't, an I thought he had been valiant, and
> so cunning in fence, I'd have seen him damned ere I'd
> have challenged him. Let him let the matter slip, and
> I'll give him my horse, grey Capilet.
>
> (III. iv. 311-15)

But Toby sees to it that the duel takes place. So the two draw their swords and approach each other with farcical attitudes of fright, only to be interrupted by Antonio, who is searching for Sebastian, Viola-Cesario's twin brother. The next time that Andrew thinks he has overtaken Viola, he encounters Sebastian, who soundly thrashes both Sir Andrew and Sir Toby.

The last view that we gain of the precious pair is when they later appear before Olivia and the Duke with their heads broken. Toby is drunk and Andrew completely crestfallen. As they go off to have their wounds dressed, Sir Andrew offers to help Sir Toby out. Then Toby turning on him fires a parting shot, a final characterization of the gull: 'Will you help—an ass-head and a cox-comb and a knave—a thin-faced knave—a gull?' (v. i. 212-4).

Sir Andrew then is a gull—Shakespeare's composite of Matthew and Stephen, Jonson's city and country gulls. He is derided, exposed, and ejected from the company of the wise and the sane, as are all ridiculed figures in satire of any sort. But Shakespeare's lampooning of Sir Andrew is utterly devoid of malice. The gull entertains every audience in the same hilarious fashion in which he entertains Sir Toby. His folly is inoffensive. No one expects or desires his reform. We cannot share Sir Toby's final disgust with his dear manikin. We hope that he has run away only to return to amuse us on another day. At no point is the difference between the comic art of Jonson and that of Shakespeare more obvious than in their conception of their gulls. Jonson's Matthew and Stephen are personifications of an eccentricity—frank caricatures. Sir Andrew is just as farcically drawn, but always a human being, even when he is most idiotic. His follies may be wild exaggerations of human foibles, but they never completely obliterate the silly man.

VI

In his characterization of Malvolio, Shakespeare approaches much closer to Jonson's satiric methods. Malvolio is a humor figure in being, as Olivia tells us, 'sick of self-love,' or as Maria puts it, 'The best persuaded of himself, so crammed, as he thinks, with excellencies, that .it is his ground of faith that all that look on him love him' (II. iii. 155-8). His self-conceit so puffs him up with false dignity that he thinks simple fun of every sort utterly, exasperatingly trivial. This lofty scorn leads Maria to say, 'Marry sir, sometimes he is a kind of Puritan'—a remark that has misled many critics to imagine that in Malvolio Shakespeare satirizes the Puritans. But they fail to notice that Maria immediately takes back her suggestion. 'The devil a Puritan that he is,' she says, 'or anything constantly but a time-pleaser [that is, time-server]' (II. iii. 159-60).

Malvolio's self-love has filled him with an ambition presumptuous in one of his lowly social position. 'Art thou any more than a steward?' asks Sir Toby contemptuously, when

Malvolio rebukes him and Sir Andrew for their riotous noise in the hall. Maurice Evans in his recent production of *Twelfth Night* made Malvolio's social inferiority immediately obvious to his audiences by the anachronistic device of giving the steward a cockney accent. This established him at once as a rank social outsider. His aspiring to be Olivia's husband is therefore colossal presumption, gross and palpable self-conceit.

The plot which Maria devises to drive his humor into exaggerated display is quite properly based on his faith that Olivia has but to look on him to love him. Maria explains in detail the nature of the trap in which she is to catch the booby, and even describes the grotesque struggles in which he will indulge when securely caught in the toils. She will drop in his path some obscure epistles of love which he will imagine come from Olivia. She knows he will then act most like the 'affectioned ass' he is. In no humor play is the conventional device for exhibiting the fool made more obvious or its mechanism more carefully described.

In *Twelfth Night* the rogues have a valid motive for wishing to humiliate Malvolio. Unlike Lemot in Chapman's comedy, they are not professional entertainers who plan to show off the fools merely to amuse their mistress. They have a good reason for resenting Malvolio's officious pretensions. They see in him an enemy to everything in life which they enjoy. They know he would gladly destroy their cakes and ale. They are thus enthusiastic participants in Maria's scheme which will revenge his officiousness. Maria's device is also of great value to the satire, because it effects an exaggerated display of Malvolio's self-love and social presumption. He enters practicing courtly behavior to his shadow, imagining how he will act when he becomes Count Malvolio. In this mood he picks up Maria's letter and gulps down the bait.

The full revelation of his fatuous self-love comes when he

appears before Olivia in yellow stockings, a color she abhors, and cross-gartered, a fashion she detests—both adornments peculiar to serving-men, social underlings. As he smiles with empty-headed insistency, kisses his hands, and acts out with great care every one of Maria's instructions, Olivia becomes more and more certain that his mind is touched. This gives Toby his chance to improve upon Maria's plot. He has Malvolio bound and imprisoned in a dark room in the vaults of Olivia's house. There the rogues, with the help of Feste, torture Malvolio in a way which seems cruel to modern spectators, but to an Elizabethan audience was merely a hilarious form of deserved purgation. For Malvolio is purged; at least for the moment he seems to be washed clean of his ambition to marry Olivia and of the crudest of his social affectations.

Twelfth Night, however, does not close, as did *Every Man in His Humour,* with a merry ceremony in which the humor figures take joy in their reformation and are welcomed back into the company of the psychologically balanced and socially competent, by a Dionysiac celebration. Malvolio appears in the final scene to learn all about the plot of which he has been the victim. He is neither amused nor purged. Instead he rushes off the stage in a passion of anger and wounded pride, shouting, 'I'll be revenged on the whole pack of you!' And he is followed by the scornful laughter of satire.

Malvolio is Shakespeare's representative of the upstart, who was the butt of all the satirists, formal and dramatic, of the 1590's. Like the rest of the writers of the age, Shakespeare takes the conservative side in the struggle of the new classes for social recognition. Malvolio is a 'coystril.' Having no right to bear arms, he is regarded by the gentlemen as a menial and therefore an impossible husband for the lady Olivia. Shakespeare clearly agrees with them that the steward's hope to marry his mistress is consummate impudence.[12]

In another respect Shakespeare seems to take sides against

Malvolio.[13] He is the major-domo of the Tudor country house, and, as the official responsible for the economy of Olivia's establishment, he is dead against the extravagances which are relics of life in the medieval castle. He quite properly regards Sir Toby as an anachronism, as a debased representative of the armed retainers who once defended the castle from its foes and in return were given their board and keep. Though when off duty they brawled indoors and out, they were tolerated because of their help in time of trouble. Sir Toby contributes as much uproar to Olivia's household as his forebears used to do, but he performs no other service. Yet he demands all the cakes and ale that he can swallow and the right to introduce his boon companions into the hall to roister when and how they please. To this conduct Malvolio objects. He is an enemy to the time-honored English hospitality and liberality because of the strain it puts upon his lady's purse. He detests Toby's revelry, not because it is wicked, but because it is both indecorous and expensive. Shakespeare is obviously against this upstart of the new social dispensation.

Hall and the other satirists of his day, and indeed most Elizabethan writers, bewail the passing of the days of the free table, of the lavish dispensing of hospitality. To them such entertainment was the cornerstone of Merry England. To Shakespeare, also, this change in social custom was something to lament. He believed that the security of gentle folk was endangered by the transition going on in noble households like that of Olivia. Consequently he makes the merchant-minded enemy of the good old days a kill-joy, a conceited ass, an inept social parvenu.

Malvolio is thus elevated above the artificial simplicity of the typical humor figure. In the process he has become an almost pathetically ridiculous human being. In spite of this transformation Shakespeare puts him through the conventional satiric routine of a man caught in the toils of his humor and forced to struggle and grimace there for our amusement. It is Malvolio's routine that forms the center of the robust comic sub-plot of *Twelfth Night*. It provides merry interludes to the sentimental story of Viola, Orsino, and Olivia. It also enables Shakespeare to employ satiric conventions established by Chapman and Jonson in a way to create the most vivid and human of all the humor figures in Elizabethan comedy.

No humor characters appear in any of Shakespeare's plays written after *Twelfth Night*. His satiric impulses flowed into other dramatic channels. This bright comedy was followed by Shakespeare's so-called dark comedies and by his great tragedies. In these tragi-comedies he clearly adopted many of the constructive principles of Ben Jonson's comical satires, the first of which was *Every Man Out of His Humour*. In his tragedies the mocking figure of the malcontent frequently seizes control of the protagonists and utters the savage contempt for folly and sin which his poisonous mind continually distils. These speeches of Shakespeare's version of the malcontent form a searing and brutal satire different in kind from that found anywhere else in the literature of the western world.

V

The 'Dark Years'

ABOUT the year 1600 Shakespeare turned to the writing of his so-called 'dark' or 'sombre' comedies and to tragedy. The explanation for this profound change in his dramatic interests has usually been found in the events of his life. The story goes that at the turn of the century Shakespeare's naturally serene spirit was clouded with gloom and swept by despair. Many and various personal experiences of the poet have been made to account for this descent into the depths. Romantic critics have suggested that the cause lay in some sort of disillusionment. Perhaps the 'dark lady' revealed her infidelity in all its starkness about this time, or his dearest hopes met a crushing defeat.

Those who detect traces of Essex everywhere in Elizabethan literature believe that Shakespeare's depression was caused by the disasters which overtook the temperamental Earl. Dover Wilson develops the hypothesis into full length fiction [1] with the following plot: Shakespeare, during the last few years of the 1590's, had fervently hoped that Essex would be nominated as Queen Elizabeth's successor. When the Earl's folly destroyed all his chances of being chosen heir-apparent, Shakespeare sank into permanent gloom, a mood which deepened to despair after his hero's execution. The great enthusiasm of his life had come to nothing and the advent of James I merely intensified his melancholy. To him the Scottish king was a pedant, a coward, and a moral weakling. Hence it was natural that his normally buoyant spirit should fall prey to cynicism. Thereafter he poured forth his

despondency in his plays with more and more bitterness, until in *Coriolanus* and *Timon of Athens* his most characteristic utterances were sick fulmination against almost everything in his world. 'Look at Shakespeare's dramatic work
from 1601 to 1608 as a whole,' exclaims Dover Wilson, 'and
the conclusion is, I think, irresistible that, for whatever
cause, Shakespeare was subject at this time to a dominant
mood of gloom and dejection, which on one occasion at least
brought him to the verge of madness.' This ingenious solu-
tion of the problem of the dark years makes absorbingly interesting fiction. But, as Professor R. W. Chambers has
shown, it is not based on fact.[3]

In all his chronicle history plays Shakespeare had expressed
his horror of civil war and had preached the sacred obligation of the country to respect hereditary rights to the English
throne. And Essex had no legitimate claim to the kingship
whatever. He was, to be sure, the Queen's cousin, but a
cousin twice-removed and on the Boleyn, not the Tudor,
side. Elizabeth would never have been so mad as to give this
volatile favorite her 'voice' before she died. Nor would
Shakespeare have been so faithless to his most deeply held
political convictions as to have surrendered to despair because a fomenter of civil war, a traitor without a shred of
right to the throne, had been disinherited and condignly
punished. Nor did all England, including Shakespeare, suffer a spiritual decline when James came to the throne. His
accession was the triumph of legitimacy and common sense.
The entire country heaved a great sigh of relief that the
question of succession, over which it had agonized for years,
had been settled so easily. Bacon wrote that England was 'as
a man that awaketh out of a fearful dream.' If the temper
of the first years of James's reign was joyous, there is no
reason to assume that Shakespeare alone moped. Obviously
some explanation other than that offered by Dover Wilson
must be found for the sombre nature of Shakespeare's dark

comedies. Hence critics less biographical in their interest
have suggested that these plays of Shakespeare's reflect the
skepticism and pessimism which overtook many thoughtful
men of his generation. That feeling was more than a re-
surgence of medieval contempt of the world. It was fed by
other sources. Humanistic learning had made all students
familiar with many conflicting philosophies of antiquity.
This widening knowledge produced a conflict between intellectual loyalties. The age constructed no such all-embracing
and harmonious system of thought as that presented in the
Summa of Saint Thomas Aquinas. Truth that used to be
had for the asking now seemed beyond the reach of every
man.

In particular the new astronomical theories called into
question man's deepest convictions about the nature of the
universe in which he lived. He learned with dismay that
created matter above the moon was not, as he had been
taught, free from change and corruption. Decay was the law
of the universe and man the slave of mutability. His feet
were placed on shifting sands. Moreover, the earth and all
the creatures inhabiting it were rapidly becoming senile.
Since the world had completed nearly all of the six thousand
years of its allotted span, it was pitifully old, and man, whose
life kept even pace with that of the universe, was becoming
degenerate.

These ideas produced in many thoughtful men a profound
pessimism—a feeling Shakespeare may well have shared. At
least, Hamlet's melancholy falls into the moulds which Renaissance skepticism and pessimism had formed. And it is
possible that Shakespeare's personal feelings found release in
some of Hamlet's speeches and in those of other characters
in his tragedies and dark comedies. Indeed the pessimistic
tone of many of his plays written during the first decade of
the seventeenth century probably does reflect the philosophic
temper of the age.

However, it is a naïve assumption that a man who writes
comedies is habitually merry or that the writer of tragedies
is always sad. Moreover, the difference in temper between
Shakespeare's works written before 1600 and those written
after that date has been greatly exaggerated. The problem
of evil is vividly presented and deeply pondered in *Titus
Andronicus, Henry VI, Richard III, Richard II,* and *King
John,* all written when Shakespeare is supposed to have been
filled with 'Tudor gaiety of spirit.' [4] To be sure, the tragedies
probe more deeply into the ways of evil and its attendant
suffering. That is because they treat, not as do the historical
plays the 'relations of man to man, but the relations of man
to his creator,' [5] and partly also because they were written
at the height of Shakespeare's transcendant powers of mind
and spirit. It is true, as Walter Raleigh says, that if Heminge
and Condell 'asked for a comedy when he [Shakespeare] was
writing his great tragedies they got *Measure for Measure* or
Troilus and Cressida'. [6] But not all the causes contributing to
the bitterness of these comedies or to the even more distress-
ful spirit of *Timon of Athens* and *Coriolanus* were either
psychological or social. Each one of these plays had been constructed on a satiric model and subjected to a strong infusion
of the satiric spirit.

In *Troilus and Cressida* and *Measure for Measure* Shakespeare extends his imitation and adaptation of the plays in
which Ben Jonson effected a union between comedy and
satire. He continues to exhibit, expose, and deflate fools and
knaves in the manner which Jonson employed in *Every Man
in His Humour.* But he also begins to avail himself of some
of the startling innovations which first appear in *Every Man
Out of His Humour.* These dramatic novelties are closely
related to the new developments in the satiric movement of
the 1590's which I have already briefly described.

Almost immediately after the Bishop's issue of the restraining order of 1 June 1599,[7] Jonson devised *Every Man Out*

of His Humour in such a way as to incorporate into it as many of the distinguishing characteristics of the proscribed satire as he could. He advertised his project by calling his dramatic experiment 'a comical satyre.' Being too strong a classicist to strike out into utterly untried paths, Jonson found in classical critical theory a guide to follow in the construction of his new dramatic edifice. In *Every Man in His Humour* he had already established some of the features of a carefully articulated program of ridicule, admonition, and correction. And Shakespeare, as we have seen, had borrowed and developed many of them with his own characteristic originality in *Twelfth Night*. But Jonson's second humor play differs from the first in tone and in construction. The plan of *Every Man in His Humour* is Plautine and Italianate.

The plot is invented and directed by the clever servant Brainworm, who devises his time-worn tricks of disguise and deceit in order to help his young master win the lady of his choice. The derided figures are all attached loosely to this central plot. Their final deflation and reformation is brought about by a wag, a justice in motley called Dr. Clement. In this jovial mood he also clears up all the complications of the plot. The critical spirit of this justice is utterly different from that of the satirists like Hall and Marston and from that with which Jonson informed *Every Man Out of His Humour*.

This second of his humor plays Jonson decided to make as close a dramatic equivalent of formal or poetic satire as he could. His first problem was to invent a dramatic character to serve as a substitute for the author of formal satire. In other words, Jonson had to fill the indispensable post of commentator. In the interest of dramatic variety he divided the duties of this office among two characters, Macilente and Carlo Buffone.

Macilente (the lean fellow) is a kind of disguise of the

sturdy moral teacher, of Jonson himself, who in this play calls himself Asper. Macilente, as his name suggests, is the embodiment of envy. He thus expresses a belief as old as Plato that envy stimulated just the right combination of intellectual keenness and bitterness in a man to render his laughter satiric. Both allegory and formal satire written in England before 1599 had taught the audience just what to expect of a character like Macilente. It would have been prepared to hear him make two sorts of speeches. Since the objective expression of envy was scorn they would expect him to deal in vituperation. In the second place, when his scorn turned inward and provoked meditation, they would expect him to voice a deep philosophical pessimism—to become, in the language of the time, a malcontent.

Macilente did not disappoint any of these expectations. Evil men he attacks savagely and directly. Of Sordido, the conscienceless hoarder of grain, the creator of artificial famine, he says:

> O here's a precious dirty damned rogue

and comments on his wickedness in this spirit of high indignation. But the mere fools he treats with less moral disdain. He contrives ways for them to amuse the audience by inventing plots which drive them into supreme exhibition of their follies. He thus becomes, in the technical language of the critics, a wit-intriguer, the inventor and director of the comic action.

Carlo Buffone, the second official commentator, is a buffoon; that is, he is a detractor, a scurrilous railer, 'who will rather lose his soul than a jest.' His derision aims at no reform in the persons against whom it is directed. He designs it only to yield him ill-natured amusement, to serve as an empty display of his coarse humor. In particular, he delights in the invention of ribald figures of speech so that his comments on the various fools form an anthology of exuberant but vulgar similes. Yet each in its context possesses a kind of preposterous relevance that makes the audience laugh.

For example, when he looks through a key hole and sees Sogliardo trying to smoke tobacco according to the instructions of his teacher Shift, Carlo Buffone explains, 'We might see Sogliardo sit in a chair, holding his snout up like a sow under an apple tree, while the other [Shift] opened his nostrils with a poking-stick to give the smoke a more free delivery.' His comment on the pseudo-gallant Brisk is equally extravagant: 'He looks like the colonell of the Pigmies' horse, or one of those motions in an antique clock, he would show well upon a habber-dasher's stall at a corner shop.' Such sallies as these are the comments of the author-satirist made, as it were, through an amplifier which grotesquely distorts both his thought and his expression. Carlo is the source of much of the laughter in this comical satire. Both he and Macilente had a numerous progeny in the satiric plays which followed the appearance of *Every Man Out of His Humour*. One may say that the pair became the distinguishing feature of such dramas. They pelted every other character with hostile comment and kept alive in the audience a strong spirit of mockery. That is the attitude which satire tries early to establish and to intensify as the poem or play moves toward its climax.

In *Every Man Out of His Humour*, Jonson also perfected points in his dramatic construction which he first essayed in his first humor comedy. In the second play his commentators paint more sharply outlined satiric portraits at the beginning of the action and they establish more immediately and more effectively the satiric atmosphere. However Jonson did not succeed in this, his first comical satire, in placing his derided figures in a well-constructed plot. Yet he was able to break up the single line of fools and knaves who march stiffly through formal satires into groups stratified on the basis of their social competence. He thus made it natural for the creatures composing a group to stimulate and to aggravate each other's follies. At such times the commentators could rest from their arduous labors and let the characters escape from their surveillance long enough to resemble human beings.

Finally, *Every Man Out of His Humour* established more firmly the conventional ending of a satiric play. Whatever devices the author uses, he must leave the audience in a state of mind completely different from that produced by the denouement of a comedy. At the close of a romantic comedy the spectators feel relief at the untying of all the knots of a complicated plot, and joy over the anticipated happiness of hero and heroine. When ridicule is liberally inserted into the conventional Plautine plot, the spectators also experience a kind of comic catharsis. They feel vicariously purged of their own impulses toward folly.

The professed aim of writers of satire was different. In place of the unmixed serenity supposed to follow the denouement of a comedy, they offered deep ethical satisfaction. The reform of the knave established order in man's moral world and the return of the fool to sanity cleansed his social life from absurdity. In reality, however, *Every Man Out of His Humour* and other plays cast in the same dramatic mould do not produce the advertised emotional and aesthetic effect. They tend rather to leave the audience and the reader in an intensified state of scorn at human folly and futility. The laughter, though often corrective and salutary both to the characters in the plays and to the spectators, remains derisive and turbulent even after the last actors have left the stage.

After completing *Every Man Out of His Humour* Jonson wrote two other 'comical satyres,' *Cynthia's Revels* (1600) and *Poetaster* (1600-1601). They were both produced before *Troilus and Cressida*, Shakespeare's first imitation of the form, appeared. In his second and third comical satires Jonson extends his innovations, accommodating them to different types of play. Marston, too, in three of his early satiric plays, *Antonio and Mellida, Jack Drums Entertainment,* and *What You Will,* wrote comical satires of his own. Shakespeare was probably familiar with all of these dramas. But the features which he developed in his satiric plays written after 1600 had all been clearly drawn in *Every Man Out of His Humour.* This first comical satire was the play which partly determined the structure of *Troilus and Cressida* and contaminated its spirit.

VI

Troilus and Cressida

THE form of *Troilus and Cressida* has perplexed critics from the time of its first editors Heminge and Condell. They could not decide how to classify it. On the title page of the first quarto edition it is described as a 'Famous Historie,' but in the preface to this same edition it is repeatedly referred to as a comedy. The editors of the First Folio, however, entitled it *The Tragedie of Troylus and Cressida* and planned to give it a place in their volumes among the tragedies immediately after *Romeo and Juliet*. But while the edition was going through the press, they apparently realized that *Troilus and Cressida* was not comedy, tragedy, or history, if the terms be used in a conventional sense. 'They therefore,' says Charles Knight, 'placed it between the Histories and Tragedies, leaving to the reader to make his own classification.' [1] The quandary of the first editors has reappeared in the work of every critic of this play, so that Professor Tatlock in 1916 could with propriety call the nature of *Troilus and Cressida* 'the chief problem of Shakespeare.' [2]

Fortunately most of this sense of confusion disappears if the play be regarded as Shakespeare's conscious imitation of the comical satires of Jonson and Marston. For Shakespeare wrote *Troilus and Cressida* in 1601, when the vogue for comical satire was at its height. As usual he treated his models in so original a way that the structure of his play has very little in common with the stiff schematism of *Every Man Out of His Humour*. Yet it will become evident that Shakespeare's work retains all the features which most clearly

98

distinguish dramatic satire from the three more usual dramatic forms. This is particularly true of the love story. To be sure the events of the war form much more than a setting for the relations of Troilus with Cressida. They exhibit a characteristic clash of Renaissance political philosophies and Renaissance ethical systems. And from this conflict Troilus emerges firmly set upon the path which is to lead him to frustration both as a warrior and as a lover.

The philosophical character of the play, no less than the tone of its satire, was partly determined by the nature of the audience for whom the piece was written. It could not have been designed for the popular theatre. Any spectators gathered there would have been bored by its lengthy undramatic discussions of political and moral problems. Nor would *Troilus and Cressida* have pleased an audience assembled at Whitehall. The speeches bear too heavy a load of vulgarity and vituperation for the ears of the Queen and her courtiers, male and female. The characters in the play more than once turn directly to the audience and address it in scurrilous terms. Pandarus's final speech is both gross and insulting. Facing the spectators he beseeches all the bawds among them to weep for his discomfiture:

> Good traders in the flesh, set this in your painted cloths,
> As many as be here of Pandar's Hall,
> Your eyes, half out, weep out at Pandar's fall.
>
> (v. x. 46-7)

Shakespeare would have been out of his senses to have hurled this indecent speech at the court as the final lines of his drama.

If not for the London populace or the court, for what special audience might *Troilus and Cressida* have been designed? Peter Alexander has recently suggested that it was written for a crowd of benchers gathered for some festive occasion at one of the Inns of Court.[3] The scurrility which

would have been offensive to the Queen and her court was
nicely calculated to amuse a crowd of gay and dissolute barristers. Students of the law would have been interested in
the presentation of conflicting theories of the state and entertained by the employment of such terms as 'the law of nature
and of nations' in the precise signification that they had
recently been given by Alberico Gentili, since 1587 Regius
Professor of Civil Law at Oxford.[4] Obviously a play cast in
unconventional dramatic form would have been more easily
understood and more readily accepted by an audience of
barristers than by a crowd filling the Globe Theatre.

Shakespeare's most obvious satiric intention appears in his
treatment of the love story. The tale of Troilus and Cressida,
from its first appearance in Benoît's *Le Roman de Troie,* has
provoked a satiric attitude in almost every author who has
treated it. Benoît introduces the pair at the moment of their
final parting. Appearing only in nine widely separated sec-
tions of the poem, the lovers form a digression from the main
plot. They relieve the monotony of the war narrative and
give the author an opportunity to make conventional satiric
comment on woman's infidelity. The nature with which
Benoît endowed his Briseida has clung to her successor Cressida wherever she has appeared in subsequent literature. By
the time of Shakespeare the heroine had become a creature
to deplore and to deride. Troilus, by a similar process of
degeneration, had become a warrior ruined by an unworthy
love for a wanton, and Pandarus had turned into a leering
pimp. Where could Shakespeare have found characters better
suited to that excoriation and derision of sexual indulgence
which the English satirists of the sixteenth century had made
a literary fashion?

II

By Shakespeare's time all the heroes of the *Iliad* had suffered a similar degeneration. Both the Greek and the Trojan

host was weak in intellectual and moral fibre. The sources from which Shakespeare derived his information about the Trojan war would have led him to believe that the Greeks were cowards, braggarts, and bullies, and that the Trojans were dastards, utterly unable to obey the dictates of either conscience or judgment.[5]

Shakespeare's treatment of these two armies forms similar pictures of social chaos. The Greeks come to disaster because, though accepting the conventional stoic position in ethics and politics, they thwart socially reasonable action by the indulgence of personal emotion or mere whim. The Trojans meet the same fate for a different reason. They profess knowledge of the theory that to follow Nature in both social and personal life is to follow Reason, but they deliberately choose a Machiavellian philosophy. They decide to make trial of the unorthodox theory that to follow Nature is to follow Will. Shakespeare clearly adheres to the time-honored view and so presents both deviations from Reason as leading the armies and the individuals who compose them to disaster.

Ulysses in his great speech on degree enunciates the ethical and political laws which a man may break only at his peril. He describes the properly constituted state as a carefully articulated system of allegiances and subordinations. And he warns his fellow warriors that when once degree—his name for the principle which binds this system together—is abandoned, the entire social system disintegrates.

> O, when degree is shak'd
> Which is the ladder to all high designs,
> Then enterprise is sick! . . .
>   .   .   .
> Take but degree away, untune that string,
> And, hark, what discord follows!
>   (I. iii. 101-3, 109-10)

The action in the drama, so far as it concerns the Greek host, illustrates this text. It presents a political situation like that appearing in the last two parts of *Henry VI* and in *Richard II*. Because the king or supreme leader is unable or unwilling to exercise his 'speciality of rule,' the state disintegrates into social chaos. In the historical plays the confusion leads to a conventional tragic catastrophe—the death of the king. In *Troilus and Cressida* the principal characters defy the sound political theories which they expound with so much eloquence. As a result, their action becomes futile and fills the audience with cynical amusement, the emotion most appropriate to satire.

The Greeks know that they should follow the sage advice of Ulysses, but they cannot do so because, as Thersites says, they are creatures of 'too much blood and too little brain.' Achilles is presented as the chief victim of subversive emotion. He skulks in his tent because his self-love has been wounded. Ulysses devises a scheme to purge Achilles of his pride and his obstinacy. His plan is to have the Greeks pretend that in their opinion the blockish Ajax would make a worthier antagonist for Hector than Achilles. That pretence, he says, using the satiric language of purgation, 'will physic the great Myrmidon.'

The first step in Ulysses' program is to manipulate Ajax into a mood in which he will be eager to fight Hector. He succeeds so well that he drives Ajax into a supreme exhibition of his imbecility and renders the fatuous boaster completely ridiculous. Then he begins to work upon Achilles. He causes the Greek warriors to file by their sulky comrade, each making contemptuous gestures in his direction. This scorn from his former comrades produces the desired effect. He takes counsel with himself. 'Whither has fled my reputation?' he asks in a soliloquy which becomes a deeply philosophical pondering of the question.

The first part of Ulysses' plot to purge Achilles has succeeded. It has filled the recalcitrant leader with distaste for his petulant selfishness. His mind responds eagerly to the philosophical arguments which Ulysses now advances with persuasive seriousness. His first argument is that a man who flouts the good opinion of his fellows cannot keep alive his necessary self-respect. His second argument is that a heroic reputation dies when heroic action ceases. Time soon destroys the memory of past achievements, however glorious. This truth Ulysses expresses in one of the most profound of the philosophical lyrics in which the play abounds:

> For Time is like a fashionable host,
> That slightly shakes his parting guest by the hand,
> And with his arms outstretch'd, as he would fly,
> Grasps in the comer. The welcome ever smiles,
> And farewell goes out sighing. Let not virtue seek
> Remuneration for the thing it was!
> For beauty, wit,
> High birth, vigour of bone, desert in service,
> Love, friendship, charity, are subjects all
> To envious and calumniating Time.

> (III. iii. 165-74)

This is one of the most memorable expressions of the Renaissance preoccupation with mutability, or the Triumph of Time. It is the real subject of most of Shakespeare's sonnets. It is what Mark Van Doren describes as 'swift-footed terrible Time that writes death on faces, roots out the work of masonry, fades roses, brings winter after spring and makes in general the music to which all the world marches groaning to its end.' [6] The fact that passages of philosophical and imaginative fervor appear during the exposure of folly distinguishes *Troilus and Cressida* from all other comical satires. These poetic triumphs offer welcome relief from the scornful temper of satire and ally the program of personal reform with the highest issues of the individual life, in its relation both to society and to eternity.

The speeches of Ulysses convince Achilles that his conduct

has been folly. He realizes how deep an injury he has done his good name:

> I see my reputation is at stake;
> My fame is shrewdly gor'd.
> (III. iii. 227-8)

His reason is convinced. But now he explains that his refusal to fight has resulted from other considerations than wounded vanity. He is in love with one of Priam's daughters, and the code of chivalric love forbids him to seek the death of her kinsman. Reason, therefore, must give way to the irrational demands of an artificial code of amorous behavior.

~ Shakespeare takes this way of ridiculing a decadent survival in Elizabethan life of one of the ideals of chivalry. He satirizes what Professor W. W. Lawrence describes as the 'fantastic exaggeration of medieval *fine amor* in the manners of Elizabeth and her court.'[7] More specifically he is turning his attention to exhibitions of the cult as it appeared in the adventurers and military leaders among the great lords and lesser nobility of his age. The extravagant protestations of devotion made in medieval romance by the lovers to their ladies were repeated by many Elizabethan courtiers, of whom Essex himself furnished some of the most absurd exhibitions. For example, it is reported that when he was campaigning in the peninsula, he thrust his pike into one of the gates of Lisbon, 'demanding aloud if "any Spaniard mewed therein durst adventure forth in favor his mistress to break a lance." There was no reply.'[8] The irrational obligations to the service of love, which the warriors in *Troilus and Cressida* constantly recognize, would thus serve as satiric comment upon a contemporary folly.

The purgation and reform of Achilles hoped for by Ulysses and expected in a comic-satiric ending does not take place. Only the tempest of grief and rage aroused by the murder of Patroclus drives him back to battle. Then he acts not like a soldier but like a man wild with anger. So Ulysses' nicely devised plan to force Achilles to resume his social duties fails. The outcome, as in the case of all the plans of the other characters, whether wise or foolish, is futility, and was meant to awaken the scornful laughter of satire.

Attached to the Greek story is Thersites, whom Shakespeare could have found in Homer, supplied with all his scurrility. Indeed it has been suggested that all the abusive characteristics which he reveals in *Troilus and Cressida* are merely Shakespeare's dramatic expansion of Homer's brief description of Thersites as translated by Chapman.[9] However, the discovery of the source of his explosive nature does not explain his dramatic function. Consequently the critics have never ceased in their efforts to define and clarify his role. Their usual explanation is that he is a combination of clown and chorus. Brandes calls him 'a kind of satyr-chorus.'[10] But Thersites is neither a chorus nor a clown. A chorus suggests classical drama or English Senecan tragedy, both utterly unlike *Troilus and Cressida* in form. Moreover, a chorus presents the moral or religious principles of the author, or at least the values by which he wishes his characters to be judged. Or it may be the ally of the stage-manager, recounting events which cannot be crowded into the two hours' traffic of the stage. Thersites fills none of these offices. His voice is not the voice of Shakespeare. The spectators as well as all the characters in the play realize that his opinions are worthless, that his sentiments are as odious as the man himself.

Thersites is more like a court fool, for he is attached to the entourage of Ajax as a kind of licensed jester. Drayton Henderson believes that he is a descendant of Erasmus' 'wise fool' designed to represent the very essence of Folly.[11] But this figure, of whom the Fool in *King Lear* is a notable example, always uses his apparent nonsense as a cover from which to shoot at his victims arrows that are barbed with common sense.

Thersites differs from these conventional figures in making opprobrious speech an end in itself. He is a railer, a detractor, and a buffoon in exactly the same sense as was Carlo Buffone, and he makes an identical contribution to the satiric spirit of the drama. Like Carlo he designs his speeches so that they will evoke at the same time amusement and aversion. This form of derision, by lightening scorn with comfortable laughter, gives the play comic substance. The following description of Ajax shows how, like the buffoon, Thersites is addicted to bold 'adulterate similes':

> Why, 'a stalks up and down like a peacock—a stride and a stand; ruminates like a hostess that hath no arithmetic but her brain to set down her reckoning; bites his lip with a politic regard, as who should say 'There were wit in his head, an 'twould out.' And so there is; but it lies as coldly in him as fire in a flint, which will not show without knocking.
>
> (III. iii. 251-7)

Some of his satire which sounds like pure billingsgate to us would have seemed to an audience of Elizabethan benchers to contain the right Juvenalan fervor. In particular, when scourging sexual abnormalities an author might speak with some of the savagery that Marston had made popular. Thersites' description of Patroclus as Achilles' 'masculine whore' would not seem too foul an expression for so detestable a truth. And his further railing against Patroclus, the effeminate dandy, would have seemed to be couched in the correct satiric key:

> . . . thou idle immaterial skein of sleave-silk, thou green sarcenet flap for a sore eye, thou tassel of a prodigal's purse . . . Ah how the poor world is pestered with such water-flies—diminutives of nature!
>
> (V. i. 35-9)

When his appetite for detraction drives him to lampoon Agamemnon and Menelaus, it seems less justified. Then it becomes a part of his Carlo-like role of 'common jester, a violent railer.' His comments on the meaning of the events and the individual follies that drive the action to futility run the gamut from intelligent comment to foul billingsgate. When he says of Achilles and Patroclus, 'With too much blood and too little brain, these two may run mad' (v. i. 52-3), he is presenting Shakespeare's thesis and providing the audience with a standard by which to judge the conduct of the pair and to understand its utter vanity. But when he sums up the Trojan War in such phrases as, 'All the argument is a cuckold and a whore' (II. iii. 78-9) and 'Lechery, lechery; still wars and lechery; nothing else holds fashion' (v. ii. 195-7), though he may permanently jaundice the eyes of all beholders, he must be regarded as playing his role of buffoon, to their delight. It is quite different when he descends to spouting long passages of spiteful execration and becomes no more than a foul-mouthed railer.

Many critics have called Thersites 'the most un-Shakespearean figure' in all the dramatist's works. This does not mean that he represents an uncharacteristic mood of the author, that Shakespeare designed him to be the mouthpiece of a deep personal despair. The real explanation is much less subjective. It is merely that the poet tried to transform the Homeric Thersites into one of the conventional, well-nigh indispensable characters of the new satiric comedy. The figure successfully performs all the various offices of the railer and buffoon. If he is offensive in the discharge of his dramatic duties, that is because Shakespeare's higher emotional intensity and superior imagination lend to the characters qualities that, endurable in the art of lesser men, are aesthetically unacceptable when coming from the hand of a genius.

III

The Trojans in *Troilus and Cressida* fare little better at the poet's hands than the Greeks. They too forsake Reason, not through yielding to the temptations of irrational passion, but through deliberately abandoning the traditional identification of Reason with Nature. Instead they adopt one of the most dangerous heresies of the Renaissance. As we have seen, the Trojans probably came to Shakespeare from the pages of Caxton's *Recuyell,* where they were depicted as ignoble. However, there are some critics who believe that the Trojans represent some sort of ideal values. G. Wilson Knight, for example,[12] believes that they stand for intuition, and assumes that Shakespeare shared his opinion. Such a notion would have been utterly foreign to Elizabethan habits of thought. But the point that Shakespeare made the audience for whom he wrote the play would grasp at once. They would see that the Trojans in rejecting the orthodox stoic position in both politics and ethics were embarking upon a perilous course of action. In abandoning the thesis that to follow Nature is to follow Reason, and adopting as their political creed the Machiavellian heresy that to follow Nature is to follow Will, they were inviting disaster.

The Trojans first appear in a council of war like that held by the Greeks. They are discussing whether they should return Helen to her husband and bring the war to an end, or hold her and continue the bloody slaughter. Hector stands for the conservative point of view. He argues that both Reason and the

> Moral laws
> Of nature and of nations speak aloud
> To have her back return'd.
>
> (II. ii. 184-6)

Hector's attitude however provokes a wild protest from Troilus:

Nay, if we talk of reason
Let's shut our gates and sleep. Manhood and honour
Should have hare hearts, would they but fat their thoughts
With this cramm'd reason. Reason and respect
Makes livers pale and lustihood deject.

(II. ii. 46-50)

Troilus wishes to substitute Will for Reason, for what, he asks, is 'aught but as 'tis valued'? And, he continues, whatever a man has obtained through Will, Honor demands that he retain. Honor, thus, is the ideal that restrains and directs desire. It prevents Will from becoming utterly flighty and unreliable. Hector vigorously opposes this unsound doctrine, asserting that to make individual desire the standard of value is mad idolatry. To divorce one's Will from Reason is, in his opinion, to become the slave of one's appetites. But the young rebel is unconvinced and is confirmed in his error by Paris, who urges that the irrational demands of Honor are more compelling than those of Reason. Such heresy brings a severe rebuke from Hector to both of the youths. He says that they talk like those immature men:

Whom Aristotle thought
Unfit to hear moral philosophy.

(II. ii. 166-7)

And he warns them of the dangers that lurk in the adoption of this skeptical philosophy:

The reasons you allege do more conduce
To the hot passion of distemp'red blood
Than to make up a free determination
'Twixt right and wrong, for pleasure and revenge
Have ears more deaf than adders to the voice
Of any true decision.

(II. ii. 168-73)

These wise words prove to be prophetic. Troilus follows unreasonable pleasure and becomes the slave of the wanton

Cressida. He follows turbulent, irrational courses of revenge and is left rushing wildly and futilely after his rival, whom he is doomed never to overtake.

But Hector, in spite of his eloquent advocacy of the orthodox way of life, suddenly decides to put the principles of Troilus into effect. It is as if he said, 'We know all the old arguments about the identification of Reason with Nature, but since our Honor seems to require us to keep Helen, let us adopt the Machiavellian view of Nature and follow whither our Wills lead.' [13]

In taking this position he yields his rational leadership to a democracy of conflicting wills and takes the fatal step which leads to the ruin of himself and his army. We must not forget, however, that Troilus is 'the prime mover' of the Trojans to this desperate course of action. In his activities as a warrior he early professes himself to be a truant from reason. And a young man who forswears his allegiance to reason can be confidently expected, when he falls in love, to let his blood rule his safer guides. Troilus the warrior and Troilus the lover thus represent different aspects of a life which has deliberately freed itself of all rational control.

IV

Most critics find it hard to believe that Shakespeare intentionally derides the lovers and their story. Like other mortal men and women, they love a lover and are convinced that Shakespeare has depicted both Troilus and Cressida sympathetically. Nevertheless it seems clear that he meant their adventures to exemplify lust and, therefore, certain to lead them both to deserved disaster.

Cressida has naturally had fewer apologists than Troilus, for by Shakespeare's time literary tradition had fixed her as a wanton in the minds of everyone who could read. However, Shakespeare obviously does not treat her with the moral

fervor which Henryson showed in *The Testament of Cressid.*
The earlier poet depicted her at the end of her life as a piti-
able beggar afflicted with leprosy. There is nothing leprous
about Shakespeare's Cressida. Her seductiveness is never exerted on a low physical plane. Herford is right in asserting
that 'she has a certain girlish air of grace.' [14] She is a sinner
endowed with charm, and she appeals to her lover with all
the resources of her complicated nature.

Even if all this be true, Cressida should not be characterized in Tucker Brooke's words as exhibiting a 'daintiness
reaching vainly after nobility.' [15] Nor is she supposed to
arouse our pity or make us lament the human waste in her
defection from virtue. The obvious sexual charm of this
enchantress must not make us forget that Shakespeare designed her as a kind of villain of his piece and meant his
audiences to reject her.

Troilus, too, is depicted as a slave of passion. Yet many
critics have thought of him as an inexperienced young ideal-
ist who is seduced and ruined by a sensual and calculating
woman. W. W. Lawrence believes him to be a boy made
heart-sick by the faithlessness of the unworthy woman to
whom he has given his first love. Professor Boas sees him as
a 'chivalrous adorer,' [16] and Wilson Knight makes him a
metaphysical lover who is continually seeking to make desire
infinite, an emotion which is a 'slave to limit.' [17] But Troilus
early in the play declares himself a servant of his 'Will' and
one of the Elizabethan meanings of the word was physical
desire. And Troilus at the very beginning of his affair with
Cressida betrays himself to be an expert in sensuality. The
prospect of an assignation with his desirable lady makes him
dizzy with excitement:

> I am giddy; expectation whirls me round.
> The imaginary relish is so sweet
> That it enchants my sense. What will it be,
> When that the wat'ry palates taste indeed

> Love's thrice repured nectar? Death, I fear me,
> Swooning destruction, or some joy too fine,
> Too subtile-potent, tun'd too sharp in sweetness
> For the capacity of my ruder powers.
> I fear it much; and I do fear besides
> That I shall lose distinction in my joys.
>
> (III. ii. 19-28)

Troilus is beset with the sexual gourmet's fear lest the morsel which he is about to devour will be so ravishing to his taste that thereafter he will lose all sense of nice distinction in sexual experience. In this speech Shakespeare's audience would see only refined and calculated sensuality. Few would have any doubts about the sort of meeting he was licentiously anticipating.

On the remote chance that some of the spectators might still be left in the dark, Shakespeare brings in Pandarus to comment on the assignation in a way that makes its character unmistakable even to a 'thrice repured' mind. Pandarus takes an old libertine's delight in telling the lovers how to act:

> An'twere dark, you'ld close sooner. So. So: rub on
> and kiss the mistress. How now? a kiss in fee farm?
>
> (III. ii. 50-53)

In other words, 'What are you doing? Giving her a kiss that will last forever?'

Cressida plays the temptress with obvious skill. She knows how to use the arts of coquetry in a way to tease and intensify most successfully her lover's ardor. She wishes to enjoy his passion only when it has reached its highest intensity. Troilus responds to her efforts in the key of his first sensuous soliloquy. His mind runs on sexual experience:

> This is the monstruosity in love, lady, that the will
> is infinite and the execution confin'd, that the desire
> is boundless and the act a slave to limit.
>
> (III. ii. 87-90)

Speeches like these are designed to excite Cressida as her coquetry does Troilus, when she says,

> . . . Sweet, bid me hold my tongue.
> For in this rapture I shall surely speak
> The thing I shall repent. See, see, your silence,
> Cunning in dumbness, from my weakness draws
> My very soul of counsel! Stop my mouth.
> TROILUS. And shall albeit sweet music issues thence.
> [kisses her]
> PANDARUS (aside). Pretty, i' faith.
> CRESSIDA. My lord. I do beseech you pardon me.
> 'Twas not my purpose thus to beg a kiss.
> I am asham'd. O heavens! What have I done?
>
> (III. ii. 137-48)

When these amorous preliminaries have sufficiently enflamed the pair, Pandarus all but puts them to bed on the stage.

This scene is a masterful exposure of the refined licentiousness of both Troilus and Cressida. With the help of Pandarus and his grinning comments, Shakespeare makes the encounter of these two adepts in love-play both ridiculous and evil. He succeeds in awakening both derision of their sin and aversion to it. No one with any understanding of contemporary satire would expect a happy sequel to this sensual meeting.

We next see the pair the following morning. Like Romeo and Juliet, they sing an *aubade*. But their matutinal exchange is accompanied, not by the sweet notes of the lark, but by the cawing of ribald crows. Cressida is petulant. She accuses Troilus of being tired of her. Men never stay long enough. Troilus, now released from the enchantment of his Circe, replies realistically that she had better be prudent—put more clothes on, one infers—or she will take cold and curse him for it. This is not the morning after an experience of the rapture of perfect married love. It is the fretful dialogue of two sated sensualists. The scene must have aroused derisive laughter among the worldly-wise young barristers who witnessed it. To point and prolong their enjoyment, Pandarus bustles in with a mouthful of suggestive comments.

Everyone in the audience confidently expected Cressida's infidelity. So Shakespeare artfully prepares the audience to accept derisively her awaited perfidy. He has her answer with another shrill vow of eternal faithfulness the first summons to return to her father and the Greeks. To an audience realizing her frailty, her protestations produce effective dramatic irony. Almost immediately she loses even the shallow dignity that the utterance of the oath gives her for an instant. She promises that, at the coming moment of parting from her lover, her grief shall be exhibited in a manner which she believes is prescribed for a romantic lady in distress. She cries:

> . . . I'll go in and weep.
>
> *   *   *
>
> Tear my bright hair and scratch my praised cheeks,
> Crack my clear voice with sobs and break my heart
> With sounding Troilus. I will not go from Troy.
>
> (IV. ii. 113-15)

The next speech of Troilus closes with a fine poetical expression of his grief at parting from Cressida. Yet nothing in his beautiful figurative language adds any nobility to his love or to the woman who has aroused it:

> Injurious time now with a robber's haste
> Crams his rich thievery up, he knows not how.
> As many farewells as be stars in heaven,
> With distinct breath and consign'd kisses to them,
> He fumbles up into a loose adieu,
> And scants us with a single famish'd kiss,
> Distasted with the salt of broken tears.
>
> (IV. iv. 44-50)

However, Shakespeare does not permit Troilus to leave the stage with this exalted strain of poetry ringing in our ears. He puts into his mouth absurdly reiterated demands of

'Be thou true.' Cressida at first answers, 'But I'll be true,' but finally rebels at her lover's repeated exhortation. 'O heavens "Be true" again?' she exclaims after he has besought her for the fourth or fifth time. Everyone familiar with the tale knew that she could not and would not 'be true.' So the phrase 'Be true' becomes the ironic leit-motif of the extended dialogue and awakens throughout its course sardonic amusement.

From this strained antiphonal, Cressida goes directly to the Greek camp, and kisses all the men, with an abandon much greater than the liberal customs of Elizabethan salutation prescribed. Ulysses, one of the commentators, is conveniently at hand to keep the audience clear on that point:

> Fie, fie upon her!
> There's language in her eye, her cheek, her lip;
> Nay, her foot speaks. Her wanton spirits look out
> At every joint and motive of her body.
>
> (IV. v. 54-7)

So incorrigible a coquette and wanton clearly disappoints no dramatic expectation when she takes Diomed for her lover. He is a much more suitable mate for her than Troilus was, for he is a cynical realist, without romantic ideals which she must try to actualize. He does not put either her feelings or her vocabulary under any undue tension. In a pair of simple, flippant couplets she explains her transfer to Diomed's bed and board:

> Ah, poor our sex! this fault in us I find,
> The error of our eye directs our mind.
> What error leads must err. O, then conclude
> Minds sway'd by eyes are full of turpitude.
>
> (V. ii. 109-12)

Some critics argue that Troilus' actual observation of Cressida's infidelity is presented as a deeply 'tragic situation'—'one of the most poignant scenes of eavesdropping in all

Shakespeare.' But Troilus' discovery of his lady's faithless-ness inspires him to no nobility of thought or action. It merely stimulates him to indulge in what he himself calls 'madness of discourse':

> This she? No, this is Diomed's Cressida!
> If beauty have a soul, this is not she.
> If souls guide vows, if vows be sanctimonies,
> If sanctimony be the gods' delight,
> If there be rule in unity itself—
> This is not she. O madness of discourse,
> That cause sets up, with and against itself!
> Bifold authority! where reason can revolt
> Without perdition, and loss assume all reason
> Without revolt: this is, and is not, Cressid.
>
> (v. ii. 137-46)

Emotions endowed with tragic potentiality do not employ language so grotesquely tortured as this. Shakespeare's tragic heroes in great crises never confuse their passionate and imaginative utterance with such dialectical exercise. Troilus, in attempting to preserve his characteristic self-deceit in the face of contradictory objective fact, forces his logical machine to perform feats of prestidigitation that make it creak ridicu-lously. Yet its work enables him to persist in his substitution of a passion-spun distortion of fact for actuality. Thus he loses, for good and all, his hold on reality. Henceforward he acts like one distracted. The disordered lover all too easily becomes the disordered warrior. Crazy with disappointed passion, he futilely pursues his rival, Diomed, with shrill threats of 'venom'd vengeance.' And Hector's death only leads him to shake his fist more wildly in the direction of the 'vile abominable tents' where tomorrow he will franti-cally rush upon the 'great-siz'd coward' and wreak revenge.

Troilus' nature is always in a state of emotional tumult. A chaotic personality of his sort espouses folly as easily when in love as when in battle. Thersites points out the connection between the two fields of Troilus' conduct, by commenting on the 'young Troyan ass, that loves the whore' and on his violent 'clapper-clawing' of Diomed. He thereby prevents attribution of any nobility to their private squabble over a 'dissembling luxurious drab.' Like all buffoons, Thersites calls right things by wrong names. He tells the truth, however awry the form and spirit of his expression.

Pandarus acts as the official commentator for the love story just as does Thersites for the events of the war. Though not exactly a buffoon and a railer, Pandarus maintains as successfully as his fellow commentator a derisive attitude on the part of his audience. No one who attends his speeches is in danger of mistaking for noble emotions the calculating passion of Cressida or the sensuality of Troilus. Pandarus' every utterance is designed to keep the hostile laughter awake. Even his tears at the imminent parting of the lovers would seem to be either crocodile drops or tokens of the disappointment of a pander at the loss of the office that gave his senile licentiousness a vicarious satisfaction. The last lines of the play are devoted to his mock lament over the wretched rewards of a bawd. They show conclusively that it was his spirit that brooded over the love story.

v

The finale of *Troilus and Cressida* is a subtle variation of the approved end of the characters derided in dramatic satire. Throughout the play Troilus' infatuation is presented in a way to provoke mingled feelings of revulsion and amusement. This complicated emotion Shakespeare maintained and accentuated in the last scene of the play. Two kinds of denouement had become conventional in the comical satires of Jonson and Marston. The characters chosen as butts of ridicule were either purged and reformed, or scornfully ejected from the comedy. Victims of social folly could be

exposed in such a way as to make their amendment and reform seem natural. But moral delinquency was too much
a part of the culprit's essential nature to be easily corrected
and discarded. It deserved to be pursued to the very last by
the scornful laughter of both author and audience.

The formal satirists adopted this last method, ejecting evil
men and women from their poems with exclamations of
fierce disdain. Jonson, too, had treated vicious characters in
just this way. Shakespeare himself at the end of *Twelfth
Night* had sent Malvolio running off the stage shouting, 'I'll
be revenged on the whole pack of you,' and the frantic steward had been pursued by the jeers of the enemies who had
exposed him, and by the scorn of the audience.

Troilus and Cressida, too, are dismissed with similar mockery. The critics should then not be troubled that the woman
has not been condignly punished for her infidelity or that
her lover has not been slain before the eyes of the audience
in single combat with Achilles. Such poetic justice would
have given each of the lovers the dignity of a tragic figure;
and nowhere during the action had they attained such stature. If we insist upon following Troilus beyond the limits of
the play, after hearing his hysterical threat to haunt Achilles
'like a wicked conscience still,' we may, if we are discerning,
anticipate his fate. But, as a victim of uncontrolled passion
for a wanton, he did not deserve the dignity of a death on a
field of battle. And Cressida deserved a similar moment of
nobility still less. Futility, Shakespeare clearly believed, was
the proper end for characters designed to fit into the intellectual and structural conventions of dramatic satire.

However, in spite of the fact that Shakespeare employed a
firmly established literary convention in fashioning the close
of *Troilus and Cressida,* the ending has seldom been understood. The reason seems to be that in the play Shakespeare
divested the convention of all its obvious features. Troilus
has been caught in no booby trap. His sin and folly have

brought him to no obvious disaster. His catastrophe is of a more profound and less tangible sort. In accepting Will instead of Reason for his guide in public affairs as well as in the private life of his emotions, he has disrupted his entire personality and rendered himself distraught and futile. That is the meaning of Troilus' last frantic exit, but no commentator is at hand to interpret it. Pandarus, who might have performed this service for us, instead flings at the audience unsavory jests about the disappointments and disabilities of a pander's trade. Had Shakespeare designed *Troilus and Cressida* for a popular audience, he would never have put the final vile speech into the mouth of Pandarus. But this tirade, perfectly suited to the taste of a crowd of benchers, enhanced for them the meaning and the temper of the play they had just seen.

Nor in all probability would Shakespeare have made so continuous an intellectual demand upon his hearers if he had been writing for a popular audience. The debates on political philosophy and ethical principles are much longer and more subtly constructed than the pattern of the main action demanded. But intellectual men at the turn of the century were greatly interested in the effect of the various new philosophies upon traditional political and ethical codes. They would have followed the careful presentation of the case for both the old and the new with rapt attention. And the chaos in the state and in the little world of man which followed the adoption of the heretical positions would have gained enormously in significance when regarded as the natural consequence of the abandonment of Reason—the plain way of Nature. However, the uninstructed reader, even though he is enthralled by the eloquence of Ulysses, Hector, and Troilus, is often at a loss to discover the relation of this persuasive rhetoric to the story of Troilus and Cressida. The intellectual foundations of the action are laid too deep for the understanding of a cursory reader or an inattentive spectator.

The profundity of the tone in which Shakespeare has all the characters express themselves also obscures the satiric thrust of his drama. It sicklies o'er with thought the half-grim, half-derisive mood demanded of an author of satiric plays. This severity has persuaded the critics either that Shakespeare began to write a tragedy which he never finished, or that in the year 1601 he himself was making a rendezvous with despair and doom.

These inferences are both unsound. If *Troilus and Cressida* is a kind of satiric play it can be judged by definite artistic standards. It need no longer be regarded as a confused and incomplete tragedy. Nor need it be condemned for the author's failure to adopt all the principles of the new comicall satyre. In *Troilus and Cressida* Shakespeare shows his unfailing independence of his models. He combines his satire of the vices of power politics and of lust with a long philosophical and lyrical debate. In his way he has produced a play filled with a new beauty and new significance. In one sense then the work establishes the standards by which it must be judged. But modern readers can best catch and cherish the magnificent values of *Troilus and Cressida* if they realize that the play is Shakespeare's highly original version of a recently devised form—the comicall satyre of Jonson and Marston.

Measure for Measure

Measure for Measure has been nearly as much of a puzzle to critics as *Troilus and Cressida*. Quiller-Couch states the usual opinion of the play when he asserts that there must be something wrong with it—otherwise the critics would not so 'entangle themselves in apologies and interpretations.' [1]

Since the original sin of the drama is usually thought to lie in the story itself, it will be well to have the plot clearly in mind at the beginning of this discussion. It runs as follows: The Duke of Vienna temporarily abandons his office and names Angelo to serve as deputy in his absence. Reputedly a man of severe moral principles, Angelo zealously enforces statutes that had long been ignored, and is particularly hot to give effect to obsolete laws against sexual irregularity. His first victim is Claudio, a young man who has lived with Juliet, his betrothed, as her husband. Reviving an ancient law, 'fourteen years out of date,' Angelo has him arrested and condemned to death. Claudio's sister, Isabella, a 'votarist of St. Clare,' visits the self-righteous Angelo and pleads with him to spare her brother.

Ironically, this saintly woman awakens in the austere deputy the first passion he has ever known, and he basely agrees to save her brother if she will yield her honor to him. She rejects his proposal and shows only disgust and amazement when Claudio urges her to sacrifice herself in order to save him from the death he abjectly fears. At this point the Duke, who, disguised as a Friar, is now observing the whole affair, advises Isabella to pretend to consent to Angelo's demand, but in the darkness and secrecy of the meeting to substitute for herself a certain Mariana, to whom Angelo had been publicly betrothed, but to whom he had turned unfaithful upon learning that she has lost her wealth. By way of excusing himself, he has given it out that her reputation has been smirched. After the substitution of Mariana for Isabella in the nocturnal meeting has taken place, Angelo breaks his promise and orders Claudio put to death. But the Duke again intervenes to save the condemned man and to expose Angelo's villainy. Through Isabella's plea Angelo is pardoned and forced to marry his abandoned Mariana. Claudio is united with Juliet, and the Duke and Isabella make the third marriage with which Elizabethan romantic comedies conventionally closed.

Shakespeare's dramatization of this tale the romantic critics found nauseous, and they expressed their aversion in no uncertain terms. Coleridge declared: 'The play is to me the most painful part of his genuine works . . . The comic and tragic parts equally border on the hateful—the one being disgusting the other being hateful.' [2] Good Dr. Furnival speaks of 'the stifling air of this drama.' Only Hazlitt among the romantics has a good word for the play. He sees that 'This is a play as full of genius as of wisdom.' Yet even he is enough child of his time to think it necessary to object to the frank sexual nature of the story. 'There is,' he adds, 'an original sin in the nature of the subject which prevents us from taking a cordial interest in it.'

Contemporary critics, released from the obligation to be modest in public, often recognize the great virtues in the play. John Masefield maintains that *Measure for Measure* is constructed 'closely and subtly for the stage' and is 'one of the greatest works of the greatest English mind.' R. W. Chambers in a charming and wise essay waxes merry over the fact that this sex-obsessed age of ours is too prudish to endure the old story of the substituted bride. He argues that in *Measure for Measure* Shakespeare has dealt with sin and its forgiveness in a spirit of exalted Christianity. Isabella's pleas to Angelo express Shakespeare's own conviction, for, says Chambers, 'Never does Shakespeare seem more passionately to identify himself with any of his characters than he does with Isabel, as she pleads for mercy against strict justice:

> . . . O, it is excellent
> To have a giant's strength, but it is tyrannous
> To use it like a giant.
> . . . But man, proud man,
> Drest in a little brief authority,
>   .   .   .
> Plays such fantastic tricks before high heaven
> As make the angels weep.
>   (II. ii. 107-9, 117-18, 121-2)

These 'marvellous and impassioned pleadings, unsurpassed anywhere in Shakespeare, are based on her Christian faith and upon the Sermon on the Mount.' [3]

Thus a play that to Coleridge was merely disgusting, a hundred years later seems to R. W. Chambers a work full of the holy passion that is the essential spirit of Christianity. No revolution in taste could be more complete. It is obvious that such critical contradictions as this must reflect contradictions in the play itself. And a few critics have tried to discover the nature of the aesthetically confusing incongruity.

W. W. Lawrence in his excellent *Shakespeare's Problem Comedies* suggests that all the strange emotional inconsistencies of the play come from Shakespeare's treatment of naïve and traditional narrative conventions in a serious realistic manner.[4] The old tale completely disregarded psychological truth, yet Shakespeare treats the important crises in the careers of the three main characters as revelations of the souls of subtly conceived individuals. According to this theory all the puzzles in the play are the result of a continuous struggle between artificiality and realism.

Other critics have found the trouble to lie in the fact that the story is incompatible with the conventions of comedy, indeed with its very genius. The villainy of Angelo and the cowardice of Claudio, set in a Vienna morally rotten from top to bottom, form a strange basis for any sort of merriment. Nor does calling *Measure for Measure* a 'dark' comedy, or recognizing it as the product of a pessimistic spirit, provide a chart for safe aesthetic sailing. E. K. Chambers solves the problem no more successfully by sagely remarking that the structure of the play 'indicates uncertainty of dramatic invention.' Mark Van Doren begins his analysis of the play by admitting that it is unsatisfactory, though certainly not from a lack of serious attention on Shakespeare's part. 'The reason is rather that it goes against his grain to make comedy out of such matter.' [5] But one may well ask why Shakespeare should ever deliberately write a play 'against his grain.' Surely so experienced a playwright would hardly labor to create a comedy out of material he felt unadapted to the dramatic form. Later in his essay Mr. Van Doren himself gives a strange answer to this question. 'Perhaps,' he suggests, 'in this year [1604] Shakespeare was not up to tragedy'—although he was almost surely at work on *Othello* at about the time when he was fashioning *Measure for Measure.*

The following paragraphs offer a different explanation of the aesthetic confusion caused by the drama, an explanation which does not attribute mythical woes to the author or find in him resented inner or outer compulsions to fashion a comedy out of unsuitable material. It is simply that *Measure for Measure* is Shakespeare's second attempt to adapt to his genius some of the conventions of comical satire.

According to this view Angelo was first designed as clearly as Malvolio or Troilus to serve as an object of ridicule. The Duke was as certainly a satiric and moral commentator as were similar figures in earlier dramas of Jonson or Marston. Isabella's first duty, then, was to serve as the main agent in the exposure and derision of Angelo. The Viennese background of corruption and moral filth is as harmonious with the sin of the principal culprit as was the disorganization of the Greek and Trojan hosts with the passion which destroyed Troilus and Cressida.

This satiric structure is now obscure because Isabella completely outgrew the role in which she was first cast. A modern audience is properly much more concerned for her fate than for her success in laying bare the hypocrisy of Angelo. Consequently the play does not end as a satire should. Angelo is exposed but not ejected from the play with a final burst of derision. Instead he is shown as purged of his sin, repentant, and ready to make atonement for it. This fact enables Shakespeare to put into Isabella's mouth a final plea for the mercy for which she has stood during the entire drama. Once the Duke has granted this prayer, Shakespeare has lost his chance for an effective denouement. So he falls back upon the conventional ending of romantic comedy, a marriage for both the deserving and undeserving. This offers no proper resolution of the emotions aroused by the characters and is a perfunctory and aesthetically unsatisfactory close to the complicated action. For Angelo deserves not a wife, but scornful ridicule. The nature of Isabella and of her problems on the other hand have carried us to the deepest springs of human conduct. They have all along trembled on the verge of tragedy. Her promised marriage to the Duke provides a completely unsatisfactory conclusion to such a dramatic career.

II

Let us examine then the fundamental satiric structure and temper of the drama. As in *Troilus and Cressida* the social world in which the characters live is in a state of chaos and for the same reason: 'The specialty of rule hath been neglected.' The Duke, as he himself confesses, has disregarded his plain duties as magistrate:

> We have strict statutes and most biting laws
> (The needful bits and curbs to headstrong steeds),
> Which for this fourteen years we have let sleep,
> Even like an o'ergrown lion in a cave,
> That goes not out to prey. Now, as fond fathers,
> Having bound up the threat'ning twigs of birch,
> Only to stick it in their children's sight
> For terror, not to use, in time the rod
> Becomes more mock'd than fear'd; so our decrees,
> Dead to infliction, to themselves are dead,
> And liberty plucks justice by the nose;
> The baby beats the nurse, and quite athwart
> Goes all decorum.
>
> (I. iii. 19-31)

The last lines of this speech are strikingly like some in Ulysses' famous speech describing the chaos that overtakes a society in which 'degree is shaked':

> Strength should be lord of imbecility
> And the rude son should strike the father dead.
>
> (I. iii. 114-15)

The social disintegration in *Measure for Measure* is of a somewhat different sort from that depicted in the earlier drama. Here the Duke's incompetence has resulted in moral chaos. Mr. Van Doren's trenchant description of the poisonous immorality of Vienna cannot be improved. 'The city,' he writes, 'stews in its vices; bawds and pimps swarm in the streets, the prisons are crowded with moral vermin, and the gentle folk have lost their goodness. Goodness exists; Isabella, if one likes, is a saint; but it is forced to be unwholesomely conscious of itself, and the universal consciousness of evil puts a certain bitter perplexity into everyone's voice.' The serious-minded are sore perplexed, but the careless and thoughtless are cynical and irresponsible in the face of the vice and license which flourish around them. Shakespeare, following the earlier satiric dramatists, obeyed a sound aes-

thetic instinct in setting the characters whose vices he satirizes in a morally chaotic milieu.

The Duke, fearing to be thought tyrannical if he should
now begin to correct his people, has chosen Angelo to be his
deputy. He disguises himself as a friar in order to observe
Angelo's actions. Indeed he intends to conduct a kind of
experiment on the fellow in the hope of discovering if his
cloistered virtue and untried purity will remain unchanged
under the stress of real temptation. The Duke's subsequent
actions, however, show that his real dramatic purpose is not
to probe Angelo's nature but to expose the man's unconscious hypocrisy and to hold it up for derision.

John Marston had made conventional the casting of a deposed and disguised Duke in the role of satiric commentator.
Malevole, who plays this part in *The Malcontent* (1600), is
Altofronto, the deposed Duke of Genoa. In *The Fawn* (1602)
the ironic commentator is Hercules, the disguised Duke of
Ferrara, who has followed his son abroad to watch the young
man's wooing of the Princess Dulcimel and to manipulate
events as he chooses. The first commentator which Marston
introduced into one of his plays was Feliche. He appears in
Antonio and Mellida (1599), not, to be sure, as a disguised
duke, but as no less of a hanger-on at the court. He, like Altofronto, seems to hold a roving commission to ferret out the
evils of life there. Now the Duke in *Measure for Measure*
bears a close relationship to these figures of Marston. He is
also a commentator, one who utters the condemnations of
his author as clearly as do Marston's characters. He too, like
Hercules in *The Fawn,* manipulates events in such a way as
to drive the derided figures into exaggerated displays of their
follies.

The Duke, playing the part of a friar, appropriately
couches his denunciations of vice in the solemn and elevated
language of a churchman. He lashes the bawd Pompey in a
tone of suitable indignation:

Fie, sirrah! a bawd, a wicked bawd!
The evil that thou causest to be done,
That is thy means to live. Do thou but think
What 'tis to cram a maw or clothe a back
From such a filthy vice. Say to thyself
'From their abominable and beastly touches
I drink, I eat, array myself, and live.'
Canst thou believe thy living is a life
So stinkingly depending?

(III. ii. 20-28)

His comments on the rancid condition of his city maintain the critical and sinister tone that Shakespeare desires his play to possess. It is the proper atmosphere for a satiric drama.

There is so great a fever on goodness, that the dissolution of it must cure it. Novelty is only in request; and
it is as dangerous to be aged in any kind of course, as it
is virtuous to be constant in any undertaking. There is
scarce truth enough alive to make societies secure; but
security enough to make fellowships accurst. Much
upon this riddle runs the wisdom of the world.

(III. ii. 235-42)

At the end of the play, just as he is about to remove his disguise, the Duke returns to this general condemnation of the social corruption in Vienna:

. . . My business in this state
Made me a looker-on here in Vienna,
Where I have seen corruption boil and bubble
Till it o'errun the stew; laws for all faults,
But faults so countenanc'd that the strong statutes
Stand like the forfeits in a barber's shop,
As much in mock as mark.

(v. i. 318-24)

This is sound comment, grave and reverent.

➤ To keep laughter awake, even though it be the sneering sort proper to satire, Shakespeare associates with the Duke a rogue named Lucio, a representative of the second or buf-

foonish commentator who had become conventional in satiric
plays. Lucio is a gay and ribald cynic like Carlo Buffone and
all his successors. His talk bristles with extravagant and
bawdy figures of speech, and his satiric portrait of Angelo is
a scurrilous and unsavory caricature:

> LUCIO. A little more lenity to lechery would do no
> harm in him. Something too crabbed that way, friar.
> DUKE. It is too general a vice, and severity must cure it.
> LUCIO. Yes, in good sooth, the vice is of a great kindred
> —it is well allied; but it is impossible to extirp it
> quite, friar, till eating and drinking be put down.
> They say this Angelo was not made by man and
> woman after the downright way of creation. Is it
> true, think you?
> DUKE. How should he be made then?
> LUCIO. Some report a sea-maid spawn'd him; some,
> that he was begot between two stockfishes. But it is
> certain that, when he makes water, his urine is con-
> geal'd ice; that I know to be true. And he is a mo-
> tion generative; that's infallible.
> DUKE. You are pleasant, sir, and speak apace.
>   (III. ii. 103-20)

Lucio is a much more credible human being than any of
Ben Jonson's buffoonish commentators, and much more credible than Thersites, whose censure is frank calumny. Though
a gentleman, Lucio has contact with the bawdy underworld,
which frequently erupts into the main action. Sexual pro-
miscuity to Lucio is a joke, and a merry one. This attitude
lends to all his comments a careless and cynical tone appropriate to a buffoonish satirist.

In creating this figure Shakespeare seems again to be indebted to John Marston. In his play *What You Will* (1601)
Marston presented as an ideal satiric commentator a character called Quadratus [Four Square], a keen-minded de-
bauchee, a gay ribald fellow of whom Pietro Aretino was
the prototype and patron. Marston believed that the satiric

attitude of his Quadratus was a happy union of the tradi-
tionally severe spirit of correction with the traditional gaiety
of comedy. Lucio in these respects clearly resembles Quadratus, but he has a more secure place in the plot than Marston's commentator. His appetite for cleverly expressed detraction leads him to slander the Duke to his disguised face
and to keep it up with perverse insistence. 'The Duke had
crotchets in him,' he confidentially informs the Friar. 'He
would be drunk, too, that let me inform you . . . The
Duke, I say to thee again, would eat mutton on Fridays. He's
not past it yet: and I say to thee, he would mouth with a
beggar, though she smelt brown bread and garlic. Say that
I said so. Farewell.' (III. ii. 134-6, 190-95.)

The Duke leads Lucio on, to the amusement of the audience, with the clear purpose of exposing him. When Lucio
plucks off the Friar's hood and discovers the Duke, the im-
pudent buffoon also accomplishes his own exposure. He then
tries to sneak unobtrusively away, but is arrested and held
before the Duke for sentence. Although threatening Lucio
with whipping and hanging after he has married the punk
whom he has got with child, the Duke relents and remits all
the 'forfeits' except his marriage with the courtesan. This
deflation of the careless cynic and liar is in exactly the right
key. An audience which has been entertained by this genial
rascal throughout the play would have been outraged to see
him severely punished. But it would accept the libertine's
forced marriage to the harlot as an excellent joke. Moreover
the sentence arouses in nice proportions the laughter of both
comedy and satire.

III

The satiric treatment of Angelo is conducted in a much
more serious mood. The portrait of him which the Duke
draws in the very first scene of the play lacks firm outline.
Though he knows the fellow's obvious characteristics, he

seems perplexed by them and brings them to the bar of general ethical principles for judgment:

> Angelo,
> There is a kind of character in thy life
> That to th' observer doth thy history
> Fully unfold. Thyself and thy belongings
> Are not thine own so proper as to waste
> Thyself upon thy virtues, they on thee.
> Heaven doth with us as we with torches do,
> Not light them for themselves; for if our virtues
> Did not go forth of us, 'twere all alike
> As if we had them not. Spirits are not finely touch'd
> But to fine issues; nor Nature never lends
> The smallest scruple of her excellence
> But, like a thrifty goddess, she determines
> Herself the glory of a creditor,
> Both thanks and use.
>
> (I. i. 27-41)

Later, in a dialogue with the Friar, he clears up some of the obscurity in his portrait:

> Lord Angelo is precise
> Stands at guard with envy, scarce confesses
> That his blood flows, or that his appetite
> Is more to bread than stone.
>
> (I. iii. 50-53)

Angelo, he says, follows strictly the dictates of conventional morality. He is an ethical formalist and proud of his way of controlling sexual impulse by ignoring its existence. However, it is Lucio who in his extravagant way makes Angelo's constricted nature clear to the audience. He calls him:

> . . . A man whose blood
> Is very snow-broth; one who never feels
> The wanton stings and motions of the sense
> But doth rebate and blunt his natural edge
> With profits of the mind, study and fast.
>
> (I. iv. 58-62)

By the time Lucio has made this speech, we understand Angelo so well that we detect the irony in the description and are prepared for the ribald characterization which has already been quoted. The semi-tragic action of the play is devised, then, not so much to test Angelo's undisciplined virtue as to expose the folly of his confident self-righteousness.

Measure for Measure thus begins as a satiric play should. The character who is to be exposed and shamed appears at once. Almost immediately the two contrasted commentators familiar to comical satire reveal their identities. If Shakespeare had adopted the most approved mechanism of the new dramatic type, he would have made the Duke knowingly tempt Angelo by sending Isabella to him. But by the year 1604 he had freed himself from the extreme formalism of the conventional structure of such plays. Besides, Isabella is too noble a character to serve as anyone's puppet. Lucio the buffoon does suggest that she seek an interview with Angelo and beg for her brother's life. But his purpose is to save Claudio, not to expose Angelo.

The subtle plan of tempting the austere Angelo, not through the calculated wiles of an experienced wanton like Cressida but through the cold beauty of an all but dedicated woman, is Shakespeare's own. Angelo, through his utter failure to understand the power of Claudio's temptation, has shown that he is ignorant of one whole range of human experience. For this reason he has developed no defenses against the allurements of Isabella. When he first feels himself aroused, his self-righteous astonishment awakens in us just the sort of scornful amusement that the satirist tries to evoke. He is amazed that he, a kind of saint, should be like other men!

> What is't I dream on?
> O cunning enemy, that, to catch a saint,
> With saints dost bait thy hook! Most dangerous

Is that temptation that doth goad us on
To sin in loving virtue. Never could the strumpet,
With all her double vigour—art and nature—
Once stir my temper; but this virtuous maid
Subdues me quite. Ever till now,
When men were fond, I smil'd, and wond'red how.

(II. ii. 179-87)

He knows no way to conquer passion. He can only exclaim, 'Blood thou art blood,' and in spite of reason, in spite of all his moral pride, follow headlong wherever passion leads. After he has committed the crime, he is no nonchalant villain, neither does he feel the stings of remorse. He has, to be sure, been made 'dull to all proceedings,' but he is so certain of his unspotted reputation that he does not fear detection:

But that her tender shame
Will not proclaim against her maiden loss,
How might she tongue me! Yet reason dares her no;
For my authority bears so credent bulk,
That no particular scandal once can touch
But it confounds the breather.

(IV. iv. 25-30)

At about this time the Duke in his role of manipulator takes charge of the action. Mark Van Doren voices the opinion of many critics when he says that the Duke is 'tortuously slow' in making everything turn out right. He feels that the Duke's 'hands are sluggish in the manipulation of the dummies whose predicament he has wantonly created.' [6] But if the main purpose of the action is, like that of all satiric plays, to expose and humiliate the foolish and evil characters, the Duke's manipulation of events is not wanton. He is neither a spectator nor a *deus ex machina*. He is rather acting as the author's agent in displaying and unmasking Lucio and Angelo. He thus performs the duties of an intriguer in such plays as this. He sets the traps for the fools and knaves.

It is true that the Duke seems to be sometimes omnipotent

and sometimes merely an over-clever stage-manager. At least he seems to delight in tying tangled knots for the mere sake of the strong theatrical effects he can produce while untying them. This is an undoubted flaw in the structure of the play. But the Duke's complicated plotting has the supreme merit of laying bare the ugly scars in Angelo's nature.

When Angelo realizes that it is the Duke who has observed all his wickedness and hypocrisy, he is at first stunned. Then, collapsing with shame and contrition, he begs for immediate punishment:

> O my dread lord,
> I should be guiltier than my guiltiness,
> To think I can be undiscernible,
> When I perceive your grace, like power divine,
> Hath look'd upon my passes!
>
> (v. i. 371-4)

The Duke acts as though he were to carry out Angelo's wishes. He orders Angelo to marry Mariana and condemns him 'to the very block where Claudio stooped to death.' But both Mariana and Isabella plead for his life, the latter because she feels that she has been the innocent cause of his fall. She confesses:

> . . . I partly think
> A due sincerity governed his deeds,
> Till he did look on me: since it is so,
> Let him not die.
>
> (v. i. 450-53)

However, Angelo's remorse, particularly over his execution of Claudio, is so deep that he continues to crave 'death more willingly than mercy.' And he persists in this feeling until the Duke unmuffles the supposedly dead Claudio. This is the last trick in his program of mystification and correction. Only then does Angelo wish to live, only then does he show that he has been thoroughly purged of his sin. The Duke, too, is satisfied that his craftiness has produced the results he sought. 'Well, Angelo,' he remarks, 'your evil quits you well. Look that you love your wife, her worth worth yours.' Thus is Angelo cleansed from his evil impulses and pronounced fit to play his part in the triplicate mating at the close of the comedy.

Except for its ending, the plot, as thus far described, is exactly like that of the typical satiric drama. But Shakespeare's development of the character of Isabella and the theatrical skill with which he has written the scenes in which she appears obscure the basic satiric anatomy of the work. This fact has led many commentators to mistake her position in the action. Structurally she is the author's device for bringing Angelo's unsound nature to the judgment seat. In this sense alone is she 'the main-spring of the whole action.' [7] Poetically she does become the heroine of the play, because her impassioned pleas for mercy are the vehicle for the principal ideal values expressed in the drama. In almost all her appearances in the first three acts, she transcends her appointed service to the plot. This independence has led many critics to charge Shakespeare with failure to make Isabella a consistent character. Like many of Shakespeare's figures she comes to life in the course of the play and escapes from the narrow limits assigned her as a creature of the plot. Her liberation is responsible for much of the perplexity which afflicts most persons who pronounce judgment on *Measure for Measure*.

IV

Shakespeare makes us realize very early in the play that the essence of Isabella's nature is her innate austere purity. Unless all her actions were dominated by this instinct for chastity, the irony of her becoming to Angelo an irresistible temptation to lust would be lost. Though Lucio's tribute to her:

> I hold you as a thing enskied and sainted,

may be, as Quiller-Couch suggests, merely 'the sentimental homage which vice pays to virtue,' the buffoon voices the opinion which Shakespeare wished his audience to form at once. Her speeches in the interviews with Angelo and Claudio, all of them subtly and skillfully composed for the stage, possess an elevation and a moral intensity which cynical moderns often mistake for harsh declamation. Most literary critics of our age are contemptuous of any author who places his women on pedestals of any sort. They hold austere sexual restraint in particular disfavor, putting it down at once as springing from emotional starvation or pathological frigidity.

It must be admitted that Shakespeare has placed Isabella in a dilemma which is excessively cruel. This is a relic of archaic plotting. Medieval story was prone to subject its heroines, in particular, to extravagant trials of virtue. What could be more extreme than the choice which the novice of the sisterhood of St. Clare is forced to make? She must decide whether she will be the innocent cause of her brother's death, or consent to the sacrifice of her virtue and so lose her soul. The choice for the sainted Isabella is inevitable:

> Better it were a brother died at once
> Than that a sister, by redeeming him
> Should die forever.
>
> (II. iv. 106-8)

As her dilemma is extreme, so is the language immoderate with which she rejects the temptation to sell her soul at the dictates of human affection:

> Then Isabel, live chaste; and, brother, die!
> More than our brother is our chastity.
>
> (II. iv. 184-5)

The abuse which she rains upon Claudio for asking her to yield to Angelo also seems to us unjustified. The difficulty, however, is not that her chastity is rancid, but that she meets the test to her virtue with too adamantine a hardness for our taste.

Some of Isabella's tirades, which have been denounced as the cries of a termagant, are designed to sustain the satiric temper of the drama. Some of them are direct attacks on the hypocrisy of Angelo. Sometimes her speeches are unmitigated rebuke, as when she says:

> I know your virtue hath a license in't,
> Which seems a little fouler than it is
> To pluck on others.
>
> (II. iv. 145-7)

or:

> O perilous mouths
> That bear in them one and the selfsame tongue,
> Either of condemnation or approof,
> Bidding the law make curtsy to their will,
> Hooking both right and wrong to th' appetite
> To follow as it draws.
>
> (II. iv. 172-7)

Sometimes her speeches are mere abuse. More often what she says is revelant to more than the immediate situation and rings with universal meaning. Such is her censure of Angelo's misuse of authority, a symptom of a morality unrestrained by any understanding of human frailty:

> Could great men thunder
> As Jove himself does, Jove would ne'er be quiet,
> For every pelting petty officer
> Would use his heaven for thunder—nothing but thunder!
> Merciful heaven,
> Thou rather with thy sharp and sulphurous bolt
> Split'st the unwedgeable and gnarled oak
> Than the soft myrtle. But man, proud man,
> Drest in a little brief authority,
> Most ignorant of what he's most assur'd
> (His glassy essence), like an angry ape,

> Plays such fantastic tricks before high heaven
> As make the angels weep; who, with our spleens
> Would all themselves laugh mortal.
>
> (II. ii. 110-23)

More exalted still and less related to the correction of
Angelo's immorality are her appeals for mercy:

> ANGELO. Your brother is a forfeit of the law.
>   And you but waste your words.
>   ISABELLA.   Alas, alas!
>   Why, all the souls that were were forfeit once,
>   And he that might the vantage best have took
>   Found out the remedy. How would you be
>   If he which is the top of judgment should
>   But judge you as you are? O, think on that!
>   And mercy then will breathe within your lips
>   Like man new made.
>
> (II. ii. 71-9)

After the end of the third act, Isabella is almost wholly
occupied with fulfilling the dramatic purpose for which she
was created. She serves as the Duke's pawn in the elaborate
plot which he devises to expose Angelo. She obediently
makes an assignation with Angelo and just as obediently induces Mariana, his trothplight wife, secretly to take her place
in the darkness. In arranging this substitution she is no
wanton procuress, but a friend helping the rejected Mariana
to consummate a union which the authorities of both Church
and State in Shakespeare's day recognized as legally valid. It
is true that Mariana's willingness thus to trap her fiancé into
marriage may now be considered, as Schucking asserts, a
complete sacrifice of her dignity as a woman.[8] But the Elizabethans did not so regard it. They would have seen in what
W. W. Lawrence calls the 'bed-trick' an act of poetic justice
for the hypocritical way in which Angelo had abandoned
Mariana, and they would have applauded the deception.

Isabella's execution of this part of the Duke's plot does not seem so inconsistent with her saintly nature as her willingness to announce before an assemblage of almost all the *dramatis personae* that she has yielded to Angelo. Here, as often in the last two acts, the character of Isabella, as Shakespeare has built it up in the earlier big scenes, seems to go to pieces. In other words she reassumes the role for which she was created, faithfully discharging her dramatic duty to shame Angelo and force him to repent. She forswears her eloquent expositions of Christian doctrine to become the principal element in the craft which the Duke announces he 'must apply against' Angelo's wickedness.

v

We can perhaps best understand *Measure for Measure* if we regard it as a form of comical satire designed for a popular audience, as *Troilus and Cressida* was the version of the type suited to the taste of an intelligent audience of barristers. The two plays are alike in possessing a background of social disintegration which forms an appropriate milieu for the individuals who are to be satirized. They are alike in attacking lust, the vice against which all the satirists directed most of their barbed shafts. They are alike in the method by which the central figures are presented to the audience.

However, the dramas are in some ways as unlike as the different spectators for which they were written. The complicated structure of *Troilus and Cressida* and the many long passages devoted to the elaboration of ethical and social theory were too heavy for a popular audience. Consequently Shakespeare made the plot which exposes Angelo simple in structure and contrived the philosophical speeches of the Duke and Isabella in such a way that they too advance the plot. Moreover, an ending like that of *Troilus and Cressida* would have confused a popular Elizabethan audience, as it has confused almost every modern reader, just because it is so resolutely consistent with the temper of satire.

Shakespeare took no such chance of perplexing his spectators with the denouement of *Measure for Measure*. Instead of ending it on a note of savage scorn, he gave the drama a conventional close, one that forces satire to effect a self-effacing compromise with comedy. It ends with the inevitable three marriages. None of these is a logical consummation of any part of the story, nor does any one of them give off the slightest aroma of romance. The marriages merely announce to the audience in familiar terms that the play is finished. This pseudo-romantic denouement ought not to divert intelligent spectators from their interest in the exposure and humiliation of Lucio and Angelo. An attentive audience should continue to recognize the correction of the knave and the scamp as the central theme of the drama.

The occasional expansion of Isabella's role forms a more serious barrier to a complete understanding of Shakespeare's purpose in composing *Measure for Measure*. During the first three acts she threatens to make her dilemma the dramatic center of the play. However, the author does not permit her to succeed. The manipulations of the Duke relieve her of the obligation to decide whether to be the innocent cause of her brother's death or to sacrifice her maiden honor. Either of these courses of action would have carried her down the road to a tragic ending. But Shakespeare allows the Duke to save her virtue and at the very end of the play to offer himself to her as a husband. The dramatist, therefore, takes ample precaution against our elevating Isabella into the role of a heroine. He undoubtedly thought that he had given her dramatic career an ending perfunctory enough to keep our interest in her secondary to our concern for Angelo. However as in the case of Cressida, he did not foresee the hypnotic effect that a beautiful woman, whatever her position in the plot, will inevitably make upon sentimental masculine critics.

When the woman is also noble and fallen into undeserved distress, she possesses unlimited power to steal the interest from other characters more important for the structure of the work of art.

VI

The primary purpose of this analysis of *Measure for Measure* has been to put Isabella back into her proper place in the plot. The diminution of her importance need not diminish our delight in her eloquent ethical tirades, or our admiration for the technical skill with which Shakespeare has made these speeches contribute to the mounting suspense of her great scenes with Angelo and Claudio. This fairer conception of her part in the play does, however, deprive her of the role of heroine, and proves that in *Measure for Measure* there is neither heroine nor hero.

For Angelo cannot fill the hero's place left vacant by Isabella. Her retirement restores him, to be sure, to the central place in the drama, but it is a bad eminence, on which a rain of ridicule falls without intermission. His predicament there should enable us to see that *Measure for Measure* is a comedy which is more than half satiric. We can now recognize it to be Shakespeare's second original development of the distinctive features of the new type of satiric play which Ben Jonson had invented in *Every Man in His Humour*.

Hamlet and Other Malcontents

THE term 'malcontent' we have already applied to Jaques. We found he was a representative of the type called 'malcontent traveller.' That is, he was a man who had been rendered so melancholy by his sojourn on the Continent that when he came home he found everything in England worthy only of disdain. But Jaques is an imperfect example of what Shakespeare's contemporaries described as a malcontent. Elizabethan dramatists, in particular, came to attach a much more precise and limited meaning to the word.[1]

William Rankins seems to have been the first to define the term. In 1588 he calls the word 'the new found name' and describes malcontents as 'these enchanted sort of people' who '. . . contemne their superiors because they are above them, their equals, because their insolency brooketh no equality, and their inferiors, because their weighty mindes pressent them lower than their estate of itself doth debase them. So that they appear now never content.'[2] In other words, to Rankins a malcontent was a person utterly discontented with his situation in the world.

The pessimism of a man thus badly adjusted to life was no mere pose. It was one phase of what the Elizabethans called unnatural—but we should name it pathological-melancholy. All those afflicted with this malady were subject to alternate seizures of hysterical excitement and deep depression. So when the malcontent was in the trough of dejection, he was overwhelmed with a causeless sadness, one that 'shut up the heart as it were in a dungeon.'[3] Such despair took the form of a radical dissatisfaction with all the conditions of human life.

When the malcontent turned his jaundiced eyes upon man and his concerns, he inevitably poured vials of bitter scorn upon everything that he saw. Sometimes his discontent took the form of brooding hatred of the corruption which he saw poisoning the very springs of life. Sometimes he fell into a macabre mood, in which his gloom was seasoned with a kind of sneering amusement at human futility. Then he found relief in sportive jesting at the fools about him.

John Marston was the first playwright to call one of his characters a malcontent. He gives this name to Malevole, who is the professional commentator in his drama entitled *The Malcontent*. Malevole is the disguise assumed by Altofronto, the deposed Duke of Genoa, when he wishes to linger incognito in the environs of the court and there lay plans to recover his dukedom. The character, as the Duke plays him, is a bitterly disillusioned courtier habitually filled with hatred of vice, the prevalence of which produces in him disgust with life and contempt of mankind. His habitual mood is one of mockery, which he expresses in the set speeches of a professional cynic. His censure is always general. It is seldom directed against any character in the play and almost never issues from a specific dramatic situation. It is usually a comment on the desperate state of all mankind.

His utterances, often deliberately uncouth and obscure, embody what Renaissance critics believed to be a necessary characteristic of satire. Since most satirists held the curious notion that their art was a development and an imitation of the scornful cries of satyrs—rough wild creatures of the primitive Greek forests—they believed that their work should always exhibit a certain awkward roughness. Moreover, the inchoate form in which Lucilius cast his satires and the mannered obscurity of Persius confirmed Marston and his fellows in their conviction that all satires should appear in uncouth garb. Malevole, therefore, complicated the irritation which his speeches aroused by keeping his victims uncertain of the full implication of his insults.

II

Malevole's vigilant hostility to folly and evil was identical with that which the English formal satirists had assumed. It is not surprising then to find that John Marston, the author of a collection of satires called *The Scourge of Villainy* (1598), is blood brother of Malevole. In his poems he often anticipates the derisive criticism which he later put into the mouth of his most famous dramatic figure. Marston fully realized that Melancholy nourished his satiric impulses as surely as it was to foster those of Malevole and his fellow malcontents. In his 'Proem' to the first book of *The Scourge of Villainy* he writes:

> Thou nursing mother of fair wisdom's lore,
> Ingenuous Melancholy, I implore
> Thy grave assistance: take thy gloomy seat;
> Enthrone thee in my blood; let me entreat,
> Stay his quick jocund skips, and force him run
> A sad-paced course, until my whips be done.[4]

When Marston the satirist contemplates the world in which he is compelled to live, he, like the malcontent, finds it utterly vile. He cries:

> Now rail no more at my sharp cynic sound
> Thou brutish world, that in all vileness drowned
> Hast lost thy soul: for nought but shades I see—
> Resemblances of men inhabit thee.
> (Satire VII. 139-42)

This universal corruption, so he believes, shows its ugliness most shockingly in the sins and perversions of sex. All the English satirists of the 1590's imitated a striking feature of

their classical models in their preoccupation with sexual immorality. And Marston was fairly obsessed by it. His repeated
excoriation of lewdness seems to offer him a kind of protec-
tion from his unhealthy interest in the subject. In particular,
Juvenal's violent attack upon women's lust and debauchery
fascinated all the English satirists, but Marston most of all.
The Latin poet's fierce indignation established the tone
which Marston adopted in treating the subject. This is his
way of announcing his theme:

> O split my heart, lest it do break with rage,
> To see the immodest looseness of our age!
> Immodest looseness? fie, too gentle word,
> When every sign can brothelry afford,
> When lust doth sparkle from our females' eyes,
> And modesty is roosted in the skies.
>
> (Satire II. 104-9)

He follows this agonized outcry with shocking examples of
both male and female licentiousness, pornographic details
that might well be entitled 'What every old roué should
know.'

The emotion that Marston most often affected when exposing evil was a kind of exasperation, a counterpart of
Juvenal's *saeva indignatio*. His critical mood, like that of his
great Latin model, was deliberately severe. Yet his method
of attack was often far from simple or direct. He cultivated
a style of complicated allusiveness and indulged in a kind of
tangled obscurity that he believed was the cherished manner
of Persius. The first satire of *The Scourge of Villainy* begins
with lines that baffle the reader. Let him fathom their meaning if he can!

> Marry, God forfend! Martius swears he'll stab
> Phrygio, fear not, thou art no lying drab,
> What though dagger-hack'd mouths of his blade swears
> It slew as many as figures of years

Aquafortis eat in't, or as many more
As Methodist Musus killed with hellebore
In autumn last.

(Satire I. 1-7)

Now when Marston created Malevole, he endowed him
with all the mental characteristics which he himself had
shown as author of *The Scourge of Villainy*. And they were
those which he believed every authentic satirist should possess. Consequently Malevole became in a very real sense Marston's dramatic mouthpiece. But since he was obliged to take
part in a play, he deviated in important ways from the established literary line of the traditional satirist. He sought not
to reform his fellow characters, but merely to vex them. This
impulse was a natural result of frustrated purpose. Altofronto had been driven from his dukedom by the plots of
Pietro Jacoma, and so found himself unable to exercise his
accustomed powers. The forced inaction drove him into
melancholy and soured him on his little world. That is to
say, his unhappy experiences turned him into a malcontent.

In the very first scene of Marston's melodrama Pietro carefully describes the role that Malevole is to play. The malcontent's greatest delight is 'to procure others vexation and
therein he thinks he truly serves heaven, for 'tis his position
whosoever in this earth can be contented is a slave and
damned; therefore does he afflict all in that to which they
are most affected . . . Now shall you here the extremity of
a malcontent: he blows over every man' (I. i. 31-5, 41-2).

From his first appearance Malevole speaks plain truth to
every member of Pietro's court. The more deeply he wounds,
the happier he is. To Guerrino he says, 'Now, signior Guerrino, that thou from a most pitied prisoner should'st grow
a most loathed flatterer' (I. i. 107-9). Then he turns upon
another courtier, Equato, with ' 'Tis pity that thou, being
so excellent a scholar by art, should be so ridiculous a fool by
nature' (I. i. 113-15). But he reserves his most poisonous shaft

for the usurping Duke himself: 'Blirt o'rhyme, blirt o'rhyme!
Maquerelle is a cunning bawd; I am an honest villain: thy
wife is a close drab; and thou art a notorious cuckold. Farewell, Duke' (I. i. 130-32).

Often his maddening attacks are couched in figurative language, deliberately obscure. He astonishes the old panderess
Maquerelle by calling her an 'old coal. Aye old coal: me-
thinks thou liest like a brand under these billets of green
wood. He that will inflame a young wench's heart, let him
lay close to her an old coal that hath first been fired, a panderess, my half-burnt lint, who though thou canst not flame
thyself, yet art able to set a thousand virgins' tapers afire
(II. ii. 4-9).

The malcontent's spirit of mockery relates him closely to
the Vice—a familiar stock character in earlier English drama.
As we have already seen, this professional rogue's delight in
making a laughing-stock of other characters in a play was one
of the sources from which Shakespeare's earliest satiric figures
derived their business. The Vice, however, was moved
neither by malice nor by discontent. He was merely so eager
to entertain himself and his lord that he spared no one. It is
greatly to the enrichment of the malcontent that the stage
representative of the type borrowed from the tradition of
the mocking Vice. The melancholy scoffer, as conceived by
Marston, thus acquires a title to some of the easily recognized
garments of the familiar hero of many an interlude, with the
result that Elizabethan audiences found it easy to accept the
new dramatic figure and to understand what he was about.

However, many of Malevole's tirades have a larger scope
than attacks on any individual. They are outcries against
general human depravity. These outbursts are a symptom of
pathological melancholy, and have their source in the deep
well from which rises the black cloud that lies between the
hero and all that he sees and hears. The corrosive evil that

he detects everywhere in society is the same one that outraged Marston, sexual immorality:

> Why, methinks I see that signior pawn his footcloth,
> that metreza her plate: this madam takes physic, that
> t'other monsieur may minister to her: here is a pander
> jewelled; there is a fellow in shift of satin this day,
> that could not shift a shirt t'other night: here a Paris
> supports that Helen; there's a Lady Guinevere bears
> up that Sir Lancelot: dreams, dreams, visions, fanta-
> sies, chimeras, imaginations, tricks, conceits—[To Pre-
> passo.] Sir Tristram Trimtram, come aloft, Jack-an-
> apes, with a whim-wham: here's a knight of the land
> of Catito shall play at trap with any page in Europe;
> do the sword-dance with any morris-dancer in Chris-
> tendom; ride at the ring till the fin of his eyes look as
> blue as the welkin; and run the wildgoose-chase even
> with Pompey the Huge.
>
> (I. i. 91-105)

Women, to Malevole as to Marston, are most incorrigibly
addicted to this form of vice. And the malcontent rails
against them at the top of his voice:

> Women: nay, Furies; nay worse; for they torment
> only the bad, but women good and bad. Damnation
> of mankind! . . . rash in asking, desperate in work-
> ing, impatient in suffering, extreme in desiring, slaves
> unto appetite . . . their words are feigned, their eyes
> forged, their sighs dissembled, their looks counterfeit,
> their hair false . . . their blood is their only god: bad
> clothes and old age, are the only devils they trouble at.
>
> (I. ii. 85-102 passim)

On rare occasions Malevole's pessimism strikes a still more
hopeless note. He then damns the earth as a foul and ugly
pit, and all its creatures as mere crawling slime:

> Think this:—this earth is the only grave and Gol-
> gotha wherein all things that live must rot; 'tis but the
> draught wherein the heavenly bodies discharge their
> corruption; the very muck-hill on which the sublunary

orbs cast their excrements: man is the slime of this
dung-pit, and princes are the governors of these men;
for, for our souls, they are as free as emperors, all of
one piece; there goes but a pair of shears betwixt an
emperor and the son of a bagpiper; only the dying,
dressing, pressing, glossing, makes the difference.

(IV. ii. 141-51)

III

Now most of the tragedies which Shakespeare wrote during the first decade of the seventeenth century are vehicles
for at least incidental satire, most of it coming from the
mouths of characters who are, in some sense, malcontents.
In *Hamlet, Othello,* and *King Lear* the protagonist falls into
a malcontent mood only on occasions. But in *Timon of
Athens* and *Coriolanus* the mood dominates the central character and so completely shapes the dramatic structure that
each of these two strangely bitter tragedies becomes a kind
of tragical satire.

Hamlet frequently displays most of the distinguishing
traits of a malcontent-satirist. Many years ago Professor E. E.
Stoll advanced the theory that Jaques is a sort of malcontent
and that Hamlet is a highly sophisticated version of Malevole. I have already given what seems to me a more natural
explanation of the origin of Jaques. The resemblances which
Stoll points out between Malevole and Hamlet are without
doubt striking. However, since we cannot be sure that Marston's play was written before *Hamlet,* we ought not to assume that the supreme creation of Shakespeare's genius is
merely a development of the invention of one of his lesser
contemporaries. For we are now in a position to know that
Hamlet's resemblance to Malevóle can be explained more
simply by realizing that each of the characters belong to a
satiric tradition older than either of them.

Many recent critics have tried to fathom Hamlet's mystery
by proving that he was intended to be one of the psycho-

logical types carefully differentiated by Elizabethan writers on ethics or medicine. But none of these efforts has been successful. Hamlet is much more than a representative of a clearly defined melancholy type. His career is also much more incalculable than the case history of a man in whose nature one of the emotions is allowed to take its destructive course. The ravages of grief are not sufficient to explain his tragedy. Nor does a sick tendency to brooding self-analysis account for his dilatory approach to the inevitable catastrophe. Hamlet hitherto has escaped all attempts at classification as surely as do the most highly organized human beings.

The purpose of this essay is certainly not to explain Hamlet by showing that he is a malcontent—not even a malcontent subtilized in the manner of which no one but Shakespeare was master. If such an attempt could succeed, it would destroy all the richness of Hamlet's nature and reduce the complexity of the dramatic action to a simplicity as jejune as it would be unreal. Yet, it is indeed true that at certain moments in the course of the action Hamlet displays the distinguishing characteristics of the newly established type. At such times he parries the heaviest blows of adversity by wielding the familiar weapons of the mocking satirist.

IV

Shakespeare's greatest play is, as everyone knows, his version of an older drama, now always designated as the *Ur-Hamlet*. This lost work was probably a crude, though an enormously popular, melodrama. Shakespeare transformed the early blood-and-thunder play into great tragedy largely by endowing its principal characters with human subtlety and complexity. On Hamlet these gifts were bestowed in richest measure. The poet wrought his artistic miracle partly by inserting into Hamlet's role all the well-known manifestations of melancholy which he believed would enhance the richness of his hero's nature.

We have already seen that many of the Elizabethan writers who described the symptoms of abnormal melancholy were struck by the rhythmic fashion in which depression and hysterical excitement alternated in controlling the patient's mood. Shakespeare saw that if Hamlet's mind were to swing like a pendulum between these extremes of emotion, his actions would be rendered incalculable and inexplicable to himself as well as to every other character in the tragedy. What principle of both aesthetic and psychological structure could make a dramatic figure more fascinating or add more constant suspense to his actions than this? In a somewhat different way Hamlet's malcontent moods also served to enrich his character. And the satire which they prompted him to pour forth contributed its own particular emotional note to the tragic symphony of the drama.

Abnormal melancholy, or so the Elizabethan doctors thought, was caused by many sorts of experience and took many different forms. All the authorities agreed that one of its causes was frustration produced by forces independent of the patient's will and hostile to it. Polonius and Claudius are thus on the right track in searching for the cause of Hamlet's melancholy in some defeat of his dearest hopes. Polonius' insistence that the young man's malady had its origin in disappointed love, and Claudius' belief that thwarted ambition is the cause of the Prince's distemper are errors of judgment only because they do not probe deep enough into the hidden realities of Hamlet's situation. It is largely because he cannot rush headlong to his revenge that he falls victim to the ravages of melancholy.

The dominant emotion produced by this sense of frustration is a deep and savage exasperation. Under its stress Hamlet turns in disgust or contempt upon everyone whom he believes to be responsible for blocking an exit from the labyrinth in which he is lost. The King, the Queen, Polonius, Rosencrantz and Guildenstern, Osric, even poor Ophelia, at some time or other becomes the object of his brutal irony or his cruel invective.

At least twice Hamlet releases his inner tension in highly conventional satiric tirades. While deriding and perplexing Polonius he confessedly employs the terms in which satirists for generations had shown their contempt for old age:

> The satirical rogue says here [that is, in the book which he pretends to read] that old men have grey beards; that their faces are wrinkled; their eyes purging thick amber and plum-tree gum; and that they have a plentiful lack of wit, together with most weak hams. All which, sir, though I most powerfully and potently believe, yet I hold it not honesty to have it thus set down; for you yourself, sir, should be old as I am, if like a crab, you could go backward.

> (II. ii. 198-207)

Polonius' aside, 'Though this be madness, yet there is method in't,' shows that the thrust has gone home and tempts the audience to accept Hamlet's invitation to a burst of derisive laughter.

The insults which Ophelia's one-time lover heaps upon her are painful revelations of the pathological inflammation of his whole nature. His exasperation with all human existence drives him to wound even where he has garnered up his heart. Whenever he is with her, he makes of her a scapegoat for all women. Though most of his attacks penetrate far beneath the surface of woman's nature, in one passage Hamlet draws his ammunition from the storehouse of weapons wielded for centuries against all forms of social affectation. He joins an ancient satirical fraternity when he turns scornfully upon Ophelia to cry:

> I have heard of your paintings too, well-enough.
> God hath given you one face and you make yourselves
> another. You jig, you amble, and you lisp; and nick-
> name God's creatures and make your wantonness your
> ignorance. Go to, I'll no more on't! it hath made me
> mad.
>
> (III. i. 148-53)

This tirade has little importance for the plot of the play. For
a moment a malcontent interrupts the action to present a
satiric interlude in a form which any Elizabethan audience
would grasp at once.

Most of Hamlet's attacks on both Ophelia and his mother
are the familiar accusations of lust—stock material of satirists,
ancient and modern, down to Shakespeare's own day. Yet the
terms in which he phrases this age-old scorn when speaking
to Ophelia sorely perplex the poor innocent girl. He begins
his excursion into satire with what he calls a paradox: 'The
power of beauty will sooner transform honesty [chastity]
from what it is to a bawd than the force of honesty can translate beauty into his likeness' (III. i. 111-14). But he soon
abandons confusing generalities for direct attack ostensibly
upon Ophelia, but really upon all women:

> Be thou as chaste as ice, as pure as snow, thou shalt
> not escape calumny. Get thee to a nunnery. Go, fare-
> well. Or if thou wilt needs marry, marry a fool, for
> wise men know well enough what monsters you make
> of them.
>
> (III. i. 140-44)

Often Hamlet contemplates sexual indulgence with a savage disgust that approaches physical revulsion. What more
cruel than his association of the conception of an unmarried
woman with the 'sun breeding maggots in a dead dog!' His
mother's incest naturally seems to him the foulest of sexual
sins, and he excoriates her vile trespass with the most sadistic
of his phrases. To be married to the bloat King is to Hamlet

to live
In the rank sweat of an enseamed bed,
Stewed in corruption, honeying and making love
Over the nasty sty!

(III. iv. 91-4)

Diatribes such as this have led many critics to assume that Shakespeare when writing *Hamlet* was himself suffering from sex-nausea. The Freudian interpreters, on the other hand, have taken such lines as these as proof that Hamlet was the victim of a mother fixation. That she, even she, should have sexual relations, not only with his father but also with a second man—and with one whom he execrated—aroused in the unhappy young man a pathological jealousy which, as the Freudians think, found relief in outrageous expressions of loathing. There is not a remote possibility that either of these psychiatric explanations would have occurred to Shakespeare or to any other Elizabethan. The intelligent among the audiences who first saw the tragedy would have recognized Hamlet's fierce disgust as the proper attitude for a satirist to assume toward sins of sex.

Indeed it is strikingly like Marston's point of view in *The Scourge of Villainy*. The differences between the effects produced by the two poets are due to the greater subtlety of Shakespeare's mind and the higher reaches of his art. Such phrases of Marston as 'to snort in filth' or 'the snottery of our slimy time' pack as much aversion into a few words as any of Hamlet's similar diatribes. But Shakespeare's phrases are seldom pure unadorned invective. They all contain some harvest of a widely ranging imagination. In some of the passages already quoted he brings together ideas normally as remote from each other as Hamlet's love for the fragile Ophelia and the notion of the sun's breeding maggots in a dead dog. The vast difference in the imaginative reach of the two dramatists strikes the reader with full force when he sets side by side Marston's 'snort in filth' with Hamlet's 'honeying and making love over a nasty sty.' Each phrase expresses intense loathing. But in Shakespeare's art the bold figure of speech has sublimated disgust into superb poetic irony.

Hamlet's wit turns vivacious and lightning-quick whenever he has need to protect himself from anyone who would intrude upon the secret places of his heart and mind. He is particularly skillful in fending off Rosencrantz and Guildenstern:

> HAMLET. Do not believe it.
> ROS. Believe what?
> HAMLET. That I can keep your counsel and not mine own. Besides, to be demanded of a sponge, what replication should be made by the son of a King?
> ROS. Take you me for a sponge, my lord?
> HAMLET. Ay, sir; that soaks up the King's countenance, his rewards, his authorities.
>
> (IV. ii. 9-17)

With Horatio his wit takes the form of mocking cynicism. His satirical thrusts then penetrate the hard surface of many an apparently harmless situation to reveal its ugly essence. To Horatio's remark that the Queen's marriage followed hard upon the death of her first husband, Hamlet exclaims:

> Thrift, thrift, Horatio! The funeral baked meats
> Did coldly furnish forth the marriage tables.
>
> (I. ii. 180-81)

Even in the midst of the most sincere expressions of his deep need for Horatio's friendship he lets his love sleep for a moment while he flings a sneer at flatterers:

> Nay, do not think I flatter,
> For what advancement may I hope from thee,
> That no revenue hast but thy good spirits
> To feed and clothe thee? Why should the poor be flattered?
> No, let the candied tongue lick absurd pomp,
> And crook the pregnant hinges of the knee
> Where thrift may follow fawning.
>
> (III. ii. 61-7)

The grave-digger's chop logic drives Hamlet to an amused comment on the precision of the old fellow's talk. The humble clown becomes a parlous social phenomenon, for he is fatuously imitating those far above him in the social scale. 'That is natural,' remarks Hamlet, for 'the age is grown so picked [refined] that the toe of the heel of the courtier galls his kibe [takes the skin off his chilblains]' (v. i. 151-3). This is an expression of hostile criticism that appeared on almost every page of the English satirists. It is a reflection of their conservative reaction to the social results of the economic revolution which took place in England during the latter part of the sixteenth century. Inflation had reduced the real income of many landed gentlemen and had given the merchant a chance to buy himself a higher place in the social scale. Time-honored class barriers were broken down, to the regret and alarm of all those attached by sympathy or self-interest to the old regime. Perhaps the most influential of the opponents of the new order were the satirists. They reiterated their displeasure so often that they had apparently created an appetite for this particular form of satire. At any rate Shakespeare believed that a passing fling at social climbers would bring a ready and grateful response from his audience.

The most ridiculous of the would-be gentlemen of the age of social readjustments were the affected courtiers and the sons of prosperous merchants who imitated their showy manners. Such an 'affectioned ass' is Osric. Hamlet parodies the upstart's flamboyant way of talking, and he deflates Osric's elaborate politeness by wryly remarking, 'He did comply with his dug before he sucked it.' With our minds full of this picture of the baby Osric bowing to his mother's nipple before putting it into his mouth, we are ready to laugh him out of the play with a derision that is both merry and scornful.

IV

Hamlet also follows the malcontent into the lowest depths of pessimism. Even the passages which contain what everyone has regarded as Hamlet's most profound philosophical speculation are a master's variations on themes crudely announced by Malevole. Everyone who has heard Marston's creature exclaim, 'This earth is the only grave and Golgotha wherein all things that live must rot,' will read as a sublimation of this cynical utterance Hamlet's famous speech to Rosencrantz and Guildenstern:

> I have of late—but wherefore I know not—lost all
> my mirth, foregone all custom of exercises; and indeed
> it goes so heavily with my disposition that this goodly
> frame, the earth, seems to me a sterile promontory;
> this most excellent canopy, the air, look you, this
> brave o'erhanging firmament, the majestical roof fret-
> ted with golden fire—why, it appears no other thing to
> me than a foul and pestilent congregation of vapors.
> What a piece of work is a man! how noble in reason!
> how infinite in faculty! in form, in moving how ex-
> press and admirable! in action how like an angel! in
> apprehension how like a god! the beauty of the world,
> the paragon of animals! And yet to me what is this
> quintessence of dust?
>
> (II. ii. 307-21)

All the familiar monologues in which Hamlet contemplates suicide contain passages as clearly in the malcontent's manner as the familiar lines:

> How weary, stale, flat and unprofitable
> Seem to me all the uses of this world.

Careful readers of the famous 'To be or not to be' soliloquy have remarked that many of the asperities of life from which Hamlet longs to escape could never have touched him. The oppressor's wrong, the proud man's contumely, the law's delay, the insolence of office—Hamlet, Prince of Denmark, had never felt the sting of any of these afflictions. That they weigh as an intolerable load upon his spirit is proof of his profound dissatisfaction with the entire human situation. That is, Hamlet in his moments of deepest gloom finds the malcontent's sick aversion to life a perfect reflection of his own troubled spirit.

Hamlet's most bitter expression of contempt for human existence issues from a macabre mood. Then the essence of man seems to him merely the quintessence of dust, choice food for worms. He perversely thinks of the dead Polonius as at supper, 'Not where he eats, but where he is eaten. A certain convocation of politic worms are e'en at him. Your worm is your only emperor for diet. We fat all creatures else to fat us, and we fat ourselves for maggots' (IV. iii. 20-24).

This gruesome mood unites pessimism and mockery most effectively at the beginning of the fifth act, while Hamlet and Horatio stand watching the grave-diggers at their work. The heap of skulls and other ignoble relics of mortality which the workmen shovel up prolongs Hamlet's preoccupation with all the wormy circumstance of death and dissolution, until his disgust issues in flippant derision of human life even at its most dignified and glorious. The noble dust of Alexander or imperious Caesar might conceivably be transformed to earth, to loam, finally to become the stopper of a bung-hole:

> Imperious Caesar dead and turned to clay,
> Might stop a hole to keep the wind away.
> (v. i. 236-7)

Such a mixture of horror and jest is not to modern taste, yet it is the malcontent's most striking form of mockery. Hamlet's soliloquies among the skulls are only Shakespeare's finer imaginative apprehension of what lies dormant in many of Malevole's flings at despicable humanity. 'This earth is the only grave and Golgotha wherein all things that live must rot,' intones Malevole. And he takes horrid pleasure in telling a minion of the court, 'I ha' seen a sumptuous steeple turned to a stinking privy . . . nay, most inhuman, the stoned coffins of long-dead Christians burst up and made hog's troughs: *hic finis Priami*' (II. iii. 195-9).

Hamlet, of course, dwells in a realm of the imagination infinitely higher than the very mundane sphere of Malevole. Marston's creature is little more than a satirist thrust into a melodrama for the sake of the incidental pleasure that his contemptuous merriment could give to an Elizabethan audience. His pessimism bears only the most superficial relationship to his character or to his dramatic role. Hamlet's melancholy, on the other hand, is the direct result of the exasperation which dominates him when circumstances prevent his rushing to revenge. Frustration of his most vital emotional drives floods his nature with cosmic bitterness. Every derisive expression is, of course, satire, making the distinctive aesthetic appeal of the literary form; but it is also part of the structure of the tragedy. Hamlet's irresistible impulse toward mockery delays the catastrophe and so prolongs and complicates the suspense.

But it serves an even more important end. Hamlet's bursts of righteous indignation help Shakespeare to create the illusion that Hamlet is endowed with an infinitely rich and sensitive nature. What in Malevole is the railing of a disappointed, ill-natured cynic becomes in Hamlet the deepest and the most moving philosophical lyricism in all literature. In this way Shakespeare's genius transformed a dramatic figure who was at once the essence and the culmination of the spirit of the English satirists into the greatest of tragic characters. For Hamlet during the process of transfiguration has become as various, as inscrutable, and as appealing as the finest human being, and as beautiful as only the highest artistic creations can be.

V

Iago, Lear, and Timon are also malcontents of a sort.[5] Each one of them suffers from a profound sense of frustration, from the baffling of a vital impulse. Each is the prey to complete disillusionment; each finds the world a place where only evil flourishes and only sin triumphs.

The cause of Iago's melancholy is consistent with the theory enunciated by one of the keenest of seventeenth-century students of personality. Earle in his famous *Micro-cosmographie* (1628) explains what he believes to be the origin of the atrabilious temperament. He asserts that a high-spirited man, if fortune fails to recognize his worth, is likely to turn 'desperately melancholy' at the realization that his hopes have been denied.[6] This is precisely what has happened to Iago. When he realizes that his ambitions for a successful career in the army have been thwarted once and for all, he turns malcontent. He feels only scorn for all idealism and only contempt for all mankind. From the moment he hears that Othello has promoted the gracious gentleman Cassio to the position which he coveted, Iago plots villainy and speaks mockery.

Because he is the villain of the piece, his exasperation expresses itself most often in his evil designs. His disappointment is eased through his delight in the disasters which he brings to beauty and virtue. It is only when a brief pause is forced on his malign activity that he finds leisure to indulge in the fleering satire of a malcontent. Even then his derision is written in a different key from that of a noble malcontent like Hamlet; for Iago's censure is not directed against either folly or vice. Like one of his forebears, the Vice, the tempter of mankind in the morality plays, Iago scoffs at virtue and idealism in a tone of coarse and sneering raillery. He is filthily merry over Desdemona's marriage with a Moor, whom

he persists in regarding as a Negro. The figures of speech
which he employs to describe the miscegenation are as foul
and preposterous as those of the buffoon. When Brabantio
rebukes him for the hubbub he makes in reporting Desdemona's elopement, the villain seasons his exasperation with
mordant wit:

> Because we come to do you service, and you think
> we are ruffians, you'll have your daughter covered with
> a Barbary horse; you'll have your nephews neigh to
> you; you'll have coursers for cousins, and gennets for
> germans. [Spanish horses for kinsmen]
>
> (I. i. 109-14)

Speeches like this have gained Iago the reputation with all
his acquaintances of speaking home, of being an amusing
though disillusioned critic of human behavior. Even Desdemona takes pleasure in his shockingly frank satire of women.
To pass the time merrily, she and Emilia join in provoking
the sallies which spring from his scandalous opinion of every
sort of woman. 'What have you to say about a woman who is
fair and foolish,' asks Emilia, and Iago replies,

> She never yet was foolish that was fair
> For even her folly helped her to an heir.
> DESDEMONA. These are old fond paradoxes to make
> fools laugh in the alehouse. What miserable praise
> hast thou for her that's foul and foolish?
> IAGO. There's none so foul, and foolish thereunto,
> But does foul pranks which fair and wise ones do.
>
> (II. i. 137-43)

Such an encounter as this makes it clear that the authors
of many of the tragedies produced during the first decade
of the seventeenth century deliberately wrote into the part
of the malcontent a kind of bitter comic relief to the mounting pity and terror. Yet unlike any form of gay laughter, this
derision neither interrupts nor dilutes the tragic tone of the
drama. On the contrary, the malcontent's searing pessimism,

even while it amuses, saturates the atmosphere of the piece with sinister gloom.

The cynical conviction of this ubiquitous commentator that evil determines the course of all human conduct intensifies the tragic spirit of these dramas in yet another way. It gives them philosophical depth, even though it digs a pit beneath the action instead of spreading a sky above it. This is the effect of Iago's speeches. Detraction is the informing spirit of nearly all of them. Cassio's soldiership is 'mere prattle, without practice.' Fidelity to a master is asinine stupidity:

> . . . You shall mark
> Many a duteous and knee-crooking knave
> That, doting on his own obsequious bondage,
> Wears out his time, much like his master's ass
> For naught but provender; and when he's old, cashiered [dismissed].
> Whip me such honest knaves.
>
> (i. i. 44-9)

Love to Iago is merely 'a lust of the blood and a permission of the will' (sexual desire). The silly Roderigo is a 'snipe' upon whom he would not spend a moment of his time except for 'his sport and profit.'

Why multiply examples of Iago's vicious slander of men and their motives? At his every appearance it underscores his hard cynicism. Though his mockery, while familiar to everyone, has seldom been recognized as satire, it none the less shows most of the characteristics of the satirist's art as developed during the years immediately preceding 1604, the probable date of the composition of *Othello*. For Iago's diatribes produce a far-off distorted echo of laughter. They are always sport to him, sometimes sport to other characters in the play, and usually a kind of perverted and painful sport to an audience. The disdain which his early sallies both reveal and communicate is an emotion dear to satirists from the dawn of their art. However, as the action of the tragedy moves nearer and nearer to inevitable catastrophe, Iago's contemptuous hatred of all men but himself and his cynical disbelief in virtue merge into the terror which holds us more and more firmly in its vise-like grip. His contemptuous laughter at human idiocy becomes cynical devotion to evil doing. The frustration which must inevitably turn a man into a malcontent has in Iago driven the afflicted soul through hostile laughter and barbed satire to the commission of a horrible crime.

VI

It will doubtless be surprising to many to discover old King Lear among the malcontents. His tragic career takes place in imaginative regions far from the confined world of folly, meanness, and sin in which the satirist lays about him with his corded whip. Shakespeare has set Lear's tragedy against a back-drop of eternity.

Yet it is true that Lear has certain traits of a malcontent. He, too, finds all the current of his being dammed up, or at least forced to flow along the shallows of pompous ceremonial and public adulation. The resulting starvation of his inner life produces in him the familiar state of exasperation. But his early irritation at slights to his dignity becomes, as the play progresses, a much less personal and a much more agonizing emotion. He stands for man, mere 'unaccommodated man,' who is embarked upon a frantic search for his soul. In his mad desire to divest himself of all unessential trappings he tears the very clothes from his body. This insane violence accomplishes no more than to bare his flesh to the pitiless assaults of the storm, convincing him that Nature has no peace or security to bestow upon the human spirit. Only when he is united with Cordelia does he discover the secret of happiness which he has been seeking with utter desperation. Love, unselfish love of one human soul for another, is the solvent of all unhappiness. Upon the sacrifice to love of all that the world has to offer 'the gods themselves throw incense.' Lear's death at the moment of his great discovery thus becomes a transfiguration.

It is strange that the voice of the malcontent should be heard in the course of this sublime morality play. But it no longer sounds querulous. Shakespeare has contrived to make Lear's conventional diatribes pathetic revelations of his frenzy. They burst wildly from one after another of his mad illusions. Bolts of lightning to his disordered brain are bailiffs sent from God's own court to summon the wicked to judgment. At these chimerical fugitives from justice, Lear points with triumphant disdain:

> . . . Tremble, thou wretch,
> That hast within thee undivulged crimes
> Unwhipped of justice. Hide thee, thou bloody hand;
> Thou perjured, and thou simular of virtue
> That are incestuous. Caitiff, to pieces shake
> That under covert and convenient seeming
> Hast practised on man's life.
>
> (III. ii. 51-7)

Perhaps not every member of an Elizabethan audience would recognize the accents of a malcontent satirist in this tremendous Jeremiad. But no one could fail to catch familiar echoes in Lear's brutal attack on women's lust:

> Behold yond simp'ring dame,
> Whose face between her forks presageth snow,
> That minces virtue, and does shake the head
> To hear of pleasure's name.
> The fitchew nor the soiled horse goes to't
> With a more riotous appetite.
> Down from the waist they are centaurs,
> Though women all above.
> But to the girdle do the gods inherit,
> Beneath is all the fiend's.
>
> (IV. vi. 120-29)

Lear's assault on hypocrisy and the miscarriage of justice is almost equally severe and throws almost as white a light upon the old King's distraction:

> . . . A dog's obey'd in office.
> Thou rascal beadle, hold thy bloody hand!
> Why dost thou lash that whore? Strip thine own back.
> Thou hotly lusts to use her in that kind
> For which thou whip'st her. The usurer hangs the cozener.
> Through tatter'd clothes great vices do appear;
> Robes and furr'd gowns hide all. Plate sins with gold,
> And the strong lance of justice hurtless breaks;
> Arm it in rags, a pigmy's straw does pierce it.
>
> (IV. vi. 163-71)

Each of these speeches is conventional satire filled with the symbols of judicial punishment—the lash, the whip, the strong lance of justice—which were the stock in trade of Hall, Marston, and their fellows. But neither of these philippics is the inartistic intrusion of Shakespeare the man, unable to suppress the painful symptoms of his sex-nausea. Both harangues have been skillfully woven into the fabric of the play. Lear, the dispossessed, fancies that he is again dispensing royal justice. Speeches of no other sort could have furnished so convincing evidence of his madness.

Like all insane men, Lear is at the mercy of that part of his mind which he has most resolutely thrust down into his subconscious—and the most turbulent of civilized man's suppressed impulses are likely to be those of sex. So erotic images, often distorted and polluted by their long imprisonment in the deep well of the unconscious, flood the mind which reason has ceased to control. Thus a great artist transforms the malcontent speeches of King Lear into picturesque but terrifying evidence of his madness.

Perhaps it is the cosmic pessimism of the desperately melancholy man that best serves Shakespeare's double purpose of mockery and characterization. When Lear first meets the

blinded Gloucester he does not recognize him. The block in
his normal paths of association make Gloucester's hollow
sockets seem a phenomenon unrelated to anything in his unhappy memory. He imagines that old Gloucester is Cupid
squinting and winking at him. Again the erotic association!
In any case Gloucester's blindness is a matter of no importance. The ways of the world are so outrageous that 'a man
may see how the world goes with no eyes. Look with thine
ears.' But at last Lear is able to identify the face of his old
friend behind the cruel disfigurement. Then he expresses the
sympathy that he vaguely feels, indirectly by way of the
familiar satiric conception of the world as a great stage for
fools. He cries:

> Thou must be patient. We came crying hither;
> Thou knows't, the first time that we smell the air,
> We wawl and cry. I will preach to thee. Mark.
> GLOUCESTER. Alack, alack the day!
> LEAR. When we are born, we cry that we are come
> To this great stage of fools.
>
> (IV. vi. 182-7)

VII

From these examples it should be clear that Shakespeare
placed in Lear's mouth, even at moments of the old man's
deepest spiritual agony, some of the characteristic utterances
of the malcontent. No better evidence could be found of the
importance which the poet attached to the introduction of
satire into his greatest tragedies. He forced it to serve many
purposes. But its principal value to us is the momentary relief it offers to the pity and terror which the action arouses.
To be sure, the laughter which it provokes is never sustained,
and it is always completely devoid of merriment. Yet the
little spurts of scorn it injects into the tragedies serve to
relieve the emotional strain even while they thicken the
atmosphere of evil in which the doomed protagonists are

forced to have their being. In Shakespeare's hands the malcontent's scathing wit and mordant bitterness deepen our
interest in the tragic heroes. The uncontrollable impulse to
mock reveals the inner chaos into which the doomed creatures seek desperately and futilely to bring order. Much of
the bitterness with which Shakespeare fills his later tragedies
and much of the sharpness of the inner conflicts which these
plays reveal are then the result of the poet's development
of a traditional satiric character. Both are the product of
the scornful spirit of derision which reflect the malcontent's
exasperation with life. The pessimism in which the tragedies
seem more and more to be steeped must not be regarded as
a revelation of the dramatist's deep personal unhappiness but
as a signal of one of his most brilliant artistic achievements.

Timon of Athens

THE most furious malcontent in all of Shakespeare's work is undoubtedly Timon of Athens. Though the play to which he gives his name is called a tragedy, it is of a completely different sort from the great works which immediately preceded it. It dramatizes the making and breaking of a malcontent in so absolute a fashion that Shakespeare was forced radically to modify the structure which had served him in *Hamlet, Othello,* and *King Lear.* Timon proved to be so unconventional a tragic protagonist that Shakespeare in devising a satisfactory medium for him found it necessary to borrow so many of the devices of satire that the drama can most accurately be described as a tragical satire.

Presently we shall see that in modifying the orthodox tragic form Shakespeare followed a lead taken by Ben Jonson in *Sejanus* and *Volpone.* But first we must have in mind the strange naked plot of *Timon of Athens.* In the second scene of the play we see Timon holding court in the great hall of his mansion. To the sound of loud music played by 'hautboys' servants enter bearing in a great banquet. Soon there enters a masque of Cupid with ladies dressed as Amazons. They bear lutes in their hands, to the sounds of which they dance first by themselves, then, as was the custom of all maskers, with the banqueters. Then other servants bear in caskets of rich jewels. The guests, who are not true friends but flatterers, bring Timon sumptuous gifts such as:

Four milk-white horses trapped in silver.

He accepts these offerings with ostentatious graciousness, be-
stowing in return gifts upon his guests with even more lavish
generosity. No where else in all his work does Shakespeare
present so blazing a scene of opulence. Only Apemantus, the
professional cynic, suggests that the whole performance is 'a
sweep of vanity.'

We soon see that he speaks truth, for all Timon's display
of munificence is fatuous. His delight in scattering rich gifts
has blinded him to the falseness of his courtiers. They flatter,
even adore him, merely to line their purses. Besides, a steward presently informs us that Timon's histrionic generosity
is sheer folly, for his spendthrift bounty has already dissi-
pated his entire fortune. The gifts which we have seen him
scatter in uncontrolled profusion have all been paid for 'out
of an empty coffer':

> His promises fly so beyond his state
> That what he speaks is all in debt.
> (I. ii. 203-4)

His liberality has been in fact 'raging waste.'

In the third act we see the melancholy results of Timon's
prodigality. Finding himself impoverished, he sends to his
fair weather friends for financial aid. But they ignore his
urgent appeals. Three of them in three successive scenes refuse to lend him money for three different reasons. Then
three strangers comment on their outrageous conduct, and
we begin to mark the queer formal schematism of the work.
Timon's rage at this show of ingratitude can express itself
in no comment however violent. He has a more active way
of expressing his contempt for their conduct. He invites the
despicable creatures to a banquet. When the guests uncover
the vessels bearing the first course, they see that the bowls
contain only warm water. Before they can master their indignation, Timon seizes the dishes and throws the water full
into the faces of his guests. This action he accompanies with

a diatribe against them. He calls them 'smiling smooth, detested parasites,' 'trencher friends,' 'cap-and-knee slaves,' and
ends by announcing:

> Henceforth hated be
> Of Timon man and all humanity!
> (III. vi. 115-16)

The last two acts show us Timon outside the walls of
Athens, now in the woods, now on the sea-shore, entirely
given over to misanthropic utterance. Flavius, Alcibiades
with his two mistresses, and Apemantus come to see him in
turn. They are followed by three banditti and they by three
senators. Timon greets each visitor with a ferocious attack
upon Athens, all its inhabitants, and finally upon all human
kind. At length Timon commits suicide and is buried near
the turbulent sea.

II

Not only the curiously bare nature of the drama, but also
the condition of the text has cast doubt upon Shakespeare's
authorship. When the editors of the First Folio planned their
collection, they apparently had no intention of including
this strange play. However, while the edition was going
through the press, they decided that *Troilus and Cressida*
was no proper tragedy and so moved it out of the place reserved for it between *Romeo and Juliet* and *Julius Caesar*.
Then they looked around for a play of the proper length
to fill the empty space, and found somewhere among the
books and papers of their company the manuscript of *Timon
of Athens*. With the help of an ingenious printer they were
able to make this drama serve their turn. To be sure, they
had to omit a whole quire of the paper reserved for the book,
to use one of the pages left empty for a list of the actors'
names, and to leave one entire page completely blank. But
these changes were easy and inexpensive to make; so into

the First Folio edition of Shakespeare's plays went *Timon of Athens*. The queer condition of the copy which the editors used undoubtedly explains their hesitation to print the drama as one of Shakespeare's authentic works. To borrow Professor Kittredge's characterization, 'The text is a strange jumble of good verse, limping metre, and out and out prose.' Moreover, some of the speeches are inarticulated, almost inchoate.

The critics used to explain the wretched state of the text by assuming that it contains much work by a hand other than Shakespeare's. Some believed that Shakespeare, after having completed more than half of his revision of an older drama, abandoned his task. Others advanced the notion that he sketched the outlines of a new play and began the work of filling it in, but, finding the subject uncongenial or the material intractable, he turned his manuscript over to an inferior dramatist to finish.[1]

Differences between the two levels of composition are so great as to be obvious to the dullest of minds. In some of the finer passages Timon expresses the mood of King Lear with all the depth and eloquence of that great tragic figure. Such are the lines in which Timon beseeches Alcibiades to bring total war to Athens:

> Let not thy sword skip one.
> Pity not honour'd age for his white beard;
> He is a usurer. Strike me the counterfeit matron;
> It is her habit only that is honest,
> Herself's a bawd. Let not the virgin's cheek
> Make soft thy trenchant sword; for those milk paps
> That through the window bars bore at men's eyes
> Are not within the leaf of pity writ,
> But set them down horrible traitors.
>
> (IV. iii. 110-18)

Violent though this emotion is, the voice is that of Shakespeare as he spoke in the years 1606-9.

The inferior passages represent a lower level of attainment than that found anywhere else in Shakespeare's plays. Witness the following speech of Apemantus:

> I scorn thy meat. 'Twould choke me, for I should ne'er flatter thee. O you gods, what a number of men eats Timon, and he sees 'em not! It grieves me to see so many dip their meat in one man's blood; and all the madness is, he cheers them up too.
> I wonder men dare trust themselves with men.
> Methinks they should invite them without knives:
> Good for their meat, and safer for their lives.
>
> (I. ii. 38-46)

This passage of mixed verse and prose is too bad to be the finished work of any experienced dramatist. Not Tourneur, Chapman, Wilkins, Field, Day or any of the other men who have been nominated as Shakespeare's collaborator would have been capable of writing such inchoate stuff. These passages are more like an author's rough notes or first outlines of action and dialogue, later to be worked into final form.

E. K. Chambers has recently suggested that *Timon of Athens* was left unfinished by Shakespeare and that it is unfinished still.[2] He believes that the chaotic verse 'looks very much like rough notes, hastily jotted down to be worked up later.' He does not assume that the condition of the manuscript throws much light upon Shakespeare's normal methods of composition because he believes that the author was working at this time hurriedly and under great strain. This explanation has seemed to many critics the most satisfactory yet offered. But whether or not the theory be preferred to that of multiple authorship, the fact is that the discrepancies between the two parts of the drama are never more than those of style. The conception of Timon's character and method in which he is presented remain consistent throughout the play.

III

More important for an understanding of Shakespeare's de-
sign in composing this tragedy is the fact to which we have
already referred. The principles upon which he constructed
Timon of Athens, including his manipulation of the central
character, he modelled on those which Ben Jonson had
applied to fashioning first the tragedy *Sejanus,* and later, in
modified form, to giving the so-called comedy *Volpone* its
passionate bitterness.

Each of these works is an original extension of the experiment he had made in writing his three comical satires.
In *Every Man Out of His Humour, Cynthia's Revels,* and
Poetaster, Jonson had tried in three different ways to form
an effective union of satire and comedy.

But he was clearly dissatisfied with the reception given to
all three attempts; so in an Apologetical Dialogue affixed to
The Poetaster, the author announces that he will write no
more comical satires, but compose tragedies instead:

> Since the Comic Muse
> Hath proved so ominous to me, I will try
> If Tragedy have a more kind aspect.

At this stage of his career Jonson's mind was so bent toward
satire that any play that he wrote was inevitably steeped in
derision. For this reason, *Sejanus* was born of a union of
tragedy with satire and became what may well be called a
tragical satire. The first offspring of this union may have
been *Richard Crookback,* staged in June 1602. But since this
drama is no longer extant, *Sejanus his Fall* must be studied
as though it were Jonson's initial attempt to write a tragical
satire.

Sejanus is not the kind of tragedy one would expect from
an inveterate classicist. Jonson himself foresaw the astonishment of critics and tried to forestall it. In an 'Address to the

Readers' he confesses that he has failed to observe the sacro-
sanct unity of time and avoided the introduction of the classical chorus, 'whose Habit and Moodes are such, and so dif-
ficult' that no dramatists 'since the Auntients . . . have yet
come in the way off.' The strict observance of the rules of
the ancients, he says, is neither possible nor necessary 'in
these our Times and to such Auditors, as commonly Things
are presented.' Jonson, it appears, was enough of a practical
dramatist to know that Elizabethan audiences had no interest whatever in the rules of the ancients, but did demand
from their playwrights variety of scene and diversity of
incident.

However, he proudly affirms that though he may not have
retained the forms of classical tragedy, he has reimbodied its
essential spirit. He insists that he has preserved 'truth of
Argument, dignity of Persons, gravity and height of Elocu-
tion and frequency of Sentence.' That is, the characters are
of high estate, his style is elevated and filled with philosophical and moral aphorisms and his plot at every point is his-
torically accurate. His enormous respect for this last rule led
him to translate into dramatic idiom long passages from
Tacitus' *Annals* and from Dion's *Roman History*.

The result is a plot clogged with historical fact. As Hazlitt
remarked, *Sejanus* is little more than 'an ancient mosaic' of
'translated bits.' Though Jonson's allegiance to classical
canons betrayed him into pedantry, he persisted in his me-
ticulous historical accuracy, at least partly because he intended his play to serve as a scornful commentary on Shakespeare's *Julius Caesar*. He was clearly determined to show
the amateur in classical learning that no man with 'small
Latin' could write a proper historical play about ancient
Rome.

Almost every intelligent reader of *Sejanus* has recognized
these qualities of the play. But only a few of the most discriminating critics have remarked—and that in a cursory

fashion—the satiric features of the drama. Herford and Simpson say with truth that 'On the whole, *Sejanus* is the tragedy
of a satirist—of one who felt and saw more intensely the vices
and follies than the sorrows of men, and who, with bound-
less power of scorn, was but poorly endowed with pity.'

The same editors realize that Sejanus, a monster of arrogant evil, is not a genuinely tragic figure. His fall excites no
tragic pity. They further note that Arruntius, a figure almost
entirely of Jonson's invention, is a satiric critic in the direct
line of descent from Asper-Crites and Horace of the 'comical
satyres.' He, too, is the voice of Jonson, the irrepressible
censor of morals. What even the acute Herford and Simpson
have failed to notice is that *Sejanus,* no less than Jonson's
'comical satyres,' has been constructed on the model of a
satire.

One of the distinctive features of these dramatic unions of
satire with comedy was a derisive exposition of the principal
characters. The expositors of the central figures painted their
first portrait with a brush dipped in derision, and hostile
commentators pursued them to the very end of the drama.
In *Sejanus* Jonson retains this expository ridicule and fills it
with moral indignation. It is consistently severe and never
awakens expansive laughter. Moreover, the social and political situation which forms the setting at once for the action
and for the society of which Sejanus is the poisoned fruit is
presented in as unfavorable a light as the characters. In the
first long speech of the play, a commentator named Sabinus
takes an ill-natured fling at the base ways by which Romans
nowadays attain political power. He intimates that he and
his friends lack the slimy arts of flattery and the aversion to
crime which are essential to a successful political career in
Rome:

> We have no shift of faces, no cleft tongues,
> No soft and glutinous bodies that can stick,
> Like snails, on painted walls.

(I. i. 7-9)

Two sycophants then appear briefly for no other apparent purpose than to stimulate satiric comment from another gentleman called Silius. He points an accusing finger at these contemptible creatures, saying:

> These can lie,
> Flatter and swear, forswear, deprave, inform
> Smile and betray . . .
>   .   .   .
> Laugh when their patron laughs; sweat when he sweats;
> Be hot and cold with him; change every mood,
> Habit and garb, as often as he varies.
>
> (I. 27-9; 33-5)

Arruntius, the principal commentator, the mouthpiece of the author, immediately takes up the strain. He exclaims that men, like the times,

>   are base
> Poor, and degenerate from the exalted strain
> Of our great fathers.
>
> (I. 87-9)

These expressions of social satire are long, circumstantial, and bitter. They establish at once and irrevocably an atmosphere congenial to the career of Sejanus. His first appearance is brief. He merely passes over the stage with his retainers and clients, appearing to the audience just long enough to enable it to understand the furious satire which Arruntius and Silius hurl against him. They expose his vile past, his present tyrannical power, and his insolent ambition. This scene is a precise dramatic equivalent of the portrait which the formal satirists habitually painted in the first lines of their works.

Up to this point by far the most important characters have been the commentators. The principal actors in the drama have filed across the stage merely to give their critics a chance to pelt them with satire. Exposition of this sort establishes in every audience a deeply hostile attitude toward

Sejanus, his associates, and the vile world in which they live. Jonson knew that no protagonist thus introduced could win a bit of sympathy from anyone and that his fall would bring only relief. In other words, he knew that Sejanus could never become a genuinely tragic figure.

Nor is Sejanus better suited for the role of a villain-hero, a part which Shakespeare's Richard III played with great effect. Richard's crimes are so boldly conceived and so skillfully executed that they win our terrified admiration for the man's malign cunning. Compared to the bold-faced irony with which Richard plans and practices his villainies, Sejanus' announcement of the vices in which he will indulge is merely disgusting:

> Adultery! it is the lightest ill
> I will commit. A race of wicked acts
> Shall flow out of my anger, and o'erspread
> The world's wide face.
>
> (II. ii. 12-15)

This obscene boasting resembles not so much Richard's determination to prove a villain as the criminal impulses of Thyestes, the foulest of Seneca's creations.

Jonson introduces into this drama a few short scenes of comedy to relieve the feelings of scorn and disgust provoked by Sejanus' evil machinations. These scenes are satiric too, though not of Juvenal's temper. A colloquy between the physician Eudemus and the Princess Livia, the faithless wife of Drusus, ridicules the use of cosmetics, a favorite subject with satirists from the dawn of their art. Eudemus, evidently a skin specialist, is so eager that Livia make the most effective use of the rouge he has prescribed that he insists on applying it himself. Only through such expert aid with her toilet will she be able to hold the love of Sejanus.

In this atmosphere of derision which permeates the early scenes of the drama no tragic hero can be nurtured. And as the play develops Sejanus' villainy becomes monstrous and grotesque. He mounts through a series of crimes, each one more extravagant than the last, to dizzier and dizzier heights of wickedness, until at the beginning of the last act his self-confidence has become fantastic. He shouts exultantly:

> Great and high,
> The world knows only two, that's Rome and I.
> My roof receives me not; tis air I tread;
> And, at each step, I feel my advanced head
> Knock out a star in heaven!
>
> (v. i. 5-9)

His conquest of his human enemies has been so easy that he dares wish that the gods:

> by mixing in the cause, would bless
> Our fortune with their conquest. That were worth
> Sejanus' strife; durst fates but bring it forth.
>
> (v. i. 21-3)

This is hybris more excessive than that expressed by any character in any of Seneca's plays. It is the kind of madness with which the elder gods afflicted a man before they struck him low. Yet it is too bizarre to arouse either pity or terror. And the self-confidence of Sejanus is too egregious to make us interested in the form of the vengeance which we know the gods are sure to take.

Nemesis at once punishes his insolence. Sejanus is so blinded by his hybris that he believes he can ignore the Emperor Tiberius, whom he imagines is completely absorbed by his life of dissipation on the island of Capri. But Sejanus' enemy, Macro, has been acting as the Emperor's spy and keeping him informed of all the tyrannous deeds of his creature, and Tiberius finally strikes down the insolent fellow. He summons a meeting of the Senate, to which all the members come expecting to witness the showering of new honors upon Sejanus. Therefore they vie with each other in making flattering comments upon the great man whose power to

grant them favors is about to be enormously increased. Their
sycophancy arouses the fierce scorn of Arruntius, who directs
some of his bitterest satire against their fawning:

> Gods! how the sponges open and take in,
> And shut again! look! look! is not he blest
> That gets a seat in eye-reach of him? more,
> That comes in ear, or tongue reach? O but most,
> Can claw his subtle elbow, or with a buzz
> Fly-blow his ears.
>
> (v. x. 44-9)

The scene that follows is not effective drama. Its principal
incident is the reading to the senators of a long communica-
tion from Tiberius. The document is composed so as to confirm Sejanus and his flatterers in a sense of security, only to
make the final degree against him fall like a thunder-bolt
upon their ears. The Emperor demands 'that the offices his
minion holds be first seized by the Senate, and himself sus-
pended from all exercise of place and power.' Macro then
enters and directs his arrest and imprisonment.

Later we learn that the Senate has sentenced him to lose
his head:

> which was no sooner off
> But that and the unfortunate trunk were seized
> By the rude multitude; who not content
> With what the forward justice of the state
> Officiously had done, with violent rage
> Have rent it limb from limb.
>
> (v. x. 244-9)

The messenger then proceeds to present all the details of the
crowd's fury with more than a Senecan relish for the horrors:

> These mounting at his head, these at his face,
> These digging out his eyes, those with his brains
> Sprinkling themselves, their houses and their friends;
> Others are met, have ravished thence an arm,
> And deal small pieces of the flesh for favours;
> These with a thigh, this hath cut off his hands.

And this his feet; these fingers, and these toes:
That hath his liver, he his heart.

(v. x. 256-63)

The death of no tragic hero was ever thus desecrated and
befouled. Sejanus is literally torn out of the play in little
pieces and scattered to the winds. His end produces neither
pity nor terror. It stimulates no renewed confidence in the
dignity of the human spirit and its ability to rise above suffering and death. Like the final disappearance of all satirically conceived figures, his catastrophe produces intense satisfaction, liberally seasoned with scorn.

Furthermore, Sejanus' end has not purged the state of its
evil and cleared the way for the establishment of a sound
and healthful social order. After the death of Shakespeare's
super-villain Richard III, Richmond mounts the English
throne to end the long years of bloody civil war and to usher
in a reign of peace. In *Hamlet,* young Fortinbras plays a
similar role. Macro, the architect of Sejanus' overthrow and
his successor, is no such ambassador of concord. He is a villain
in his own right. Vicious Rome has travailed in agony but to
spawn a monster of wickedness as horrible as his predecessor.
He has the young innocent son and daughter of Sejanus
obscenely tortured and executed:

> . . . And because our laws
> Admit no virgin immature to die,
> The wittily and strangely cruel Macro
> Delivered her [the daughter] to be deflowered and spoiled,
> By the rude lust of the licentious hangman,
> Then to be strangled with her harmless brother.

(v. x. 287-92)

No wonder that Arruntius hazards the prophecy:

> That this fellow Macro, will become
> A greater prodigy in Rome, than he
> That now is fallen.

(v. x. 189-91)

Macro's rise to power will only inaugurate a new cycle of tyranny which will drive himself and the state to a catastrophe like that it has just suffered.

Then in the last speech of the play Jonson dons the priest-like robes of the admonitory author of formal satire. He has Arruntius turn to the audience and say:

> Let this example move the insolent man
> Not to grow proud and careless of the gods.
>
> (v. x. 336-7)

In this strange play, Ben Jonson's originality flowered again. By filling the mould of a typical Senecan drama with the materials and spirit of satire, he created a new type of play— a kind of tragical satire.

After this excursion into tragedy, Jonson in *Volpone* returned to comedy, but comedy written in a spirit like that which animates *Sejanus*. Volpone is almost as menacing a creature as the Roman monster, and the punishment prescribed for him at the end of the play is the most severe that a writer of comedy has ever dared mete out. The judge orders all of Volpone's wealth to be confiscated:

> And since the most was gotten by imposture
> By feigning lame, gout, palsy and such diseases,
> Thou art to lie in prison, cramped with irons
> Till thou be'st sick and lame indeed.
>
> (v. xii. 121-4)

The scorn that this sentencing of Volpone arouses dissipates with a derisive snarl the terror which has up to now permeated the drama.

Jonson in *Volpone* clearly sports not with human follies but with crimes. And he organizes his criminally minded legacy-hunters according to the scheme which he and other satirists had found most effective. He forms his knaves into a procession which passes through the chamber of Volpone's bedroom, where he pretends to be dying and where the gifts

of his duped would-be heirs are piled high. Jonson makes
this evil creature still more repulsive by surrounding him
with a household composed of distorted and deformed
wretches—a dwarf, a eunuch, and a hermaphrodite.

Each covetous sychophant proves to be a monster of cupid-
ity. Corbaccio, for example, is willing to stake his son's in-
heritance against the chance of being Volpone's heir, and
Corvino is glad to barter his wife's honor. For that he cares
nothing:

> Honour! tut, a breath;
> There's no such thing in nature; a mere term
> Invented to awe fools. What is my gold
> The worse for touching, clothes for being looked on?
> Why this 's no more.
>
> (III. vii. 38-42)

And Corvino cares no more for reputation:

> And for your fame
> That's such a jig; as if I would go tell it,
> Cry it on the Piazza! who shall know it,
> But he that cannot speak it, and this fellow.
>
> (III. vii. 47-50)

In a similar fashion Jonson deals with each one of the vicious
characters in the play.

The first effect of his method is to create fierce scorn for
each of the knaves. Moreover, his scheme of presenting them
one after another in a kind of grotesque procession carries us
beyond contempt for the individual to detestation of the
greed whose ugly features grin from the several masks which
the vice has donned. The emotions which the comedy *Volpone* produces are thus the very same as those aroused by the
tragedy *Sejanus*. Each evokes in its own way moral repulsion,
scorn, and derision. And these are the emotions which satire
in both its tragic and comic modes seeks to arouse.

IV

Many of the satirical devices which Jonson perfected in
Sejanus and *Volpone* Shakespeare adopted in constructing
from the traditional story of Timon his first tragical satire.
This view is, of course, not consistent with the conventional
opinion of the play. Most critics believe that the drama is a
tragedy cut after the pattern which Shakespeare habitually
used. Timon, so they say, resembles the protagonists in the
poet's other tragedies in being at the opening of the action a
man 'of good and gracious nature.' This essentially noble man
is converted into a slave of passion through the vicious influence exerted upon him by the diseased money-worshipping
society of Athens. Then, like other tragic heroes of his
creator, he lunges from one emotion to its extreme opposite.
As Macbeth, for example, a naturally courageous man, veers
from fear and superstition to the hideous rashness associated
with hybris; so Timon vacillates between histrionic generosity, stimulated by flattery, and savage misanthropy.

Yet even these orthodox critics find it unlikely that
Timon's conduct during the last two acts of the play will
produce the pity and terror which is the aesthetic end of
tragedy. Timon's violence in both speech and action, they
admit, alienates the sympathy of every sort of spectator. But
they try to imagine that Timon's uninterrupted torrent of
vituperation conforms to Shakespeare's conventional practice by asserting that 'Timon is cast in the psychological
mould of Lear. Like the old King on the heath:

> his wits
> Are drowned and lost in his calamities.'

Wilson Knight, after his fashion, makes the most extravagant
claims for Timon's essential fineness.[3] Timon's 'tragic guilt,'
so he thinks, is merely 'impetuous and curbless love—essen-

tial nobility unmixed with any restraining faculty of criticism. The heart's gold of Timon is alloyed with no baser
metal of intellect.' The spirit of perfected man which in-
habits him is distressed to find that love is not 'truly inter-
fused' throughout 'this beneath world.' Because it is tragi-
cally absent from Athens, his inmost soul demands that he
reject her. So he turns his back on his native land in order
to seek in Nature the emotional fulfilment which he has
vainly sought in mankind. When he flees to his cave in the
desert, Knight tells us that Timon is stepping 'from Time
into Eternity.' The emotions which he there displays are
only those suitable for the grandeurs of a limitless world.
He then dons the 'imperial nakedness of Hate,' a magical
garment which opens his eyes to 'all forms of human frailty,
moral, physical and social.'

Therefore Knight has the curious notion that Timon's diatribes all spring from his realization that 'loss of love alone
is responsible for all the ills that flesh endures.' Hence
Timon's tragedy—and it is a deeply spiritual one—derives
from the fact that a character with so much love to lavish
upon mankind has been driven away from all human associations to seek and to find his salvation 'in solitary contemplation of the infinite.' Knight does not explain just how
Timon's suicide is a form of salvation, nor does he show how
the cave, the roots, and the lumps of gold have been made
effective symbols of infinity. He does present a kind of blan-
ket explanation of these difficulties by asserting that the play
is an allegory and so 'sublimely unrealistic.' Not so sublimely
unrealistic, one is tempted to object, as Wilson Knight's interpretation of the drama, particularly to one who comes
upon the critic's metaphysical flights fresh from reading the
last two acts of *Timon of Athens,* for to the eye of common-
sense they are one protracted spasm of vituperation and vili-
fication.

Other critics offer a less transcendental explanation of the

disintegration of the tragic pattern which takes place in the
last two acts of the play. They assume that when Timon
became completely alienated from mankind, Shakespeare,
the suffering man, snatched the pen from the hand of Shakespeare, the cunning playwright. His wits, too, were drowned
and lost in his personal calamities. *Timon of Athens* thus
makes up for what it loses in tragic power through its revelation of the woe that was corroding Shakespeare's mind in the
year 1607. It becomes a lyrical expression of subjective bitterness and bleakness. Mark Van Doren, one of the ablest of
the critics who take this point of view, imagines that in
Timon's tomb—in 'a bleak open timeless space where a sea
of air broods in its vast arc above another sea whose waves
are without memory—Shakespeare buried for good and all
his bitterness toward life.'

Mr. Van Doren's eloquence is seductive, but to regard the
play merely as a revelation of the pestilent congregation of
vapors which shrouded Shakespeare's inner life is to take the
easy road from aesthetic criticism to biographical curiosity.
It is more courageous not so easily to give up the search for
a literary form which will make intrinsic to the structure of
the work those elements which have hitherto seemed deviations from the ways of normal tragedy. I believe that *Timon
of Athens* is not a tragedy wrecked in full career by the erup-
tion of the author's personal despair too imperious to be
restrained. On the contrary, most of its eccentricities will be
softened or disappear altogether if we realize that Shakespeare designed his play as a satire to be written, after the
new manner of Ben Jonson, in a tragic key.

v

A close examination of the structure of the work should
establish the truth of this hypothesis. Timon is not introduced to us as Knight believes, as 'a hero too noble for this

world.' He is from the first presented as the credulous victim
of a crowd of flatterers. Before the first scene is half over the
poet-commentator describes the fawning sycophants with appropriate satiric contempt. They:

> Follow his [Timon's] strides, his lobbies fill with tendance,
> Rain sacrificial whisperings in his ear,
> Make sacred even his stirrup, and through him
> Drink the free air.
>
> (I. i. 80-83)

This servile adoration Timon fails to distinguish from the
discriminating praise of true friends. An Elizabethan audience, vividly awake to the dangers of flattery, saw at once in
Timon's response to this adulation, not generosity but self-
satisfaction at the display of his own munificence. The be-
stowal of his largesse is touched with vanity and ostentation.
He pays the debt for which Ventidius has been imprisoned,
with a little burst of self-gratulation.

> I am not of that feather to shake off
> My friend when he most needs me.
>
> (I. i. 100-101)

With a similar pompous flourish he gives one of his old
retainers three talents as a dowry for a daughter:

> This gentleman of mine hath serv'd me long.
> To build his fortune I will strain a little,
> For 'tis a bond in men.
>
> (I. i. 143-5)

Timon's great wealth has removed him from reality into a
world where his every impulse is grandiose and a little absurd. For, as one of the commentators remarks:

> For bounty, that makes gods, doth still mar men.
>
> (IV. ii. 39)

At the end of the second scene of the play we see that
Timon loves above all else to play the role of ostentatious

benefactor. To be sure, some of these sycophants call him 'noble.' But the excellence which they discern in their patron is spendthrift generosity, the only kind of nobility to appeal to a society which worships money. The lord who at the end of the first scene in the play declares that Timon carries the noblest mind 'that ever governed man' leaves us in no doubt what he means. He means that Timon has more money to spend than any other man in Athens and that he scatters his gold about with more complete abandon. It pays to bring gifts to such a squanderer:

> He pours it out. Plutus, the god of gold
> Is but his steward. No meed, but he repays
> Sevenfold above itself. No gift to him
> But breeds the giver a return exceeding
> All use of quittance.
>
> (I. i. 287-91)

After this speech we realize that Timon's 'good and gracious nature' is but his false friends' euphemism for prodigality.

These first scenes have been constructed like a satire. The various characters are introduced not to play parts in a well-knit plot; they are arranged as a procession of individuals, each one serving as the illustration of the same vice. Their only function is, as it were, to file across the stage in the conventional costumes of flatterers. Their lavish commendations of Timon are rewarded with money. The similarity of his response to each one of these adulators in turn makes his generosity seem automatic and therefore ridiculous.

At the rear of this procession of blandiloquents appears Apemantus to play the part of a buffoonish commentator. Like all who take this role, he displays some of the characteristics of Jonson's Carlo Buffone. Like him, Apemantus expresses his bitter scorn and indignation in grotesque and extravagant terms. In this way he arouses and directs the derision of the spectators and at the same time entertains them in his characteristically preposterous fashion.

In answer to Timon's question, 'How dost thou like this jewel, Apemantus?' he replies, 'Not so well as plain-dealing, which will not cost a doit' (I. i. 215-17). He makes the flatterers both disgusting and ridiculous by pointing at their fawning postures and exclaiming:

> What a coil's here!
> Serving of becks and jutting out of bums!
> (I. ii. 236-7)

He remarks with a pointed glance at Timon: 'He that loves to be flattered is worthy o' th' flatterer' (I. i. 232-3). Finally his disgust mounts to such intensity that it can be voided only in a cry of violent misanthropy:

> The strain of man's bred out
> Into baboon and monkey.
> (I. i. 259-60)

In these four speeches Apemantus reveals the character of his mind and the nature of his dramatic function. Though a buffoon, he is not so foul-mouthed as Thersites, or so funny as Carlo Buffone. He represents the Renaissance idea of a cynic, a creature whose soul was inhabited by a snarling dog. In his 'kennel wit' there is much angry detraction and little laughter.

His remarks, along with those of less trenchant commentators, help to establish in the audience a hostile attitude toward Timon. Apemantus makes us doubly sure of the insincerity of his friends and clients. If we but listen to him, we shall not mistake Timon's strutting pride for 'true erotic richness' or for 'the flower of human aspiration.' Apemantus does not 'enlist our respect for Timon.' [4] On the contrary he keeps us from being dazzled by the deceptive splendor which might cause us to mistake pretentious parade for noble generosity.

The schematism which first appears when the suitors beg

favors of Timon becomes more obvious as the play advances. After the news of his financial failure has been spread abroad, his creditors present their bills in one, two, three order. Three friends refuse to lend him money in three successive scenes, and three come to the mock banquet. This is the method not of tragedy, but, as we have seen in our glance at *Volpone*, of satire; for a procession of figures similarly ridiculous or base shifts the emphasis from their individualities to the folly they all represent. It also makes all the figures seem like automata, and hence absurd victims of a folly or a vice, creatures to arouse at once our scorn and derision.

Timon, the man, is nothing like Jonson's Volpone. The latter's cries of delirious joy at his success in duping the sycophants, uttered from his bed, are nothing like Timon's misanthropic diatribes shouted from the mouth of his cave at the visitors who file out into the desert to get his gold. The occasions and the purposes of the two streams of satire are different; so is their form. Yet they are alike in the picturesque setting which they have been given and in their savage violence.

VI

In the last two acts of the play Timon becomes almost a caricature of the now familiar figure of the malcontent satirist. Apemantus describes Timon's malady in terms which make this relationship clear, asserting that his hatred of mankind is the result of

> A poor unmanly melancholy sprung
> From change of fortune.
> (IV. iii. 203-4)

And a little later, one of the three Banditti who visit Timon in order to seize some of the gold that he has dug up explains that 'the mere want of gold and the falling-from of

his friends drove him into this melancholy' (IV. iii. 401-3).
That is, Timon's bitter experience with the greed and ingratitude of his supposed friends has dried up all the springs
of his being. The ensuing sense of frustration issues in that
combination of wrath and disgust which ruled the malcontent. The first object of Timon's unrestrained attack is the
worship of money, which has corrupted and perverted the
entire state of Athens. Picking up a handful of gold—of yellow, glittering, precious gold—he cries:

> Thus much of this will make black white, foul fair,
> Wrong right, base noble, old young, coward valiant.
> Ha, you gods! Why this? What, this, you gods? Why, this
> Will lug your priests and servants from your sides,
> Pluck sick men's pillows from below their heads:
> This yellow slave
> Will knit and break religions, bless the accurs'd,
> Make the hoar leprosy ador'd, place thieves
> And give them title, knee and approbation
> With senators on the bench.
>
> (IV. iii. 28-37)

The theme of this diatribe is a familiar one—the love of
money is the root of all evil. But neither in this speech nor
in any of the others which Timon makes during the last two
acts does he level his scorn at any private individual. He is,
rather, aghast at the demoralization which greed has produced in all public and private relationships in Athens. The
entire social structure, contaminated by the conduct of its
leaders, has become sick. Not only has degree become 'slaked,'
as in *Troilus and Cressida,* but the authority of all moral
imperatives has been destroyed. All the restraints that keep
civilized man from reverting to brutish chaos have been lost.
Hence Athenians have no choice but to abandon themselves
to anarchy and bestiality. Timon, therefore, shouts out advice which will expedite this march to moral and social
chaos:

Matrons, turn incontent!
Obedience fail in children! Slaves and fools,
Pluck the grave wrinkled Senate from the bench
And minister in their steads! To general filths
Convert o' the instant, green virginity!
Do't in your parents' eyes! Bankrupts, hold fast,
Rather than render back, out with your knives
And cut your trusters' throats! Bound servants, steal!

. . .

. . . Son of sixteen,
Pluck the lin'd crutch from thy old limping sire;
With it beat out his brains!

(IV. i. 3-10; 13-15)

From this extravagant invitation to unrestrained disorder,
Timon turns to urging the Athenians to break their allegiance to all the principles which bind men together into
societies:

Piety and fear,
Religion to the gods, peace, justice, truth,
Domestic awe, night-rest and neighbourhood,
Instruction, manners, mysteries and trades,
Degrees, observances, customs and laws,
Decline to your confounding contraries
And let confusion live!

(IV. i. 15-21)

This last phrase is the battle cry with which Timon seeks
to inspirit all who visit him in his desert retreat. This is the
spirit that will bring devastation down upon Athens. He begs
Alcibiades to let his army be a planetary plague to the
citizens. He shouts:

. . . Spare not the babe
Whose dimpled smiles from fools exhaust their mercy.
Think it a bastard whom the oracle
Hath doubtfully pronounc'd thy throat shall cut,
And mince it sans remorse.

. . .

. . . There's gold to pay thy soldiers.
Make large confusion; and, thy fury spent,
Counfounded be thyself!

(IV. iii. 118-22; 126-8)

In a final frenzy of angry misanthropy he cries for the extinction of the entire human race. He bids Nature:

> Ensear thy fertile and conceptious womb;
> Let it no more bring out ingrateful man!
> Go great with tigers, dragons, wolves and bears;
> Teem with new monsters whom thy upward face
> Hath to the marbled mansion all above
> Never presented.
>
> (IV. iii. 187-92)

In this second stage of his career Timon enlists our sympathy even less than in the first. Shakespeare calls him a 'naked gull,' a term used over and over again by the satirists. He is completely the slave of his misanthropy. His propensity to vituperate is always beyond his control. Every human being who confronts him ignites the powder of his anger and automatically explodes it. The mechanical nature of his responses, despite their obvious intensity, deprives him of every shred of human dignity. It makes him absurd even while he is terrifying.

Moreover, the nature of his outbursts is meant to arouse strong disapproval. They are the expression of no zeal to improve social conditions or to reform individuals—the only two impulses toward satire approved by the critics. His speeches are, on the contrary, unmitigated detraction, and they are adapted to no fit time or occasion. That is, they represent all that the Renaissance critics, and Shakespeare among them, believed to be false, presumptuous, and ugly in satire.

Nor is Timon's end that of a proper tragic protagonist. He commits suicide. Hence his death is not the result of righteous indignation but the final act of an ignoble and cowardly disgust with life. His catastrophe neither reconciles the destructive forces of his nature nor brings any catharsis to the spectators. Even his choice of a grave is food for scorn. He chooses to make:

> his everlasting mansion
> Upon the beached verge of the salt flood,
> Who once a day with his embossed froth
> The turbulent surge shall cover.
>
> (v. i. 218-21)

Thus Timon seeks to be associated for all eternity with turbulence and senseless destruction. As one of the senators explains:

> His discontents are unremovably
> Coupled to nature.
>
> (v. i. 227-8)

His self-composed epitaph is an ill-natured attempt to make his scorn and hatred of man everlasting. It reads as follows:

> Here lies a wretched corpse, of wretched soul bereft.
> Seek not my name. A plague consume you wicked caitiffs left.
> Here lie I, Timon, who alive all living men did hate.
> Pass by, and curse thy fill, but pass and stay not here thy gait.
>
> (v. iv. 69-73)

In these lines Timon absurdly seeks to create a posthumous life for his misanthropic railing. Thus the end of the play merely brings to fruition the disapproval and derision which Shakespeare has systematically provoked throughout the drama. It is not an attitude appropriate to tragedy, but one which is of the very essence of satire.

VII

This view of *Timon of Athens* will at least set those who wish to approach the play sympathetically upon the right aesthetic path. They will begin by listening attentively to the many formal commentators who appear throughout the play. They will give particular heed to the buffoon Apemantus, even while he, like his prototype in Jonson's drama, at once repels and entertains them with the extravagance and foulness of his remarks. They will share his hostile attitude toward the action and all the characters. With these dramatically conventional representations of the satiric author, they will first join in reprehending the condition of Athens, where the magistrates have poisoned all its channels of power and justice by their greed. They will scorn the flatterers who deceive Timon and will revile their ingratitude. If they but heed the same guides, they will become abundantly aware of Timon's folly. They will see that the gold standards of Athens, in the scales of which Timon's false friends weigh him, have rendered him a fool of generosity and have caused him with lavish gestures to strut down the path of extravagance and adulation to his ruin.

The spectators who assume this proper critical attitude toward Timon in the first part of the play will not mistake his violent reaction to his disillusionment for indignation of a noble mind. They will see in it wild automatic surrenders to irrational misanthropy. And they will recognize in the things he says unmitigated detraction. Finally his catastrophe will seem not the tragic end of a noble man, but the welcome disappearance of an addict to violence unable to keep his powerful nature from veering between folly and madness.

Readers of the play who accept this interpretation will also understand the obscure relationship between the career of Timon and the deeds of Alcibiades. In both of Shakespeare's earlier satiric plays, *Troilus and Cressida* and *Measure for Measure,* he placed his derided characters in a decaying society. The foolish or evil figures were at least partly the product of their milieux. He adopts the same semi-deterministic principles in the construction of this drama. Timon's Athens is a completely demoralized social organization. The senators who rule the city value riches more than virtue. According to the best political theorists of the age, this was to run counter to the Divine plan. For God blessed the formation of political states, because only in the social tranquility which they achieved could man live a life of intellectual aspiration and Christian virtue. To be sure, a well-ordered society made it possible to obtain the material necessities of life. But when a state made this its main purpose, it became corrupt and perverted.

This is the condition to which the venal senators have brought Athens. And their avarice has been contagious. Private citizens have caught it from their magistrates. Timon's flattering acquaintances suffer from a most virulent form of the infection. They court him only because they covet his wealth. Timon is also a creature of the money-worshipping society. His apparent virtues are wholly dependent upon his great possessions. As soon as they go, he is stripped as bare of excellence as was Lear. His story is thus but a concrete example of the evil effects of the love of money. The vice has vitiated the life of the entire social structure 'in sequence of degree from high to low throughout.' It has also stripped Timon of all his civilized virtues and left him a savage brute.

Timon, as we have seen, pours out the vials of his wrath upon the universal lust for gold. Alcibiades aids him in exposing this vice and acts as its scourge.[5] In a speech delivered in the Senate chamber he accuses the rulers of being utterly perverted by their greed. 'Banish you dotage,' he shouts. 'Banish usury, that makes the Senate ugly.' His contempt for their materialism he develops in a soliloquy which follows this diatribe:

> I have kept back their foes.
> While they have told their money and let out
> Their coin upon large interest, I myself
> Rich only in large hurts. All those for this?
> Is this the balsam that the usuring Senate
> Pours into captains' wounds?
> (III. v. 106-11)

It is to overthrow the government which is responsible for so much public and private woe that Alcibiades marches victoriously against Athens. When he sees the Senators on the walls, he shouts:

> Till now you have gone on and filled the time
> With all licentious measure, making your wills
> The scope of justice.

(v. iv. 3-5)

These enemies of good government are the very men who indirectly have destroyed Timon. Not all are guilty; so Alcibiades does not raze the entire city. Only those set out for reproof are to fall. He will cleanse the rest by making each:

> Prescribe to other, as each other's leech.

This queer ending which compromises with both tragedy and satire is another reason for the confused aesthetic effects of the drama.

If we now understand that *Timon of Athens* is Shakespeare's first attempt to write a tragical satire, we may partly understand why he did not complete the work. We have seen that the first three acts remain a kind of unfinished sketch of dramatic action. Only the last two acts have been given a form that seems nearly final. And it is precisely these last two acts which demanded effective satiric writing. Only after Timon had become a 'naked gull' did his emotions reach the intensity which naturally explodes in angry derision. Naturally in these parts of the drama Shakespeare found a chance to test his satiric powers. Neither his imagination nor his poetic interest was fired by anything in the first three acts as he outlined them. He seemed unable to devise a plot which could become the natural history of the development of a figure who like Timon was at once tragic and ridiculous. In *Coriolanus* he found a story better suited to the complicated demands of a tragical satire. So he turned to that tale of ancient Rome and left *Timon of Athens* in its present fragmentary form.

But to understand these facts about the drama will not remove all sense of confusion from the minds of those who read the play. The author's mood is not dramatic even in the last two acts. As Mark Van Doren remarks, our interest is concentrated upon 'the things his hero says rather than upon the meaning of the fact that he says them.' [6] He believes that Timon's speeches are in the lyric mode and therefore an expression of Shakespeare's personal feelings and not of his theme. But according to our hypothesis, Timon's declamations are not personal lyrics but vituperative satire. The one, however, can be just as undramatic as the other and just as disturbing an interruption to an audience's interest in a play.

For satire is almost as personal a form of expression as lyric poetry. However, the difference between the two is of great importance. In satire the feeling, without losing any of its intensity, is completely objectified. This is the reason that Timon's speeches are terrifying even while they render him absurd. And it is the union of feelings of absurdity with those of terror that gives Shakespeare's two satires written in the tragic mode their strange baffling quality. The two emotions in most minds prey upon each other. The result is something like a mental convulsion. This distress cannot easily be surmounted or transformed into any sort of aesthetic feeling. So even those who realize that *Timon of Athens* is not a tragedy made chaotic by the insurrection of Shakespeare's emotions of despair and disgust will not give it their unqualified approval. Just because it is tragical satire, it is not attuned to Shakespeare's nature or to the intensities of his genius. Even those informed by historical study of the author's purpose in composing *Timon of Athens* will quite properly continue to assign it a low place in the canon of Shakespeare's works.

X

Coriolanus

IN *Coriolanus* we have Shakespeare's second and more successful experiment in tragical satire. The structure which in *Timon of Athens* was bare and almost crude has here become a suitable form in which to cast the Roman aristocrat's story. Yet the construction of this last of Shakespeare's tragedies has been almost universally deplored. Critics, realizing that its pattern is very different from the one which the poet employed in his great tragedies, have agreed to brand it as inept. A. C. Bradley, for example, believes that the author's unintentional departure from his usual practice accounts for the failure of the play to produce a sound tragic effect.[1] This usually acute critic did not allow for the fact that Shakespeare, at this time a thoroughly experienced dramatist, might have deliberately experimented with new dramatic structures.

It is natural enough to judge *Coriolanus* by the standards of conventional tragedy; in the first Folio it is entitled *The Tragedy of Coriolanus*. Bernard Shaw was one of the first to see that the play was not a tragedy at all. He solves the problem of *Coriolanus* by propounding a witty paradox. 'It is,' he asserts, 'the greatest of Shakespeare's comedies.' This perverse statement suggests the proper approach to the play. Shakespeare did not attempt to give *Coriolanus* the structure of a conventional tragedy. Neither in his presentation of the central figure nor in his construction of the plot does he follow orthodox tragic principles. Instead of enlisting our sympathy for Coriolanus, he deliberately alienates it. Indeed he makes

the figure partly an object of scorn. Instead of ennobling
Coriolanus through his fall and death, he mocks and ridicules him to the end. In brief, he fills the tragedy so full of
the spirit of derision that the play can be understood only
if it be recognized as perhaps the most successful of Shakespeare's satiric plays.

II

Shakespeare found the materials for his play in Plutarch's
Life of Coriolanus, but he gave the historical events a meaning entirely his own. For Plutarch they yielded a lesson in
political restraint and patriotism. As he tells the story continual war has reduced the plebs to dire poverty. Indeed
their misery is so great that they demand a change in their
constitution—the creation of new officers to be called tribunes, who are to redress the wrongs of the people. This agita-
tion contains a threat of revolution. But the peril is averted
because the senate is wise enough to send to the plebs 'certain of their pleasantest old men' to discuss the grievances
of the commoners. These ambassadors agree to the creation
of the new officers and induce the plebs to join with the patricians in the defense of Rome against a foreign enemy.

Shakespeare completely changes the significance of these
events. His play opens 'in the midst of a riot staged by the
mutinous masses,' who are starving because of a shortage of
wheat. For their misery they blame not the drought, which is
the real cause of the famine, but their governing class, the
patricians, and, in particular, Coriolanus, the leader and
mouthpiece of the aristocrats. They hate him for the contempt he has always shown them. Coriolanus in his very first
speech proves that their charge is just, for he addresses them
as: dissentious rogues
        That, rubbing the poor itch of your opinions,
        Make yourself scabs.
                                    (I. i. 168-70)

This unsavory figurative language is characteristic of most of the utterances of the haughty patrician. On the occasion in question the vituperative torrent is interrupted by a messenger who brings Coriolanus an order to lead the Roman army against the Volscians and Aufidius their leader. Since carnage is his natural element, he responds to this call with enthusiasm. But even the heroism he summons for the battle cannot temper his fundamental brutality. When at the first onslaught of the enemy his soldiers flee in disorder, he berates them with characteristically foul speech. By insults rather than encouragement he drives his men back into the fray, where he does deeds of superhuman valor, defeats Aufidius in single combat, and brings complete victory to his army.

On his return to the capital, the populace greets him with wild acclaim and the senators at once nominate him for consul. He craves the office, but his whole nature flares into revolt against the convention which demands that he stand in the market place and beg the plebeians for their votes. However, at the insistence of his dominating mother he submits to the humiliation of this electioneering. Though his appeal is filled with disdain, it seems to succeed. But after he has come through his ordeal and gone home, the tribunes persuade the crowd that he has mocked them. If they possess any self-respect, they will at once revoke their 'ignorant election.' This they do and drive Coriolanus into the rage which the tribunes anticipate and exploit.

When they inform him of the people's change of heart, he insults them with mounting violence, until they call in a 'rabble of plebeians' and precipitate a brawl. In the course of this uproar the people and their officers are driven off. Later they return to find that Coriolanus has been persuaded by his mother to allay their anger with fair speech. But his amenity does not divert them from their intention to drive him into one of his fits of uncontrollable rage. They call him traitor, and to the word he reacts as they had planned. He looses upon them a torrent of abuse. This stimulates the rabble to shout for his banishment, and in the words of Coriolanus they 'whoop' him out of Rome. Through his uncontrollable rage he has been manipulated into a course of action which is to lead to his self-destruction.

Then he goes straight over to the enemy, and although he treats all the Volscians with overbearing arrogance, his military genius enables him to lead their conquering army to the very gates of Rome. There various representative citizens meet him with desperate pleas to spare his native city. They find him adamant. As a last resort his mother, Volumnia, accompanied by his wife Virgilia and his small son, is sent out to confront him. She feels sure that she can force him to abandon his dire purpose, for she well knows her irresistible influence upon the man who in many respects is still her little boy. She wisely does not ask him to rejoin the Roman forces, but merely to force Aufidius to make peace. Coriolanus is deaf to his mother's entreaties but cannot hold out against her anger. He yields in the flurried terror of a frightened child.

Returning to the Volscian army, Coriolanus induces Aufidius to 'frame convenient peace.' By thus snatching the fruits of complete victory from the Volscians, he wins the undying resentment of their leader, who lays a clever trap to catch and destroy the haughty Olympian schoolboy. He knows how to stimulate Coriolanus to one of his characteristic fits of wild anger. He uses the same method which the tribunes had found effective, and insults him publicly. In the presence of a crowd of confederates he brands him as a traitor to his adopted country. The accusation has the desired effect. Coriolanus throws into the teeth of the Volscians his former triumphs over them and raises their resentment

to the killing point. Then, though the Lords of Corioli protest, the Volscian plebeians fall upon Coriolanus and kill
him.

III

From this brief resumé of the action it should·be clear that
Coriolanus, like all Shakespeare's other history plays, em-
bodies some of the author's political ideas. Some critics, to
be sure, hesitate to attribute any definite political views to
him. The idolators of the early nineteenth century and their
modern representatives are responsible for this transcendental attitude toward their hero. Shakespeare, they proudly as-
sert, was not of an age, but of all time. Of all movements in
a given era, political squabbles are the most ephemeral.
Therefore to the idolators an assertion that Shakespeare expressed positive political opinions even in his chronicle history plays was the rankest heresy. A. C. Bradley expressed
their view when he wrote, 'I think it extremely hazardous to
ascribe to him [Shakespeare] any political feeling at all and
ridiculous to pretend to any certainty on the subject.' [2] This
betrays a strange view of the dramatist's art. He, less than
any other man of letters, dares to retire to an ivory tower,
remote from the social interests of his contemporaries, in
order to allow the trade winds from eternity to blow through
his philosophic mind. Shakespeare based his profound studies
of human motive and human passion upon a realistic ap-
praisal of the various milieux in which his characters came
to life; and of all the environments in which human beings
must live, the political organization most interested Shakespeare and his contemporaries. The problems of Tudor politics obsessed them.

The usual view is that in *Coriolanus* Shakespeare expresses
his contempt for the common man and his conviction that
political power in the hands of the mob always brings disaster to the state.[3] More recently critics have looked at the

other side of the picture and discerned in Coriolanus' conduct an exposure of the brutal methods that dictators in
every age must employ to retain their absolute power.[4] Each
of these apparently contradictory views is partly correct.
Though Shakespeare is not in this play showing his contempt
for the common man, he is nevertheless expressing his vigorous disapproval of democracy. In common with all political
theorists of his age, he regarded it as the absence of all government—a form of organized disorder.[5]

But he does not lay all the blame for the social chaos on
the plebs and its leaders. To his mind Coriolanus is equally
guilty. He is a bad ruler. In the many volumes that the fifteenth and sixteenth centuries devoted to the education of a
prince, the supreme magistrate—usually the king—is admon-
ished to regard his subjects as his children and to be a father
to them. He must sympathize with their trials and dangers
and feel keenly his responsibility for their welfare. He must
follow the example set by Henry V toward his soldiers in
Shakespeare's play of that name. But Coriolanus acts in a
manner diametrically opposed. He hates the people. On almost every occasion in which he meets them face to face he
berates them and curses them vilely. Inevitably he finds them
hostile and recalcitrant to his leadership—brave and efficient
though it be in battle. Instead of correcting their faults, he
goads them to anarchy by his hostility and violence. Coriolanus is thus as much responsible as the plebs for the political débâcle.

As a political *exemplum* the play presents a case of violent
political disorder and reveals its causes. The trouble lies in
the fact that no civil group performs its prescribed duties
properly. As a result the divinely revealed pattern for the
state is disrupted and society reels toward primal chaos. This
lesson could not be clearly taught in the terms of tragedy.
With its interest concentrated upon the tragic career of Coriolanus the man, an audience might easily ignore the political

significance of the play. But the satiric form gave Shakespeare an opportunity to treat derisively both the crowd and Coriolanus, between whose 'endless jars' the commonweal was sorely wounded. A careful analysis of the play will show how skillfully the political teaching, the central theme of every Elizabethan history play, has been fitted to the satiric form of the drama.

IV

The play opens with a picture of a mutinous mob, in this way establishing immediately the atmosphere of social turmoil which is to exercise its destructive power throughout the action and to form a natural milieu for the subversive forces in the little world of Coriolanus' passions. In the midst of the uproar Menenius appears. He is the chief of the many commentators and expositors in this play who serve as Shakespeare's mouthpiece. He performs this service with a fussy garrulity that is intended to rouse our laughter. Later in the play he explains that he is 'a humorous [i.e. crotchety] patrician and one that loves a cup of hot wine with not a drop of allaying Tiber in 't . . . One that converses more with the buttock of the night than with the forehead of the morning. What I think, I utter, and spend my malice in my breath' (ii. i. 51-8 passim). The character of this speech, particularly its unsavory metaphors, stamps Menenius as Shakespeare's variant of the now familiar buffoonish commentator. Like Carlo Buffone he says right things in the wrong way, thus giving to his comments a kind of outrageous pertinence.

His first speech to the crowd only partly reveals these characteristics. In order to persuade it to cease its revolutionary uproar, he tells the fable of the rebellion which the other members of the body once raised against the belly,

> That only like a gulf it did remain
> I' the midst o' the' body, idle and unactive,

Still cupboarding the viand, never bearing
Like labor with the rest.

(I. i. 101-4)

But the belly replies that by sending rivers of blood to all
parts of the body it serves as the source of the health and the
very life of the whole organism. The belly, it appears, stands
in this parable for the senators, and for Coriolanus in particular, because in Rome he and his fellow patricians exer-
cised the functions of the king. The mutinous members of
the body represent the plebeians.

The audience would have regarded this figure of the belly
and its functions as a speech designed to characterize Menenius—to stamp him as a garrulous old man. But they would
also recognize it as a conventional way of stating a familiar
principle of current political philosophy. It would seem like
a page torn from almost any political primer. Because both
the plebs and Coriolanus disregard the principles illustrated
in Menenius' parable they bring disaster to Rome and to
themselves. The people, in seeking to exercise the functions
of a ruler, were permitting 'the foot to partake in point of
preëminence with the head.' They were instituting a form
of democracy which was universally regarded as a monstrous
body of many heads.[5] Coriolanus himself employs this figure
to describe the proletariat. As he stands outside the gate of
Rome, whence he has been driven by the mob, he exclaims

The beast
With many heads butts me away.
(IV. i. 2-3)

Elsewhere in the play he calls the plebs Hydra.[6] Through the
repeated use of such familiar figurative language the author
impressed his historical lesson upon his audience. No member of it could fail to recognize the drama as an exhibition
of the forces of democracy at their destructive work. The
most obvious lesson that the drama is designed to teach is,

then, as follows: The people should never be allowed to exercise any of the functions proper to a ruler. That way lies anarchy. But the career of Coriolanus is to constitute an equally impressive warning: No ruler must act as cruelly and brutally toward his subjects as does this man. He is more of a slave driver than a kind father. Such a magistrate is always an architect of social confusion.

V

A character cast to play such an admonitory role cannot be treated like an ordinary tragic hero. And Shakespeare deals with Coriolanus from the moment of his first appearance through the whole course of the play to the catastrophe in a manner directly opposite to the one he invariably adopted for his real tragic protagonists. In the first place he endows all his true tragic heroes with many noble traits which appear and reappear through the play. In particular he puts into the mouths of other characters words of praise for the hero as they knew him before he became a slave to one of the subversive passions. Shakespeare also puts into his hero's mouth reflective soliloquies which reveal his struggles between good and evil, and win our sympathetic understanding even while he is losing his battle with destiny. Then, as his protagonist stands at the very brink of the catastrophe, the poet allows him to utter a poignant speech which recalls to the minds of the spectators the loftiness of his nature before he had been caught in the net of his tragic fate. Finally, after the hero's death some character who has survived the holocaust is likely to utter a brief encomium or a benediction upon the soul of the dead man.

These dramatic characteristics are all clearly illustrated in the tragedy of *Hamlet*. In this play Shakespeare finds numerous opportunities to describe his hero's nature before it was overwhelmed with grief and melancholy. Ophelia's lament is the most famous of these portraits of the uncorrupted Hamlet:

> O, what a noble mind is here o'erthrown!
> The courtier's, scholar's, soldier's eye, tongue, sword,
> The expectancy and rose of the fair state,
> The glass of fashion and the mould of form,
> The observ'd of all observers—quite, quite down.
> (III. i. 158-62)

The same innate gentleness shines through Hamlet's colloquies with the friends of his youth. It comes out clearly in his talks with Horatio, and only a little less appealingly in his conversations with his renegade friends Rosencrantz and Guildenstern.

But it is on the eve of his death that Shakespeare allows the best in Hamlet's nature to reveal itself in a final burst of splendor. He generously forgives Laertes. And he appeals to Horatio's loyalty in terms of idealistic friendship. Shakespeare enriches these speeches by marrying lofty thought to some of his most inspiring verbal music. Moreover Hamlet's death is followed by Horatio's benediction, in which he invokes the deepest religious emotions to add poignancy and elevation to the feelings aroused by the passing of his friend:

> Good night, sweet prince,
> And flights of angels sing thee to thy rest.
> (v. ii. 370-1)

Coriolanus is treated in a completely different fashion. The very first comments made upon him are derogatory. The two citizens who discuss him in the opening scene are detractors. The first of them asserts that Coriolanus has served his country not from patriotic motives but only to please his mother and to flatter his own pride. The second feebly defends Coriolanus by saying, 'What he cannot help in his nature, you account a vice in him.' The first citizen, unimpressed by the notion that innate faults are not vices, replies,

'He hath faults (with surplus) to tire in repetition.' This very first expository scene presents Coriolanus' passion nakedly, stripped of all nobility. It is what Mark Van Doren calls 'an animal pride—graceless, sodden, and hateful.' This initial exposition is but the first of many conversations about Coriolanus, all contributing features to a disagreeable portrait.

The accumulation of derogatory comment does much to set the satiric tone of the play. 'Groups of people,' says Mark Van Doren, 'tribunes, citizens, servants, officers laying cushions in the Capitol, travellers on the highway, the ladies of his household—are forever exchanging opinions on the subject of Coriolanus. And the individuals who share with him the bulk of our attention are here for no other purpose than to make leading remarks about him.' [7] In other words the play is crowded with satiric commentators.

When two or three characters gather together, the subject of their conversation is always Coriolanus. And even his wife's friend Valeria and his mother Volumnia, in contriving what they think is praise of Coriolanus, reveal the savage results of his pride. Valeria's description of the little boy at play becomes a revelation of his father's heady violence. She says, 'I saw him [the boy] run after a gilded butterfly; and when he caught it, he let it go again and after it again, and over and over he comes and up again; catch'd it again; or whether his fall enrag'd him or how 'twas, he so set his teeth and tear it! O, I warrant, how he mamock't it [tore it to shreds]' (I. iii. 66-71). Volumnia's comment on this incident—made with complete satisfaction—is 'One on's father's moods.' And she is right. Irascibility and anger are the emotions which Coriolanus most often displays—and properly, for they are the inevitable results of thwarted pride.

Of all the commentators Menenius is the least obvious in his hostility. That is because, being a buffoon, he inevitably draws the fire of some of the derision. Yet in his characterization of the tribunes, his unsavory metaphors arouse laughter,

even while they furiously mock. Witness his vulgar description of the tribunes' attempt to act as judges: 'When you are
hearing a matter between party and party, if you chance to
be pinch'd with the colic, you make faces like mummers, set
up the bloody flag against all patience, and, in roaring for a
chamber pot, dismiss, the controversy bleeding, the more entangled by your hearing . . . When you speak best unto the
purpose, it is not worth the wagging of your beards; and your
beards deserve not so honorable a grave a's to stuff a botcher's
cushion or to be entombed in an ass's packsadle' (ii. i. 81-7,
95-9). This is the buffoon at his expert best.

When this 'perfect giber for the table' (and 'giber' is an
almost exact equivalent for our slang 'wise-cracker') turns his
wit upon Coriolanus, he realizes that it must combine exposition of the man's nature with his ridicule. Once while
attempting to excuse his friend's violence, he says:

> His nature is too noble for the world.
> He would not flatter Neptune for his trident
> Or Jove for's power to thunder. His heart's his mouth;
> What his breast forges, that his tongue must vent,
> And being angry does forget that ever
> He heard the name of death.
>
> (iii. i. 255-9)

The first line of his speech, torn from its context, has been
used by many critics to prove that Coriolanus' pride is the
tragic flaw in an otherwise noble nature.[8] But Menenius is
speaking not of pride, but of headlong anger. Even if the
old patrician had meant to say that the pride of Coriolanus
was the infirmity of his noble mind, no one in an Elizabethan
audience would have mistaken his opinion for Shakespeare's.
By the third act even the slowest-minded spectator would
have recognized Menenius as a sort of buffoon and his comments as food for laughter.

After this attempt to palliate his hero's anger, Menenius
returns to his more characteristic vein of comment. Such is

the tone of his description of his friend's appearance when rejecting the old man's appeal to save Rome: 'He no more remembers his mother now than an eight-year-old horse. The tartness of his face sours ripe grapes. When he walks, he moves like an engine, and the ground shrinks before his treading. He is able to pierce a corslet with his eye, talk like knell and his hum a battery . . . He wants nothing of a god but eternity and a heaven to throne in' (v. iv. 14-26 *passim*). This is bitterly derisive comment, utterly inappropriate for a tragic hero on the verge of his catastrophe, but just the sort of talk best calculated to keep alert to the end of the play the satiric attitude of an unsympathetic audience.

VI

This purpose is accomplished throughout the drama in still more direct ways. Instead of revealing a rich inner nature in profound poetic soliloquies, Coriolanus exhibits over and over again his one ruling passion—the choler which Renaissance philosophers regarded as the inevitable result of wounded pride. At every one of his encounters with the people his rage boils at their impertinence. His contempt he displays through the insults which a 'lonely dragon' or Caliban might pour upon 'rank-scented' men. When his soldiers retreat before the attack of the Volscians, he shouts:

> All the contagion of the South light on you,
> You shames of Rome! you herd of—. Biles and plagues
> Plaster you o'er, that you may be abhorr'd
> Farther than seen, and one infect another
> Against the wind a mile! You souls of geese
> That bear the shapes of men, how have you run
> From slaves that apes would beat!
>
> (I. iv. 30-36)

For this voice we can feel only aversion. Yet its vigor and its lean thrust form an almost perfect expression of the spirit of

Juvenalian satire. Indeed the bare poetic style of this play, lamented by most critics, is exquisitely adapted to the author's derisive intentions.

Understanding the easy inflammability of Coriolanus, the tribunes are able to teach the plebs just how to induce his paroxysms of anger. When thus beside himself, he becomes their easy victim: 'Put him to choler straight,' they advise,

> . . . Being once chaf'd, he cannot
> Be rein'd again to temperance; then he speaks
> What's in his heart; and that is there which looks
> With us to break his neck.
>
> (III. iii. 25-30)

By following these instructions the mob produces a rhythmical recurrence of Coriolanus' grotesque rage; and this stimulated repetition of a vice or a folly is of the very essence of satire of every sort. It turns Coriolanus into a jack-in-the-box. Every time his self-esteem is depressed, it springs back with the same choler-distorted face. This emotional automatism deprives his pride and his anger of all dignity. It makes him a natural object of derision.

Coriolanus is also his mother's puppet. Volumnia transforms him into a terrified little boy every time the two confront each other. Shakespeare may have intended her to represent an austere patrician woman of early Rome, a worthy mother of grim warriors. Yet she wins from her son not the respect of a man, but the frightened obedience of a whimpering urchin. His attitude toward her remains completely infantile.

It is Volumnia who has forced her son to become a soldier and to exult in the blood and sweat of war. Plutarch describes Coriolanus as driven to battle by an irresistible impulse of his own nature. But Shakespeare tells us that it was Volumnia, 'poor hen, who clucked him to the wars and home.' This barn-yard figure incidentally deprives the martial impulses of Coriolanus of every shred of dignity. As a soldier he was and remains his mother's creature. Her proud boast is the truth:

> Thy valiantness was mine, thou suck'st it from me.
>
> (III. ii. 129)

When he is at the front, she relieves her anxiety by imagining him wading in triumph through seas of carnage and blood.

Though Volumnia has also bred into her son his contempt for the people, she knows that he must placate them. She realizes that if he is ever to become consul, he must stand in the market place and humbly beg for their votes. So at first she entreats him to go through the distasteful ceremony merely to please her:

> I prithee now, sweet son, as thou hast said
> My praises made thee first a soldier, so,
> To have my praise for this, perform a part
> Thou hast not done before.
>
> (III. ii. 107-110)

But even for his mother's sake Coriolanus refuses to let his disposition be possessed by 'some harlot's spirit,' to turn his voice 'into a pipe small as an eunuch,' or to allow a 'beggar's tongue make motion through his lips.' His answer to her courteous pleading is a flat, 'I will not do't.'

Then Volumnia loses her temper and soundly scolds her son. Her burst of scorn and anger immediately brings him around, reducing him to the stature of a frightened child, ridiculously eager to pacify an irate parent:

> Pray be content [he almost whimpers];
> Mother, I am going to the market place.
> Chide me no more.
> . . . Look I am going.
>
> (III. ii. 130-32; 134)

The contrast between his arrogant attitude toward all other persons in the drama and his infantile cowering before his mother's severity is ridiculous, and is intended to be so.

His last scene with Volumnia, in which she finally dissuades him from leading the victorious Volscians into Rome, is a kind of incremental repetition of the interview just described. When neither her pathetic appeals, made as she kneels before him, nor his wife's tears divert him from his purpose, his mother again loses her temper. She rises from her knees, crying

> Come, let us go.
> This fellow had a Volscian to his mother;
> His wife is in Corioles, and his child
> Like him by chance. Yet give us our dispatch.
> I am hushed until our city be afire.
> And then I'll speak a little.
>   (v. iii. 177-82)

The old woman's fierce indignation again cows her son. Terrified by her anger, he cries out, like a helpless little boy:

>   O mother, mother!
> What have you done? . . .

>   O my mother, mother! O!
> You have won a happy victory to Rome;
> But for your son—believe it, O, believe it!—
> Most dangerously you have with him prevail'd.
>   (v. iii. 182-3; 185-8)

This repeated quailing before his mother deprives Coriolanus of the dignity every tragic hero must possess. He never submits to her will through conviction or a sense of duty. His surrender is never evidence of filial respect. It is always a boy's frightened submission to a domineering woman. His undeviating arrogance toward the rest of humanity thus seems to be not exaggerated self-esteem, but compensation for the fear of his mother. He never attains the mean between these two unnatural extremes of emotion, but careens wildly between them. This instability renders him at once absurd and doomed. The forebodings which seize him after his final yielding to his mother are fulfilled. They set him in the path which leads straight to his downfall.

When Coriolanus returns to the Volscian army, he finds Aufidius hostile. He has all along been jealous of the renegade Roman and now sees a chance to destroy him. Knowing how easy it is to drive Coriolanus into a fit of blind rage, he sets the stage for the undoing of his enemy in a scene which constitutes the finale of the drama. And a masterful scene it is—an admirable catastrophe for a satirically conceived tragedy. It is an almost exact replica of those in which Coriolanus has collided again and again with the Roman mob. For Aufidius knows as well as the Roman tribunes how to manipulate his foe for his sinister purpose. He stirs the commoners against his enemy by haranguing them on the subject of Coriolanus' perfidy:

> He has betrayed your business, and given up
> For certain drops of salt your city—Rome,
> (I say 'your city') to his wife and mother;
> Breaking his oath and resolution like
> A twist of rotten silk; never admitting
> Counsel o' the war; but at his nurse's tears
> He whin'd and roar'd away your victory.
>
> (v. v. 91-7)

In the course of this diatribe he taunts Coriolanus with epithets like 'traitor' and 'boy of tears,' words which drive the warrior to an almost pathological seizure of rage. Then Coriolanus, shouting insults to the crowd, stirs the Volscian populace to fury. Once aroused, they rush upon him with cries of 'Tear him to pieces!—Do it presently—He killed my son!—My daughter—He killed my cousin Marcus! He killed my father.' The lords of Corioli, aghast at the blood-thirstiness of the mob, try in vain to calm it. But Aufidius and his conspirators have aroused the masses to the killing point. With cries of 'Kill, kill, kill, kill, kill him' they fall upon Coriolanus and murder him.

This catastrophe gives final emphasis to the satiric view of Coriolanus. His automatic response to the artfully arranged provocation has at last entrapped him to his death. His end is the direct result of an over-stimulated reflex mechanism. The catastrophe of such an automaton is not tragic. It is so completely devoid of grandeur and dignity that it awakens amusement seasoned with contempt.

VII

This derision is much less absorbing than the pity and terror provoked by a genuinely tragic denouement. For that very reason a satiric play is better suited than a tragedy to present forcefully a political exemplum. In *Coriolanus* our interest is not held by the fall of a great man destroyed by forces beyond his control. It is rather caught by the picture of social and political chaos produced both by subversive forces of democracy and by a man who is temperamentally unable to be a successful ruler. The drama, then, is a satiric representation of a slave of passion designed to teach an important political lesson.

If this is true, why has *Coriolanus* never been a popular play? The principal reason is that critics and producers have invariably regarded it as a tragedy of an orthodox but greatly inferior sort. As a tragedy it lacks, as Stoll suggests, 'constructive mechanism.' Neither Fate nor a villain spins the plot. Coriolanus is destroyed by what is false within his nature. Yet we do not behold the inner emotional conflict that ends in disaster. We never see the dramatic struggle taking place within his mind and spirit. Therefore his nature inevitably seems poor and shallow. More than that, all the positive qualities which he displays are offensive. The remnants of a noble pride appear darkly through a cloud of childish impatience and uncontrolled rage. Finally, his catastrophe fixes ineradicably in the minds of all who expect a tragedy an impression

of Shakespeare's artistic ineptitude. Coriolanus is manipulated into a fatal crisis and he meets his end in a riot which
his mad fury has precipitated. No proper tragic hero moves
thus toward his end in automatic response to artfully arranged stimuli. Nor can a death which comes to a man in a
wild brawl signalize any triumph of the spirit.

These are defects only if Shakespeare intended *Coriolanus*
to be a tragedy of the usual sort. If he meant the play to be
more satire than tragedy, most of these qualities are virtues.
Shakespeare naturally avoids arousing sympathy for a man
whom he wishes to deride. For this reason he fills the early
scenes with trenchant speech of hostile commentators, whose
business is to draw a well-rounded satiric portrait of Coriolanus. Then the author traps his victim again and again so
that we may see repeatedly the writhings of his anger. Finally
he artfully designs a final scene which will make his satiric
intention unmistakable. The murder of Coriolanus is not
the moving death of a great hero; it is the deserved result of
a supreme exhibition of his folly.

The bareness of the plot of *Coriolanus* also contributes
to the satiric emphasis of the drama. True to the genius of
satire it keeps the minds of the spectators riveted upon the
ridicule of human faults. Derision, unless associated with
moral indignation, does not easily awaken aesthetic pleasure.
But in *Coriolanus* ridicule has been made to serve the teaching of sound political theory and only by a few can the de-
scriptive forces in a healthy state be strongly enough felt to
moderate the discomfort which most men feel at the persistent satire of a strong man.

Whatever the success of Shakespeare's two attempts to combine satire and tragedy, a satiric spirit continued to permeate
English tragedy even to the year 1642. It first invaded historical tragedies like *Sejanus, Coriolanus,* and *Timon of
Athens.* Then it spread to every sort of serious play, and is
at least partly responsible for the reputation of decadence

which clings to all English drama written between Shakespeare's death and the closing of the theatres in 1642. When this development has been fully described, it will become clear that the last two tragedies of Shakespeare did much to determine the character and direction of the movement.

In this volume we have been content to fix Shakespeare's relation to the satiric writing of his own time, to show that his contribution to its achievements has been substantial. Though not an innovator in the designing of satiric patterns, he richly filled the forms invented by his contemporaries, vivifying them with his own genial sense for the absurd and later with a deepening scorn of vice and folly. As the spirit of ridicule came more and more to dominate him, he found it increasingly natural to cast his plays in familiar satiric forms. Because this fact has not been recognized, *Troilus and Cressida, Measure for Measure, Timon of Athens,* and *Coriolanus* have all confused the critics. Only when they recognize that those dramas have been formed on satiric models will they be able to understand them. Only then will they grasp Shakespeare's plan of composition and appreciate the aesthetic effects he wished to produce. The plays will then stand forth as the culmination of the poet's earlier satiric impulses. Their power will, as it were, be released for the first time, and to Shakespeare's achievements as the greatest English writer of comedy and tragedy will be added triumphs in satire for the stage.

NOTES

CHAPTER I

1. For a full discussion of Kemp's relation to the clown of the *Commedia dell' Arte* compare O. J. Campbell's 'Love's Labor's Lost Restudied' in *Studies in Shakespeare, Milton and Donne,* University of Michigan Publications in Language and Literature, I, New York, 1925, pp. 34 ff. Also Louis B. Wright, 'Will Kemp and the Commedia dell'Arte,' *Modern Language Notes,* XLI, 1926, pp. 516-20.

2. W. D. Macray, ed. *The Pilgrimage to Parnassus* with Two Parts of *The Return from Parnassus,* Oxford, 1886, p. 22.

3. Cf. T. W. Baldwin, *The Organization and Personnel of the Shakespearean Company,* Princeton, 1927, p. 24. I occasionally disagree with Professor Baldwin's assignment of roles, but everyone must base his casting on Baldwin's study.

4. *Florio His First Fruites* which yeelde familiar speech merie Proverbes, withe sentences and golden sayings, London, 1578, Chapter 7, Folio 6.

5. Quoted from Frances A. Yates, *A Study of 'Love's Labor's Lost,'* Cambridge, 1936, p. 39.

6. 'Lingua' in Dodsley's *A Select Collection of English Plays,* ed. W. Carew Hazlitt, 4th edition, London, 1874, IX, pp. 370-71.

7. Henry David Gray, 'The Roles of William Kemp,' *The Modern Language Review,* XXV, 1930, pp. 261-73.

8. Mark Van Doren, *Shakespeare,* New York, 1939, pp. 126-8 passim.

CHAPTER II

1. G. P. Baker, *The Development of Shakespeare as a Dramatist,* New York, 1907, pp. 107-8.

2. J. Dover Wilson, *The Essential Shakespeare,* Cambridge, 1932, p. 13.

3. This idea, first suggested by Arthur Acheson in *Shakespeare and the Rival Poet,* London and New York, 1903, was developed (1) by Sir Arthur Quiller-Couch and J. Dover Wilson in the Cambridge edition of *Love's Labor's Lost,* Cambridge, 1923, and (2) by Frances A. Yates in *A Study of 'Love's Labor's Lost,'* Cambridge, 1936.

4. Cambridge edition, *Love's Labor's Lost,* p. xxi, note 1.

5. Very little certain knowledge of this group can now be discovered. The best account of it is to be found in M. C. Bradbrook's *The School of Night,* Cambridge, 1936.

6. 'Responsio ad Elizabethae Edictum,' passage quoted, Bradbrook, op. cit. p. 12.

7. The manuscript of this essay of Northumberland's was discovered among the *State Papers, Domestic,* by Frances A. Yates and published in her *A Study of 'Love's Labor's Lost,'* pp. 206-11.

8. G. Bruno, *Opere Italiane,* ed. G. Gentile, Bari, 1908, Vol. II, p. 287. The Italian reads, 'quelle continuelle torture, que' gravi tormenti, que' razionali discorsi que faticor i pensieri, e quelli amarissimi studi, destinati sotto la tirannide d'una indegna, imbecille, stolta e sozza sporcaria.' The translation is that of Frances A. Yates in her *John Florio,* pp. 104-5.

9. O. J. Campbell, *'Love's Labor's Lost* Restudied,' in *Studies in Shake-*

speare, Milton and Donne, University of Michigan Publications, Language and Literature, I, New York, 1925, pp. 23-44 *passim.*

10. J. Dover Wilson in 'The Schoolmaster in Shakespeare's Plays,' *Essays by Divers Hands—Transactions of the Royal Society of Literature,* 1930, Vol. IX, p. 30.

11. This peculiarity of Holofernes was suggested to me by George Gordon in his *Shakespeare's English,* in Tract 29 of The Society for Pure English, Oxford, 1928, p. 255.

12. Miss Yates, *A Study of 'Love's Labor's Lost,'* Cambridge, 1936, p. 57, believes that Shakespeare may have been satirizing one particular book of colloquies; Vives' *Linguae Latinae Exercitatio.* Eliot, in his *Ortho-epia Gallica,* London, 1593, parodies this work of the Spanish educationist.

13. Dover Wilson reminds us of this fact in a note in the New Cambridge edition of Shakespeare—'Love's Labor's Lost,' pp. 155-6. The correct beginning of the line is 'fauste precor,' not 'facile precor' as Holofernes thinks.

14. William Warburton was the first critic to suggest the identification of Holofernes and Florio. In his edition of Shakespeare (*The Works of Shakespeare . . . corrected and emended . . . by Mr. Pope and Mr. Warburton,* London, 1747, Vol. II, pp. 227-8) without presenting any evidence whatever, he made the following categorical statement: 'By Holofernes is designed a particular character, a pedant and schoolmaster of our author's time, one John Florio, a teacher of the Italian Tongue in London.' Dr. Johnson, *The Plays of William Shakespeare,* in eight volumes, London, 1765, note to 'Love's Labor's Lost,' IV, ii., seriously doubted the truth of this identification, but most of the early critics accepted it.

15. Frances A. Yates, op. cit.

16. Karl Elze (*William Shakespeare,* trans. Dora Schmitz, London, 1888, p. 37) suggested Thomas Hunt, Shakespeare's teacher at the Stratford Grammar School, 1572-7, and Abel Lefranc in *Sous le Masque de William Shakespere,* Paris, 1919, Vol. II, p. 60, put forward Richard Lloyd, the author of a manuscript play on the Nine Worthies.

17. George Puttenham, *The Arte of English Poesie,* ed. by Gladys Dodge Willcock and Alice Walker, Cambridge, 1936, p. 45.

18. *Ibid.* p. xci.

19. The rest of this paragraph is a free paraphrase of pp. 258 ff. of George Gordon's essay 'Shakespeare's English,' to which I have referred above.

20. *The Complete Works of Shakespeare,* ed. George Lyman Kittredge, Boston, 1936, p. 194.

21. Juan Luis Vives, *Vives: On Education;* a translation of *De tradendis. disciplinis* of J. L. V., together with an introduction by Foster Watson, Cambridge, 1913, p. 35.

22. Fulke Greville 'Treatie of Humane Learning,' stanza 34, *Poems and Dramas of Fulke Greville,* ed. Geoffrey Bullough, Edinburgh, 1938, I, p. 162.

23. *The Poems of Sir Walter Raleigh,* ed. Agnes M. C. Latham, London, 1929, p. 46.

CHAPTER III

1. For the text of the censor's decree, see *A Transcript of the Registers of the Company of Stationers of London,* 5 vols., ed. Edward Arber, London, 1876, III, 316.

2. Joseph Hall, *Virgidemiarum*, Sixe Bookes. Frist three Bookes. of Toothlesse Satyrs (London, 1597); The three last Bookes. Of byting Satyres; (London, 1598), lib. 5, satire 3, sig. F4.

3. *The Scourge of Villainy*, Satire 10, 1-4 (*The Works of John Marston*, ed. A. H. Bullen, London, 1887, III, 367.

4. *A Fig for Momus:* containing Pleasant Varitie, included in Satyres, Ecologues, and Epistles, London, 1595, sig. A3.

5. Desiderius Erasmus, *The Praise of Folly*, trans. by John Wilson 1668, ed. Mrs. P. S. Allen, Oxford, 1913, p. 62-6.

6. The type and its history are described in Z. S. Fink's 'Jaques and the Malcontent Traveller,' *Philological Quarterly*, XIV, No. 3, July, 1935.

7. John Marston, Satire II, 127-9, 133-6; *Works*, III, p. 276.

8. Ibid. Satire II, 139-41, 155-6.

9. For a description of the various unnatural melancholies see Chapter XVIII of Timothy Bright's *A Treatise of Melancholy*, London, 1586, pp. 110-16.

10. Cf. Timothy Bright, op. cit. p. 146.

11. Burton lists as one of the causes of melancholy 'vain libertine delight' *Anatomy of Melancholy* (London, 1896) Pt. I, Sect. II, Mem. III, Subs. XIII, I, 133.

12. For an analysis of these characters vid. O. J. Campbell's 'Jaques' in *The Huntington Library Bulletin*, No. 8, Oct. 1935, pp. 85 ff.

13. *Epigrammes and Elegies* by I. D. and C. M., London, 1593 (?), sig. A3.

14. Marston *Works*, III, 381-2.

15. Prologue 17-18, *Works* III, 428.

16. *The Scourge of Villainy*, Proemium in Librum Primum, ll. 1-4, 7-8, (*Works*, III, 307).

17. B. H. Newdigate, *The [London] Times Literary Supplement*, 3, Jan. 1929, p. 12.

18. Arthur Gray, *How Shakespeare 'Purged' Jonson: A Problem*, Cambridge, 1928.

19. The first English translation of Saviola's work appeared in 1595. Its full title was *V. Saviola his practise in two bookes. The first of the use of rapier and dagger. The second of honor and honorable quarrels* (S.T.C. No. 21788).

20. Although this volume first appeared in 1608, it is simply a record of Armin's interest in fools of various sorts.

21. 'The Works of Robert Armin, Actor (1600-1609)' in *Occasional Issues of Unique or Very Rare Books*, ed. by Alexander B. Grosart, Vol. XIV (1880), p. 39.

22. T. W. Baldwin takes this point of view in 'Shakespeare's Jester, *M.L.N.*, XXXIX, No. 8 (Dec. 1924), 454.

23. *Antonio's Revenge*, IV, ll. 37-45; *Works*, I, 158.

CHAPTER IV

1. Charles R. Baskervill, *English Elements in Jonson's Early Comedy*, Austin, Texas, University of Texas, 1911, p. 27.

2. *Every Man in His Humour*, III, i, pp. 154-8. All quotations are from the Quarto edition of 1601, the version in which Shakespeare acted. However to avoid confusion, the characters are given the more familiar names of the

Folio of 1616. In the quotation above the Folio has instead of 'bred in a man by self-love,' 'bred in the special gallantry of our time.'

3. On 11 May 1597, Henslowe enters in his Diary the receipt of a sum for the first performance of *The Comedy of Umers* [*Henslowe's Diary*, ed. W. W. Greg, 1904, Pt. II, 184]. Jonson's comedy was produced by the Lord Chamberlain's men some time in September 1598 [Maurice Castelaine, *Ben Jonson, l'homme et l'œuvre (1572-1637)*, Paris, 1907, p. 215 n.].

4. Herford and Simpson (*Ben Jonson*, Oxford, 1925, I, p. 346) have pointed out this likeness between the two characters.

5. John W. Draper in his 'The Humor of Corporal Nym,' *Shakespeare Association Bulletin*, XIII, No. 3 [July 1938] pp. 131-8, makes this interesting point.

6. M. L. Radoff in 'The Influence of French Farce in *Henry V* and *The Merry Wives*,' *Modern Language Notes*, XLVIII, 7 (November 1933) pp. 427-35 shows that this sort of foreign-language lesson thus hilariously interrupted is a convention of French farce.

7. *The Return from Parnassus*, Part Two, I, iv, [p. 92 in *The Pilgrimage to Parnassus* with two parts of *The Return from Parnassus* ed. W. D. Macray] Oxford, 1906.

8. Shakespeare's name appears first in the list of actors enumerated by Jonson in the 1616 Folio of his dramas.

9. Ben Jonson, ed. by Brinsley Nicholson and C. H. Herford, London, 1893-5 (Mermaid Series) I, p. xliii.

10. C. R. Baskervill, op. cit. p. 154, n. 1.

11. Paul Mueschke and Jeannette Fleisher 'Jonsonian Elements in the Comic Underplot of *Twelfth Night*,' *P.M.L.A.*, XLVIII, No. 3 (September 1933) pp. 722-40.

12. J. W. Draper emphasizes this point in his 'The Wooing of Olivia' in *Neophilologus* XXIII, 42-3.

13. This paragraph is greatly indebted to John W. Draper's essay 'Olivia's Household,' *P.M.L.A.*, XLIX, No. 3 (September 1934) 797-806.

CHAPTER V

1. J. Dover Wilson, *The Essential Shakespeare*, Cambridge, 1932, pp. 95-115.

2. Ibid. p. 115.

3. R. W. Chambers, 'The Jacobean Shakespeare and *Measure for Measure*,' Annual Shakespere Lecture of the British Academy, 1937, pp. 17-24.

4. The phrase appears in A. W. Pollard and Dover Wilson's 'William Shakespeare,' in *The Great Tudors* ed. Katharine Garvin, London, 1935, p. 593.

5. E. K. Chambers, *Shakespeare: A Survey*, London, 1925, p. 219.

6. Sir Walter Raleigh, *Shakespeare*, London, 1916.

7. The text of this document can be found in *A Transcript of the Registers of the Company of Stationers of London*, ed. Edward Arber, 5 vols. London, 1876, III, p. 316.

CHAPTER VI

1. *The Pictorial Edition of the Works of Shakespeare*, ed. Charles Knight, 1839, VII, p. 72.

2. *Sewanee Review*, XXIV, p. 129.

3. Peter Alexander, 'Troilus and Cressida, 1609,' *The Library*, 4th Series, IX, pp. 277-8.

4. For the proof of these statements the reader is referred to the present author's *Comical Satyre and Shakespeare's 'Troilus and Cressida,'* pp. 192-3, especially note 28.

5. I share Tucker Brooke's belief ('Shakespeare's Study in Culture and Anarchy,' *Yale Review*, XVII, 574-5) that Shakespeare derived his conception of the Trojans from Fenton's version of Caxton's *Recuyell* (1596), and his view of the Greeks from Chapman's *Homer*.

6. Mark Van Doren, *Shakespeare*, New York, 1939, p. 13.

7. W. W. Lawrence, *Shakespeare's Problem Comedies*, New York, 1931, p. 143.

8. Lytton Strachey, *Elizabeth and Essex*, London, 1930, p. 34.

9. W. B. Drayton Henderson, '*Troilus and Cressida* yet Deeper in its Tradition,' in *Essays in Dramatic Literature*, the Parrott Presentation Volume, ed. Hardin Craig, Princeton, 1935, p. 152.

10. George Brandes, *William Shakespeare: A Critical Study*, English tr., London, 1898, II, p. 207-8.

11. Op. cit. p. 154.

12. 'The Philosophy of *Troilus and Cressida*,' in *The Wheel of Fire*, Oxford, 1931, pp. 51-79.

13. I am indebted to my colleague Professor Marjorie Nicolson for this interpretation of the debate of the Trojans.

14. C. H. Herford, *Shakespeare's Treatment of Love and Marriage, and Other Essays*, London, 1921, p. 40.

15. *Yale Review*, XVII, p. 573.

16. *Shakespeare's Problem Comedies*, New York, 1931, p. 146.

17. Op. cit. p. 72.

Chapter VII

1. *Measure for Measure*, ed. by Sir Arthur Quiller-Couch and J. Dover Wilson, Cambridge, 1922, p. xiii.

2. Samuel Taylor Coleridge, *Lectures and Notes on Shakespeare and other English Poets*, London, 1888, p. 299.

3. R. W. Chambers 'The Jacobean Shakespeare and *Measure for Measure*, Annual Shakespere Lecture of the British Academy, 1937.

4. W. W. Lawrence, *Shakespeare's Problem Comedies*, New York, 1931 pp. 78-121.

5. Mark Van Doren, *Shakespeare*, New York, 1939, pp. 217 and 223-4.

6. Ibid. p. 28.

7. *Measure for Measure*, Cambridge edition, p. xxvii.

8. Levin L. Schücking, *Character Problems in Shakespeare's Plays*, New York, 1922, p. 197.

Chapter VIII

1. E. E. Stoll in his 'Shakespeare, Marston, and the Malcontent Type, *Modern Philology*, III, No. 3, pp. 281-303 (January 1906), analyzes the type with his customary keenness.

2. William Rankins, *The English Ape*, London, 1588, p. 8.

3. The phrase is one of Timothy Dwight's *A Treatise of Melancholie* (1586) *The Facsimile Text Society*, New York, 1940, p. 100.

4. *The Scourge of Villainy*, Proemium in Librum Primum, ll. 9-14, Marston *Works*, III, p. 305.

5. Harrison lists, besides Hamlet, Jaques, Lear, and Timon as Shakespeare's definitely melancholy characters. Cf. his edition of Nicholas Breton's *Melancholike Humours*, London, 1929, p. 73.

6. J. W. Draper 'Hamlet's Melancholy,' *Annals of Medical History*, New Series 9, No. 2, pp. 142-7.

CHAPTER IX

1. The view that Shakespeare rewrote a part and only a part of an older play was first presented by Charles Knight in his Pictorial Edition of Shakespeare in 1838. This idea was upheld in a scholarly article by Nikolaus Delius entitled 'Ueber Shakespeare's *Timon of Athens*,' which appeared in *Jahrbuch der deutschen Shakespeare Gesellschaft* (1869), pp. 160-97. The first important expression of the theory that an inferior hand had worked over a play which had been at least partly written by Shakespeare appeared in a paper read by F. G. Fleay to the New Shakespeare Society in 1874. This essay was printed in the *Transactions of the New Shakespeare Society*, 1874, pp. 130 ff. Fleay's thesis was elaborated by Ernest Hunter Wright in *The Authorship of Timon of Athens*, N. Y., 1910. Dixon Wecter makes an ingenious variation of the theory of multiple authorship in his 'The Purpose of *Timon of Athens*,' *P.M.L.A.*, XLIII, No. 3, pp. 701-21 (September 1928).

2. E. K. Chambers, *William Shakespeare: A Study of Facts and Problems*, Oxford, 1930, I, pp. 482-3.

3. G. Wilson Knight, 'The Pilgrimage of Hate: An Essay on *Timon of Athens*,' in *The Wheel of Fire*, London, 1930, pp. 227-62.

4. These three phrases are from Knight's essay.

5. These ideas that the social corruption of Athens infects the state and all its citizens and that the play is unified by the common cause which Alcibiades and Timon make against the greed for gold that has destroyed the city have been very effectively developed by James E. Phillips, Jr., in *The State in Shakespeare's Greek and Roman Plays*, New York, 1940, especially pp. 126-46. To this work I am indebted in this section of my chapter.

6. Mark Van Doren, *Shakespeare*, New York, 1939, p. 289.

CHAPTER X

1. A. C. Bradley 'Coriolanus. Second Annual Shakespeare Lecture' (1 July, 1912) Proceedings of the British Academy 1911-12, pp. 457-73. Hazelton Spencer in *The Art and Life of William Shakespeare* (1940) 346-50, takes a similar view. 'In *Coriolanus*,' says the critic, 'he [Shakespeare] frankly takes the line of least resistance.' The idea is that he simply followed mechanically the facts laid down in his source—'that is all.'

2. Bradley op. cit. p. 461.

3. George Brandes, for example, in a chapter in *William Shakespeare, a critical Study* (New York, 1902) emphasizes the absence in *Coriolanus* of 'any

humane consideration for the oppressed condition of the poor' and his 'physical aversion for the atmosphere of the people.' M. W. MacCallum expresses the more measured view by admitting that 'Shakespeare invariably treats crowds of citizens, whether in the ancient or modern world . . . as stupid, disunited, fickle' (*Shakespeare's Roman Plays and Their Background*, London, 1910, p. 470).

4. Serge Dinamov, *Works of Shakespeare*, 4 vols. I, xix.

5. These ideas have been thoroughly presented in James E. Phillips Jr.'s *The State in Shakespeare's Greek and Roman Plays* (N. Y., 1940) *passim*.

6. William Fulbecke in his *Pandectes of the Law of Nations* (1602) cites the history of Coriolanus to confirm his contention that the people is the 'beast with many heads.' This example he offers as part of his evidence drawn from history to prove that democracy is contrary to natural law.

7. Mark Van Doren, *Shakespeare*, New York, 1939, p. 10.

8. John W. Draper in an article called 'Shakespeare's *Coriolanus*: A Study in Renaissance Psychology,' West Virginia Bulletin (Philological Studies III Sept. 1939, pp. 22-36) develops these ideas. He believes that *Coriolanus* is a perfect illustration of the notions on this subject developed in Plutarch's *Morals*, La Primaudaye's *The French Academie*, and Thomas Adams' *Diseases of the Soul* (1616) first introduced into Shakespeare studies by Lily B. Campbell in her *Shakespeare's Tragic Heroes* (Cambridge, 1930).